ANXIETIES
OF EMPIRE
and the
FICTION
OF INTRIGUE

ANXIETIES OF EMPIRE

and the

FICTION OF INTRIGUE

Yumna Siddiqi

Columbia University Press   *New York*

Columbia University Press
Publishers Since 1893
New York   Chichester, West Sussex
Copyright © 2008 Columbia University Press
All rights reserved

Library of Congress Cataloging-in-Publication Data
Siddiqi, Yumna.
Anxieties of empire and the fiction of intrigue / Yumna Siddiqi.
p.   cm.
Includes bibliographical references and index.
ISBN 978-0-231-13808-6 (cloth : alk. paper) — ISBN 978-0-231-51086-8 (electronic)
1. English fiction—19th century—History and criticism. 2. English fiction—
20th century—History and criticism. 3. English fiction—South Asian authors—
History and criticism. 4. Intrigue in literature. 5. Espionage in literature. 6. Literature
and society—Great Britain—History—19th century. 7. Literature and society—
Great Britain—History—20th century. 8. Imperialism in literature. 9. Postcolonialism
in literature. 10. Anxiety in literature. I. Title.
PR861.S53   2008
823'.809358—dc22   2007006785

Columbia University Press books are printed on permanent and
durable acid-free paper.
This book was printed on paper with recycled content.
Printed in the United States of America
c 10 9 8 7 6 5 4 3 2 1
p 10 9 8 7 6 5 4 3 2 1

References to Internet Web sites (URLs) were accurate at the time of writing.
Neither the author nor Columbia University Press is responsible for URLs that may
have expired or changed since the manuscript was prepared.

For my parents
Asiya and Obaid Siddiqi
with all my love

Contents

Contents

Acknowledgments

So many friends, teachers, colleagues, and members of my family have helped me travel the long journey from the inception of this book as a Ph.D. dissertation at Columbia University to its publication that it is impossible to do justice to them all, but I'd particularly like to thank the following:

I was remarkably fortunate to have in my dissertation director, Edward Said, an extraordinary scholar, public intellectual, and teacher, and I am deeply sorry that he is not alive to see this book in print. The other members of my dissertation committee at Columbia University, John Archer and Steven Marcus, have also been not only my readers but also my models as scholars and teachers, and I am happy to be able to acknowledge my debt to them. I would like to give a special thanks to my colleague, mentor, and dear friend John Elder, who has helped me continue to grow and learn in the last six years at Middlebury; and to Jay Parini, whose careful reading of and unwavering support for this book have helped me see it through.

Thanks also to my other colleagues and friends at Middlebury College, especially Cates Baldridge, John Bertolini, Timothy Billings, Dan Brayton, Alison Byerly, Natasha Chang, Rob Cohen, Claudio Medeiros, Sujata Moorti, Guntram Herb, Antonia Losano, William Poulin-Deltour, Michael Sheridan, and Marion Wells for their encouragement, comments, and suggestions. Rob Nixon and Eileen Gillooly also read early versions of the manuscript at Columbia University, as did Russ McDonald, Mary Ellis Gibson, and Jennifer Keith at UNCG.

At Columbia University, I was lucky to have a cohort of talented scholars and friends, and would particularly like to express my gratitude to Pat Cahill, Joe Cleary, Jon Karp, and Lisa Makman, and to

Acknowledgments

members of the Postcolonial Collective, and the Cultural Studies dissertation writing group.

I hugely appreciate the interest, critical comments, and conviviality of my friends Hosam Aboul-Ela, Amy Carroll (who helped me think through the last chapter), David Clifford, Sarah Morgan, Shobhana Narasimhan, Kunal Parker, Gautam Premnath, Subir Sinha, Steve Striffler, Sanjay Tikku, Rashmi Varma, and Anne Waters. Thanks also to my friends and intellectual comrades in Montreal, Alia Al-Saji, Lisa Barg, Anne Bourlioux, Katie Coughlin, Jill Didur, Sharon Hayashi, Rosanna Maule, Anne McKnight, and Norma Rantisi.

One of the happenstances of being a migrant is that one adopts family in different parts of the world, and I would like to thank the many members of mine, who include Val Arnold-Forster, Lorna Mitchison, Av Mitchison, Will White, Kalpana White, Daya Varma, and Shree Mulay. A big thanks also to Peggy Sax for helping me stay sane and happy.

Thanks to John Tallmadge for his terrific editorial guidance and critical comments throughout the revision process. I am also grateful to the team who worked at and with Columbia University Press, Kay Banning, Jennifer Crewe, Lisa Hamm, Leslie Kriesel, William Meyers, Tom Pitoniak, Juree Sondker, and the anonymous reviewers of the manuscript.

An enormous thanks finally to Asiya, Obaid, Imran, Kaleem, and Diba Siddiqi, and to Imrana Qadeer, Jyotsna Dhawan, and the rest of my extended family, for their constant love and support.

Yumna Siddiqi
Middlebury, December 2007

ANXIETIES
OF EMPIRE
and the
FICTION
OF INTRIGUE

Introduction

In this book, I explore the ways in which Empire is troubled by anxieties about its own security. I investigate how these anxieties are expressed in the fiction of intrigue—fiction that foregrounds a threat to the social and political order—and particularly in detective and spy fiction. Fiction of intrigue gives voice to concerns about imperial mastery in especially pronounced ways. It responds to and in some cases partly allays these concerns through strategies of representation and narrative resolution that are characteristic of this genre. *Empire* serves as an umbrella term for the different forms of Western hegemony over the rest of the world, be it in political and military rule over an alien territory and the direct exploitation of its resources, or in the exercise of economic and cultural power in a more indirect way, through the flows of capital, goods, information, and people. To examine the nature of Empire in more specific terms, this book focuses on colonial British fiction and postcolonial fiction from South Asia.

Colonial fiction of intrigue is set in a period when Britain exerted force in more or less overt ways through a range of institutions and practices: the army, the civil service, the police, revenue collection, law and the courts, educational institutions, to name but some. The colonial regime used these institutions and practices to produce knowledge that made the so-called natives transparent and governable. Bernard Cohn writes that the imperative to "classify, categorize, and bound the vast social world that was India so that it could be controlled... shaped the 'investigative modalities' devised by the British to collect the facts."[1] Imperial writers take as their starting point the view that Britain's then control over her imperial territories is entirely a good thing; they portray threats to the colonial order as problems to be solved by putting other "investigative modalities," those of the detective and the spy, into play. Fiction of intrigue, in emphasizing a quest for knowledge and intelligence in the face of a disturbance of order, proposes a particular way of looking at the imperial world. Like imperial romances, imperial detective and spy fictions are cast as stories of adventure. However, unlike imperial romances, detective and spy stories do not represent the colonial world as enjoyably picturesque.[2] Rather, such fiction frames the imperial world as permeated with violence and intrigue; it emphasizes the mysteriousness of the Other. The protagonist's quest is not for wealth or excitement, or at least not for these alone; his ultimate aim is to secure order and intelligibility.[3]

Such a preoccupation with order and intelligibility continues to shape the West's view of the former colonial territories.[4] When I began this book, the link between discourses of police, detection, and imperialism in literature piqued my interest; yet at the time the exercise seemed somewhat academic. Then followed the catastrophic attacks of September 11, 2001, on the World Trade Center and the Pentagon. Now, anxieties about law and order, crime, police, and detection predominate in Western discussions of the Third World; one can say with little exaggeration that "terrorism" is the defining concern of the moment. Detective and spy fiction of the late nineteenth and early twentieth centuries quite strikingly anticipates contemporary metropolitan expressions of anxiety about social, political, and economic instability in former colonial territories, and current concern with making the postcolonial world an object of knowledge and control echoes that fiction's cadences.

This will to police also marks the workings of postcolonial states. Though the postcolonial fiction of intrigue that I examine is set in a period well after formal decolonization, this era has been shaped by the historical legacy of colonialism and the forces of new forms of Empire. The view that decolonization marks not a complete end to colonial relationships, especially economic ones, but merely a recasting of them, was first put forward by Marxist anti-imperialists, perhaps most trenchantly by Kwame Nkrumah, who coined the term *neocolonial* to describe this continuing subordination. Contemporary Marxist thinkers, analyzing the current era of globalization, argue that the new imperialism has still to be understood as part of the logic of capitalism.[5] More postmodern thinkers claim that the current era of globalization marks a new form of Empire, one that is deterritorialized and decentered, is characterized by new forms of sovereignty, and has generated new forms of resistance.[6] The postcolonial writers I discuss directly address the cultural and political circumstances of Empire as we know it now. They consider the ways in which power operates through a range of material structures and modes of knowledge. These writers also point to the emergence of new kinds of subjectivity and new forms of political control. They express the paradoxes of postcolonial modernity and trace the ruses and uses of reason in a world where the modern marks the horizon of hope as well as of economic, military, and ecological disaster.

Broadly speaking, I set out in this book to explore the relationship between narrative and power as it operates in the context of Empire. In the first part of the book, I probe what fiction of intrigue reveals about the discursive and material elements of Empire during the late nineteenth and early twentieth centuries, and the anxieties to which it points. In the second, I consider how fiction of intrigue serves the ideological interests of Empire by allaying these anxieties. This part of the book focuses on contemporary fiction in a persistent yet changing Empire—the New Empire. Here I argue that postcolonial fiction of intrigue takes a more critical view of the state's anxieties and the will to police that dominates this new era of Empire. I show how the current, global Empire marks and transforms fiction of intrigue, creating a demand for new modes of reading. Finally, I ask whether an analysis of fiction of intrigue in relation to the New Empire requires a rethinking of aspects of postcolonial theory. In other words, what are the implications, if any, of this exploration for the field of postcolonial studies?

It should be clear from this brief sketch that two threads tie the halves of this book together, one generic and the other historical. Both parts of this study focus on the genre of intrigue. The first part considers stories of intrigue that were written by Englishmen who were champions of the British Empire at its pinnacle. It looks at detective and spy fiction obliquely, from the angle of imperial civilization and its discontents. It is motivated by two interlocking queries: what happens to detective and spy fiction when it takes as its subject matter the imperial world; and what happens to imperial discourse when it takes the form of detective and spy fiction. The second part examines books by South Asian writers who set their novels of intrigue in societies that have liberated themselves from formal imperial control but that have also inherited the institutions and practices of imperial regimes. These postcolonial writers use narratives of intrigue to investigate the legacies of imperial occupation, as well as to explore postcolonial societies in an era of an emergent global Empire. They make critical use of the genre of intrigue, and interrogate the repressive aspects of postcolonial institutions and cultural practices. In this respect, the postcolonial writers I examine are interested not so much in "writing back" to an earlier mode of imperial representation, but in scrutinizing the repressive elements of postcolonial and global manifestations of Empire in the present. The second thread that ties this study together, then, is that of Empire in its high imperial and global aspects. While this book is not a historical study of the forms of Empire, it necessarily considers the ways in which old modes of imperialism coexist with or are replaced by new ones.

This study could not have been done without the work of Edward Said, who pioneered the study of the relationship between imperialism and culture. It is difficult to overstate the significance of Said's work for literary scholarship specifically and for the humanities and social sciences more generally. Drawing upon Foucault's exploration of the nexus between power, discourse, and knowledge, Said critiques the discursive production of knowledge about the colonized world, and the relation between this knowledge production and the more brute exercise of economic and military power by the West. If the subject of *Orientalism* was the implications of such knowledge for imperial and postcolonial hegemony, then in *Culture and Imperialism* Said also considered the manifold responses of thinkers and artists from the postcolonial world.

Said stresses the imperial will to power that marks Orientalist and imperialist writing. The first wave of scholars of postcolonial discourse paid relatively little attention to the doubts and apprehensions voiced in colonial writing, and instead largely emphasized its triumphalist tone.[7] They argued quite rightly that the relation of metropolis to colony is best characterized as one of domination. Accordingly, they stressed that colonial writing bolstered imperial rule by offering representations that validated such domination. Yet imperial power was exercised neither seamlessly nor securely. As the frequent use of the phrase "going native" suggests, imperial hegemony and imperial identity were often precarious. This instability stemmed from the contradictions and tensions that ran through imperial formations. Ann Stoler and Frederick Cooper have argued, "Colonial regimes were neither monolithic nor omnipotent. Against the power which they projected across the globe and against their claim to racial, cultural, or technological domination, closer investigation reveals competing agendas for using power, competing strategies for maintaining control, and doubts about the legitimacy of the venture."[8] And if power was successfully held, the possibility of its loss always attended its possession.[9] Even when power was maintained, the possible effect of

4

imperialism on national culture was a source of uneasiness, as the writing of the period reveals. Recent scholars have noted the ambivalence of colonial discourse. Indeed, Said too implicitly acknowledges the nexus of fantasies and fears that underpin representations of the Orient. Homi Bhabha foregrounds this ambivalence, which he locates not so much in the person of the colonizer as in the process of colonial utterance. My study, in focusing on fiction with an eye to the imperial anxieties and tensions it expresses, is very much part of a second wave of postcolonial literary scholarship.[10]

In *Culture and Imperialism*, Said examines the ways in which post-colonial writers situate themselves vis-à-vis the metropole, that is, the metropolitan center of the British Empire—England, or more narrowly, London—in what he calls "the voyage in."[11] He emphasizes the dialogic relationship between the cultural discourse of the colonized and that of the metropole. He observes that those who write from the vantage point of colonized subjects neither reproduce metropolitan discourse uncritically nor are completely detached from it; rather, writers from the periphery have a complex, angular relationship to metropolitan culture. After all, the postcolonial societies from which these writers come were not created ex nihilo; they are indelibly marked by the experience of colonial rule. The historical continuities between imperial and postcolonial societies are particularly pronounced in the domain of the state. Partha Chatterjee argues with respect to British India that the colonial state took as its ostensible project the improvement of India; this was Britain's "civilizing mission."[12] When Indian nationalists assumed power, they argued that the colonial regime's methods of improvement had not promoted the full and efficacious growth of the nation and her people, but had in fact stunted this growth. Nationalists believed that it was their mandate to use the Indian state as a vehicle for modes of development that were truly in the interest of Indians. They put in place a series of ambitious five-year plans to pursue true national development.

At the same time, they inherited the well-developed repressive apparatuses of the state, using these to control the citizenry. Hamza Alavi, one of the first scholars to use the term *postcolonial,* offers a groundbreaking discussion of the exaggerated development of the military-bureaucratic apparatuses:

[The metropolitan bourgeoisie's] task in the colony is not merely to replicate the superstructure of the state which it had established in the metropolitan country itself. Additionally, it has to create separate apparatus through which it can exercise dominion over all the indigenous social classes in the colony.... The colonial state is therefore equipped with a powerful bureaucratic-military apparatus and mechanisms of government which enable it through its routine operations to subordinate the native social classes. The postcolonial society inherits that overdeveloped apparatus of state and its institutionalized practices through which the operations of the indigenous social classes are regulated and controlled.[13]

Alavi argues that the metropolitan bourgeoisie that sets up the colonial state does not simply introduce the structures of its state, but rather has to establish apparatuses to subordinate all the social classes in the colony. Alavi's astute analysis shows how various social classes—the indigenous bourgeoisie, the metropolitan neocolonialist bourgeoisie, and the landed classes—collude and compete to produce a relatively autonomous bureaucratic military state structure, one that tends to be excessively large and powerful. These apparatuses are passed on more or less intact to the postcolonial state.

Postcolonial novels of intrigue foreground the persistence of an overblown military-bureaucratic state in the postindependence era. They underscore the abuses of power by the government and its police structures. Whereas colonial writers endorse the imperial vision of law and order, the postcolonial novelists on whom I focus use the genre of intrigue to critique the repressive mechanisms of the postcolonial state. Thus, broadly speaking, I move from a course of reading that attempts to discern the ideological currents and tensions in colonial texts, to a strategy of reading that positions postcolonial writers as participants in, rather than objects of, ideological critique.

Postcolonial novelists also explore the repressive aspects of the new global Empire, but often in more tentative ways, perhaps because the contours of this Empire are only now becoming visible and there is little consensus on how to understand it. When the United Nations General Assembly declared in 1960 the right to self-determination of all colonial countries and peoples, it articulated a principle that underpinned the decolonization of much of Africa and Asia after World War II; this decolonization of British territories continued with the independence of Zimbabwe in 1980; Belize, Antigua, and Barbados in 1981; St. Kitts and Nevis in 1983; and the reversion of Hong Kong to China in 1997. At the end of the twentieth century, the decolonization of British territories seemed a fait accompli. The question was whether imperialism had taken new forms and was now achieved by economic and financial domination. Yet with British Prime Minister Tony Blair's support for the United States–led invasion of Afghanistan and Iraq, and the touting of the principle of "preemption," the question of whether imperialism is an active and accepted practice today has a new urgency. On this global stage, the United States is clearly the dominant imperial power, with Britain taking on the role of supporting cast. It is debatable whether Western powers have reverted to old forms of imperialism, or whether we have a new species of imperialism altogether, one in which the globalized "empire of capital" is buttressed by new forms of repression. To those who see modern forms of Empire as a radical departure from the old, with novel forms of decentered and deterritorializing sovereignty, one is inclined to point out that the recent turn to violent military occupation in Iraq, Afghanistan, and Lebanon (by Israel, but with the tacit backing of the United States and the United Kingdom), is entirely in the vein of classic nineteenth-century imperial domination.

In the first part of the book, I focus principally on stories of intrigue by Arthur Conan Doyle. At first glance, Doyle does not appear to write about imperialism other than tangentially. It is only when one examines his fiction specifically through a postcolonial lens—that is, with a perspective informed by the body of criticism and theory about the relationship between culture and imperialism that emerged in the last two decades of the twentieth century—that one discerns that it is significantly marked by the experience of imperialism. The stories repeatedly figure characters from different parts of the British Empire, characters who pose a threat to order within England. Given that the period in which the stories were written and are set was one of aggressive imperial expansion, it is hardly remarkable that Empire should be represented as obtruding upon metropolitan space.[14] What is more interesting is that in Conan Doyle's mysteries, the development of plot, and the uncovering of a plot which is the moment of detective fiction, frequently occurs within an imperial framework such that different kinds of problems are imaginatively mapped onto different parts of the imperial world: Australia, India, Africa, and South America (which was subject to an informal imperialism). Read in this way, Conan Doyle's stories yield a veritable imaginative topography of Empire.

To throw the imperial subplots of Doyle's stories into relief especially sharply, and to explore the imperial dimensions of these subplots more fully, I read Doyle's stories alongside fiction by writers who more obviously contend with imperial terrain: Wilkie Collins, Rudyard Kipling, and John Buchan. I have chosen to concentrate on these writers for a number of reasons. First, they are canonical "minor" writers who have had a wide and lasting audience and cultural significance. Second, they all present fictions of intrigue in which Empire plays an important if obscure part. Third, Doyle, Kipling, and Buchan in their public lives were themselves associated with Empire, and their writing served imperial interests. This is not to say that their stories uniformly endorse imperial rule; on the contrary, they often reveal the contradictions of Empire, as I explicitly argue. But they were champions of Empire, and one must read their stories against the grain to discover anxieties about the shortcomings and dangers of imperial rule. Their fictional accounts of detection and spying not only reveal anxieties about Empire, but also tend to allay them through narratives that delineate and enact a process of ordering. Thus I argue that their writing attempts to resolve ideologically the anxieties generated by administrative policing characteristic of Empire in both its British colonial and its global manifestations.

The second part of the book focuses on contemporary postcolonial fiction by South Asian writers who refashion the genre of intrigue to interrogate the political anxieties of the present. The writers I discuss, Amitav Ghosh, Salman Rushdie, Arundhati Roy, and Michael Ondaatje, all use literary fiction to reflect critically on the large questions that face postcolonial societies: the legacy of colonialism, the nature of postcolonial identity, the significance of religion and caste, the character of political violence, and the implications of globalization and diaspora. In their novels, these writers explore the problems of economic hardship, caste and gender oppression, ethnic and communal violence, and environmental degradation. By casting their novels as stories of intrigue, they underscore the forms of "police" that operate in different domains of cultural, social, political, and economic life. They throw into relief both the repressive and emancipatory agendas of the postcolonial state.

The interpretive method that I follow is eclectic. Pierre Macherey's notion of symptomatic reading—by which he means a critical attention to textual gaps, silences, and tensions that reveal the presence of ideological matter that has been transformed through the labor of literary production—is useful in teasing out the underlying currents expressed in fiction of intrigue.[15] Macherey argues that the critic does not bring to light the meaning of a text that is obscure; rather, he or she produces a second-order text that is related to but discursively different from the literary work. In my symptomatic readings, I attempt to probe the silences and gaps in Conan Doyle's and Buchan's stories to write an account of some of the anxieties that trouble colonial texts. At the same time, as I show, in a postcolonial context of ethnic violence in which polities have been shattered, symptomatic reading can itself be problematic. The second-order text that the detective—and the critic—produces has its own ideological coloring. Ondaatje's novel *Anil's Ghost*, reflecting upon the challenges that a forensic scientist faces when thrust in the theater of political violence, repeatedly asserts, "In diagnosing a vascular injury, a high index of suspicion is necessary." The critic must be similarly vigilant, probing the tissue of the text with some sensitivity to the cultural and political traumas whose imprint it bears. The critic's narrative produces no simple "truth" either about this text or the cultural conflicts it mediates; rather, it is, at its best, a reflexive second-order narrative that represents these traumas and conflicts in a different language.

Carlo Ginzburg's conjectural paradigm is another interpretive model that I draw upon. While Macherey focuses on literary texts, and attributes an irreducible specificity to the domain of the aesthetic, Ginzburg turns his attention to historical interpretation. Ginzburg argues that the diagnostic technique of the physician and the investigative mode of the detective both exemplify what he calls the conjectural paradigm, a paradigm that the historian shares. The conjectural paradigm involves the intuitive connection of clues and traces to produce knowledge that is "indirect, presumptive." Such an approach focuses on the individual and the particular and is not scientific in the conventional sense, since it cannot be generalized or systematized. Nor is it scientific in Macherey's sense of wearing on its sleeve the rules by which it constitutes knowledge. Ginzburg argues, however, for its "flexible rigor."[16] Its role in capillary forms of control notwithstanding—Ginzburg gives the example of a British administrator of a district of Bengal, William Herschel, who laid the ground for fingerprinting when he observed the local practice of using the imprints of dirty fingers to identify individuals—the conjectural paradigm "can become a device to dissolve the ideological clouds which increasingly obscure such a complex social structure as capitalism"—and, I would argue, imperialism.[17] To tease out the "unsaid" of the novels and to elaborate on the "said," I undertake a combination of symptomatic reading and conjectural analysis.

Such an approach to interpretation is especially apposite when one tries to make sense of the social experience and representation of subaltern peoples. In "Notes on Italian History," Antonio Gramsci discusses the political situation of what he identifies as subaltern groups—subordinated groups that exist outside the aegis of the state and have a fragmented and episodic history by virtue of their marginal position. The Subaltern Studies historians have taken up Gramsci's analysis to chart a subaltern historiography, one that focuses on the marginal and subordinate: women, peasants, tribal peoples, and so on. While both Gramsci and his adherents address their remarks to the study of subordinate groups, their choice of terminology and their comments suggest ways to reconceive the nature of the dominant imperial formation. As a noun, *subaltern* can be used to denote "a person (or thing) of inferior rank or status; a subordinate; occasionally a subaltern genus; a subordinate character in a book." This is the definition invoked by Ranajit Guha and his colleagues in the Subaltern Studies series. However, the word can also be, and commonly is, used to refer to "an officer in the army of junior rank."[18] A subaltern officer is of a subordinate rank yet is an integral part of one element of the dominant group—the military.[19] It is worth considering whether, in the colonial context, members of the dominant formation shared the experience of subalternity. How, for example, would one characterize the rebellious soldiers of 1857? Given that Britain's imperial armies and administrations were to a large extent peopled by non-Europeans, a racially defined subalternity inhered in the very core of imperial regimes.[20] While Guha speaks here of indigenous groups, a similar analysis can be made of imperial regimes. Certain groups occupied a subordinate and ambiguous position in the political structure of Empire. In fact, natives too were positioned in contradictory ways as colonial subjects. Such was the case of the Indian subalterns who were forced to choose loyalties during the period of the Indian Revolt. Characters from subaltern groups appear frequently in colonial fiction. The process of conjectural reading is particularly suited to exploring the social situation of such subaltern groups because their place in the social fabric is often obscure and must be detected through their traces and by piecing together fragments of information.

The postcolonial novels that I discuss are also marked by ideological tensions and fissures, as my reading of *Anil's Ghost* in the last chapter suggests. On the whole, though, the writers of these postcolonial novels take a consciously critical stance toward Empire and its cultural and social implications. The postcolonial novels in question mount this criticism by tracing the activity of what Fredric Jameson calls the "social detective." In the essay "Totality as Conspiracy," Jameson explores the ways in which contemporary films express "the world system itself."[21] He focuses especially on "the 'conspiratorial text,' which, whatever messages it emits or implies, may also be taken to constitute an unconscious, collective effort at trying to figure out where we are and what landscapes and forces confront us in a late twentieth century whose abominations are heightened by their concealment and their bureaucratic impersonality."[22] The social detective navigates these landscapes and attempts to discover these secret forces. Often the detective indicts an entire collectivity for its involvement in a crime or a conspiracy. "Such representations are most frequently found in that older moment of a still national culture in which the function of literature includes what I have elsewhere called national allegorization, providing individual narrative representations through which the national destiny can be fantasized."[23] According to Jameson, narratives of social detection often are responses to the corrosive effects of modernity on a traditional social and moral order; they are mobilized in the service of a conservative cultural critique. Consequently,

> they are less serviceable when secularization and modernization have long since become facts of daily life—not to speak of what obtains when the new multinational organization of late capitalism problematizes the framework of the nation state along with the national cultural forms specific to it (like this allegorical one). This form, therefore, in which an individual somehow confronts crime and scandal of collective dimensions and consequences, cannot be transferred to the representations of global postmodernity without deep internal and structural modifications.

Jameson's comments are extremely suggestive in relation to the postcolonial novels of intrigue that I examine here. These novels engage precisely in a critique of the social order, but not necessarily in a conservative way. Rather, they mount a critique of both modern and traditional institutions. In these novels, the narrative follows a process of social detection, sometimes localized in a single character, at others in a more dispersed way. The protagonist, who attempts to understand the mysterious, possibly criminal events around him or her, eventually perceives the nefarious underbelly of social and political institutions. Such a narrative of social detection becomes a way of commenting on the corruption of society as a whole, and not just of individuals. Postcolonial fiction of intrigue underscores the secret abuses of power by the government and elites. As Jameson predicts, fiction of intrigue, essentially a conservative form, itself undergoes changes as it explores the contradictions of postcolonial modernity.

OUTLINE OF THE BOOK

The chapters of this book move sequentially from a consideration of detection inside the metropole, to a discussion of spying beyond the metropole in the field of Empire, and then to an examination of intrigues set in postcolonial societies. Part 1 of this book is about late-nineteenth and early-twentieth-century fiction of intrigue.

In chapter 1, I address the prevalence and the significance of anxieties of Empire. I also discuss the importance of popular fiction in expressing and shaping attitudes toward British imperialism around the beginning of the twentieth century. I then sketch the historical and theoretical context for a study of detective and spy fictionof that era, and explore the literary fashioning of the detective and the spy in relation to anxieties of Empire.

In chapter 2, I discuss a little-known but important short story by Arthur Conan Doyle, "The Mystery of Uncle Jeremy's Household." Doyle weaves into the fabric of this story of intrigue a number of the themes and concerns that I focus on in this book: ethnography, anxieties about miscegenation and hybrid identity, education, colonial desire, the return of colonial subjects from Empire to the metropole, and insurgency against British rule. At the heart of the mystery is Miss Warrender, a governess of mixed heritage who has traveled to England from India. Her identity and character raise questions about the efficacy of colonial governmentality, and the need for the proper education of colonial subjects. The story links colonial anthropology, a knowledge of the habits and customs of native subjects, directly to the project of colonial rule.

In chapter 3, I discuss a number of Doyle's detective stories in which colonial subjects return to England, where they are at the center of a mystery or crime. I attempt to unpack the cultural significance of the figure of the returned colonial in fiction of intrigue. These characters unsettle the social fabric when they appear, exposing social tensions and contradictions by their presence. I ask what ambiguities inhere in their characterization. Often they have deformed bodies, bodies that are contorted, discolored, burnt, amputated, and dismembered.[24] I consider how bodies in Empire are imbued with meaning, and specifically, how one can explain the proliferation of bodies gone awry in Empire. In the imperial context, bodies are not merely a compelling and convenient medium for mapping social concerns—there is a further reason that they assume importance. Imperial regimes were overwhelmingly concerned with controlling and extracting value from bodies and land. The viability and profitability of Empire depended on the sustained availability of appropriately productive and reproductive bodies. The appearance of unruly, anomalous, and damaged bodies in imperial fiction suggests that the imperial machinery was thought to be flawed or in jeopardy.

Chapter 4 considers Doyle's and Buchan's rhetorical treatments of a specific historical trauma: insurgency. Variously characterized by the imperial regime as a revolt, mutiny, or rebellion, insurgency marks a political threat to imperial power. It is almost a truism that the experience of imperial domination was inseparable from the phenomenon of resistance to imperial rule. Even after Britain's hegemony had been established, it was frequently challenged by violent rebellions. The most obvious cause for anxiety on this score was the fear that resistance by colonized peoples would be successful and overturn imperial rule. But this was not the only danger posed by insurgency. Periods of violent upheaval put considerable political strain on imperial formations in other, less evident ways. The Irish stand out, for instance, as a group whose allegiances were not certain in such times of turmoil. Their position in Empire was inherently paradoxical. They were, on the one hand, agents of British rule; indeed they were lionized as members of a martial race who fought valiantly for the imperial cause abroad. Yet Irish republicans in Ireland, the United States, and England were, at the end of the nineteenth century, engaged in a struggle against British occupation. Doyle reveals the paradoxical position of these colonial subjects even as he defends their imperial loyalties in the context of insurgency. The second part of chapter 4 considers John Buchan's treatment of insurgency in *Prester John* and *Greenmantle*. These novels suggest that imperial hegemony is threatened by disgruntled colonial subjects who have grand empire-building schemes of their own—in *Prester John*, a pan-African empire, and in *Greenmantle*, a pan-Islamic jihad that can be exploited by an imperialist Germany. Buchan's novels emphasize spying rather than detection as a tactic for containing these threats. A comparison of how each type of protagonist contends with insurgency highlights the differences between detective and spy fiction as responses to imperial anxieties.

I turn my attention to contemporary South Asian fiction in the second part of the book. I argue that when fiction of intrigue is transposed to the colony, its structure and topography are turned topsy-turvy in such a way as to make both the repressive and emancipatory aspects of postcolonial political sovereignty visible. In chapter 5, an intermezzo, I briefly sketch a theoretical framework for studying postcolonial fiction of intrigue. Chapter 6 examines the ways in which Amitav Ghosh turns the generic conventions of fiction of intrigue inside-out in his novel *The Circle of Reason*. While it echoes the themes of interwoven histories and migration that are prominent in his later novels *The Shadow Lines* and *In An Antique Land*, *The Circle of Reason* emphasizes the motifs of insurgency, detection, and police. Though *The Circle of Reason* is not precisely popular fiction in the way Buchan's and Doyle's stories are, the novel revisits and parodies the tropes of popular fiction of intrigue, querying its representation of social relations. By making the detective an unenthusiastic functionary of a repressive state apparatus, and his supposedly "subversive" quarry an innocent fugitive, Ghosh puts into question the ethos of surveillance that undergirds fiction of intrigue. Ghosh also examines, through the lens of parody, the legacy of Enlightenment reason in postcolonial India. His novel suggests that Enlightenment rationality has both repressive and progressive moments. The novel also makes a detour into the lives of a group of transnational migrants when it considers the difficulties and possibilities of migration for subaltern peoples.

In chapter 7, I analyze the representation of state violence in Arundhati Roy's *The God of Small Things* and Salman Rushdie's *The Moor's Last Sigh*. I argue that Roy uses a narrative of social detection to expose the violence of the state and its functionaries, the police; of social institutions such as caste; of gender relations within the family; and of the new global order and its economic policies. She suggests that small things and people are crushed by the state and its rationalities. At the same time, she identifies the domains of the erotic and of nature as spaces of possible liberation from the oppressive constraints of borders and boundaries. Rushdie explores the violence of the Hindu right in *The Moor's Last Sigh*. His protagonist, the Moor, embraces the fascism of the right; he also discovers the criminal side of his tycoon father's business dealings. The novel presents the rise of fascist violence as antithetical to the multiple and hybrid quality of India. Both Rushdie and

Roy also tangentially consider the effects of late-twentieth-century globalization on the environment, on culture, and on identity.

In chapter 8, I examine Michael Ondaatje's use of a narrative of intrigue to represent political violence in *Anil's Ghost*. Ondaatje writes of a war-torn Sri Lanka where individuals have been stripped down to their existence as bare life, victims of a genocide that has become a condition rather than an event. The writer fashions out of the political quagmire of Sri Lanka a novel that reads in many ways like a detective story. He focuses on the effects of political violence on individual bodies. At the same time, he shifts away from a juridical narrative of detection and punishment to portray violence as generalized and global. In so doing, he points to the limits of the critique of the nation-state. At the same time, he focuses on the difficulties of reading, and of hermeneutics more broadly. He repudiates the historicizing of violence, insisting on the need to read in new ways. Finally, he invokes the aesthetic as a domain of redemption in the face of brutalizing violence.

In the concluding chapter, I explore Rushdie's representation in *Shalimar the Clown* of globalization and of political violence in Kashmir, and examine Stephen Frears's film about immigrants in London whose bodies and labor are readily exploited in the interstices of a global civil society. Rushdie uses elements of the thriller to portray the bloody murder of a retired American diplomat by the husband of a Kashmiri woman with whom he has had an affair. He interweaves a story of personal betrayal and revenge with a portrait of the transformation of Kashmir, an idyllic place of great beauty and of a famed ethos of religious and ethnic tolerance, into a land ruined by internecine strife, the rise of militant separatism, and brutal repression at the hands of the Indian state. I argue that Rushdie gestures toward diasporic location and experience as an antidote to the narrow thinking of ethnic separatists and of the nation-state. Frears presents a much less sanguine view of diasporic location, and paints a harsh, macabre picture of the lives of migrants to the imperial metropolis. He uses the genre of intrigue to expose the violence to which illegal immigrants, denied full participation in and the protection of political society, are easily exploited in the trade in bodies and sweatshop labor.

The work of literary analysis undertaken here can be likened to the process of detection. My methodology is not that of the critic who explicates the great writer nor of the theorist who provides paradigms for reading, but that of the detective who investigates culture by reading clues and reconfiguring the literary and historical facts of the case into an intelligible whole. This process of discovery and reconstruction has its hazards: misreading, the use of inappropriate categories, the forcing of explanations, and the like. To avoid these pitfalls, it may be wise to follow the advice (if not always the practice) of Sherlock Holmes and avoid jumping to conclusions in the absence of evidence as well as refrain from making unwarranted assumptions. Instead, I attempt to keep my nose to the texts and make conjectures about anxieties of Empire on the basis of the evidence they provide.

ONE

Colonial Anxieties and the Fiction of Intrigue

British imperial fiction and detective fiction are, on the face of it, distinct genres of writing. Imperial fiction is usually set in Empire, and demonstrates the superiority of colonial culture and the triumph of British hegemony vis-à-vis a native Other. Detective fiction is generally set within England, and takes as its subject matter the allaying of a threat to law and order by a perspicacious policeman or sleuth. These genres overlap in late nineteenth-century fiction in interesting ways. In several mystery stories of this period, characters from the colonies enter England and bring with them violence and subterfuge. Rather than underscore the celebratory elements of imperial romance, these stories point to anxieties about the nature and effects of imperialism.

In the last decades of the nineteenth century, Britain came to see itself as an imperial nation. By 1900, Britain's power extended beyond national boundaries to over 13 million square miles and roughly 366 million people.[1] The rapid territorial expansion of the latter part of the nineteenth century, and the deepening of colonial involvement that accompanied it, brought the Empire to the forefront of the public imagination. J. R. Seeley was able to write with conviction in 1883 that the destiny of modern Britain was imperial expansion.[2] This view was not limited to the intellectual and ruling classes—it was held by large numbers of ordinary English people who followed imperial developments with great interest.[3] Public occasions such as Queen Victoria's coronation as Empress of India in 1876, and her Diamond Jubilee celebration in 1897, presented to the English a spectacle of statehood that emphasized the significance of Empire.[4] An increasingly informed and vocal public keenly supported Britain's overseas adventures, which were even thought to be "a cause through which the moral fiber of the British people would be greatly improved."[5] And as higher levels of literacy fueled a proliferation of penny papers and inexpensive journals, popular fiction became an important medium for the circulation of imperialist sentiments.[6] However, alongside this general enthusiasm for Empire, one finds in late Victorian literature a current of anxiety about incursions from Empire, and its influence upon the established pattern of English life.[7] Articulated as a concern about the instability of individual identity, the disintegration of the social and moral order, and the eruption of crime and violence, this vein of anxiety runs below the surface and emerges in certain discernible patterns in popular literature of Empire, notwithstanding its largely jingoistic tone. While the first part of this book concentrates on literature of the period of high imperialism, from 1875 to 1914, it extends before and after this period to yield a fuller picture of the culture to which such literature belongs. Popular fiction of intrigue did not just express anxieties about Empire; writers who favored this genre manipulated such anxieties for the entertainment of a wide reading public.

Detective stories by Arthur Conan Doyle typify the ways in which fiction of intrigue expresses, frames, and responds to such anxieties.[8] Novels by Wilkie Collins and Charles Dickens also weave elements of mystery with concerns about Empire, but these novels are not full-fledged fictions of intrigue, and Empire was not a central matter of concern for either writer; consequently, I consider their work only in passing.[9] As an imperialist, as well as an extremely popular writer whose stories are formative, representative, and fully crystallized versions of fiction of intrigue, Doyle is particularly suitable for this study. In his stories, a new type of protagonist emerges: a detective hero who is uniquely qualified to contend with mysteries and dangers that originate in the imperial world.[10] Sherlock Holmes is the exemplar of this type.[11] He acts within the national borders, but frequently exerts his talents to solve mysteries that originate without—he demystifies alien incursions and thus renders the national space secure.

Doyle is a somewhat neglected writer in the field of colonial studies, perhaps because his detective stories evoke an inwardly focused England in the popular imagination, and do not appear to concern themselves with questions of imperialism. In fact, his stories are replete with imperial subplots.[12] While Doyle's detective stories focus on England, and indeed on London, this is a London that is very much an imperial city, with connections to the far corners of the world. Doyle's successors Dorothy Sayers, Margery Allingham, Ngaio Marsh, and Agatha Christie, who occupied center stage during the so-called "golden age" of detective fiction, also focused on London and the English country-side, even though they wrote at a time when the British Empire was at its pinnacle. Their stories, too, might be read against the grain to explore the ways in which Empire shapes part of the "unsaid" of de-tective fiction—but that is beyond the scope of my study.

During the last decades of the nineteenth century, at the time Holmes was making a name for himself and a reputation for his author, a new popular genre emerged, cousin to the detective story: the spy thriller.[13] The spy—exemplified in John Buchan's stories by Richard Hannay—is also a type of detective hero who assures the safety of the imperial me-tropolis.[14] He becomes embroiled in international subterfuges to defuse threats to Britain and her Empire. Both kinds of hero embody strikingly similar attitudes. The detective story celebrates the mastery of disorder through the application of scientific methods and logical deduction. His perspicacious intelligence, his keen powers of analysis, and his encyclope-dic knowledge distinguish the detective. He pieces together obscure and seemingly unrelated fragments of knowledge to construct an intelligible totality. Through his efforts, identities are established and social relations are rendered transparent—he makes an increasingly bewildering social terrain knowable and hence manageable. While the detective is an agent of order—both disciplinary and epistemological—in English national space, the spy, also a guarantor of national security, goes beyond na-tional boundaries, and assumes diverse personae to gather intelligence.[15]

It would of course be a mistake to suggest that fiction of intrigue is solely an imaginative response to Empire. But the fact that so many detective and spy stories of the late nineteenth and early twentieth cen-turies have a striking pattern of reference to similar imperial motifs in-dicates that this subgenre derives from cultural exigencies specific to Empire. Other analyses—whether structuralist, psychoanalytic, Marx-ist, or humanist—assume a metropolitan frame of reference, and tend to neglect the important imperialist dimensions of this fiction.[16] In fact, many of the stories are set partially in Empire, and certain thematic and formal elements have a specific connection to imperial experience.

An examination of the anxieties and tensions of Empire provides a more accurate picture of the nature of imperial hegemony. An un-derstanding of imperial anxieties also sheds light on *the modalities of imperial domination*. There is a tendency in discussions of imperialism and colonialism to assume that the English were wielders of a self-con-stituting, autonomous imperial power, which they attempted to exer-cise on colonized peoples. This misses the point that imperial power was exercised in a highly conflicted and contested field, literally and metaphorically. The contingencies, tensions, and contradictions of this field produced anxieties that affected the exercise of power.

Social, political, and sexual codes appropriate to imperial life did not always sit well with those codes designed for the home nation. One can better apprehend the tactics and strategies of control if one appreciates how threats to a stable hegemony are imagined and where they are located. If imperial rule produced anxieties about hegemony and identity, the forms these anxieties took shaped the way power was wielded. Anxieties about Empire are clearly discernible in fiction of the late nineteenth and early twentieth centuries. Writers as diverse as Joseph Conrad, Rudyard Kipling, Doyle, Robert Louis Stevenson, Rider Haggard, Joyce Cary, and John Buchan intersperse their stories with accounts of moral depravity, political rebellion, and sexual danger. While such representations more often than not sanction European intervention and supervision, they also reflect unfavorably at times on the careers and characters of Europeans in and from the colonies. Thus imperial fiction registers apprehensions both about the influences of the Empire on the metropolis, and about the adverse effects on English character of the exercise of imperial rule.[17]

It is common to characterize late modernity in the West as an anxious age. Many have attributed the restless uncertainty of the modern world and the individual alienation that pervades it to the corrosive and destabilizing effects of capitalist economies. Others, such as Kierkegaard, have attributed the prevalence of anxiety to the decline of religious faith and the certainties that it provided. No doubt the anxieties discernible in British fiction of the late nineteenth and early twentieth centuries can in part be understood in these terms. In this study, however, I investigate the specifically imperial sources, contexts, and manifestations of cultural, political, and social anxieties as they are given narrative expression. Of course, given the intertwined nature of imperial and metropolitan culture, it is not possible to separate metropolitan from imperial anxieties very sharply. Often, in fiction, the Empire is an imaginative space onto which metropolitan concerns are projected and where they are worked through. In much the same way, the metropolis may serve to reflect apprehensions about imperial rule.

To undertake a study of the social significance of anxieties about imperial rule is to investigate the workings of ideology. Critics have employed the notion of ideology in a number of different ways. Here

I refer to ideology as a structure of values and beliefs that is intimately related to people's material circumstances, and that serves to resolve apparent contradictions in lived experience. I would contend that ideology does not completely, securely, or seamlessly resolve contradictions. Imperial anxiety can thus be understood as the effect of the seams in ideology. It may accordingly be most acute at moments and places where the structure is strained or unraveled—where the seams come apart. By exploring contradictions in experiences, values, and beliefs, one can identify certain ideological seams of the late nineteenth and early twentieth centuries that produce anxiety.

The uncertainties and difficulties that trouble imperial experience become the content of literary narratives. Anxiety is not only a latent theme in fiction of intrigue, but is a motivating force in this genre of fiction. Its status is similar to the one that Peter Brooks, in asserting a correspondence between literary and psychic dynamics, accords to desire, which he identifies as the chief propelling energy of narrative. He contends that "texts represent themselves as inhabited by energies, which are ultimately images of desire, and correspond to the arousals, expectations, doubts, suspense, reversals, revaluations, disappointments, embarrassments, fulfillments, and even the incoherences animated by reading."[18] While this account is broad enough to encompass most textual and psychic dynamics, *desire* does not capture as well as *anxiety* the sense of uneasy anticipation and relief that is elicited by fiction of intrigue. While it is difficult to pinpoint the relationship between desire and anxiety, it is useful to make a distinction between the two in describing the qualities of fiction of intrigue.

Freud argued early in his career that anxiety was the outcome of the repression of libido, but eventually rejected this explanation. His later account of anxiety suggests a certain parallel with the nature of desire: whereas desire is driven by lack, anxiety is linked to danger and to the trauma of anticipated loss.[19] In fiction of intrigue, the genealogical condition of the narrative is the trauma of a loss of order. In detective fiction, this is the originating condition of the story, whereas in spy fiction, it is a danger that is projected into the future. The reader apprehends and feels this loss of harmony. An impetus to maintain or reestablish order drives the stories at a thematic and textual level. One finds, moreover, in fiction of intrigue a tension between the impulse toward narrative closure with the establishment of order and intelligibility, and the persistence of residual, returning problematic elements that require that problems be "solved" and anxieties allayed again and again. These anxieties always exceed any relief the "solution" might provide, and so force a return to narrative.

It is important to note that literature does not in a simple, unmediated way merely reflect or express social anxieties. It plays an active role in shaping and circulating them. It does so, moreover, in a particularly compelling way: in giving them narrative form, literature imparts to cognitive frames the force of feeling that translates into attitudes and actions. To borrow again from Peter Brooks, fiction plots imperial understandings, desires, and intentions. Fiction of intrigue, in particular, generates interest in Empire by affording its readers the pleasure of mystery and mastery—it exploits cultural anxieties in such a way as to entertain a wide audience.

POPULAR LITERATURE AND EMPIRE

Both Doyle and Buchan are writers of so-called "minor fiction"—literature that is judged by critics not to be of high literary merit, but is lastingly popular and influential. Doyle's and Buchan's stories were first published in the journals and cheap editions that were the stuff of turn-of-the-century popular culture. A number of critics have demonstrated the importance of such literature in shaping and expressing cultural attitudes.[20] Popular literature, while it offers less complex representations of imperialism, provides valuable insights into how large numbers of people understood Empire in relation to their everyday lives. Moreover, while popular fiction is an important medium for the dissemination of ideology, its study can also reveal the uncertain workings of this ideology. In the late nineteenth century, this burgeoning popular literature of Empire became a crucial vehicle both for the dissemination of imperial ideology and for the expression of imperial anxieties.[21]

As fictional accounts both of criminal intrigue and of Empire, Doyle's and Buchan's stories have a double hook. In the nineteenth century, writing about crime and police was an especially popular genre. The street literature that was the staple of working-class people included broadsides, gallows literature, and ballads with woodcut illustrations, all of which detailed real crimes and purported confessions with gory relish.[22] The mass journalism that replaced this literature in the 1870s, as well as middle-class journals, "penny dreadfuls," police sheets, and novels, all trafficked in stories of crime and detection. These publications "offered a staple diet of scandal, lurid crime, upper-class intrigue, melodrama, adventure, and sin."[23] Doyle's and Buchan's stories of intrigue form part of this literature.

At the same time, the detection and espionage that dominates the narrative draws the reader into a world that is inextricably connected to Empire. Popular writing about Empire was so voluminous by the end of the nineteenth century that scholars today are able to characterize it as a body of discourse with a distinct "range of tropes, conceptual categories, and logical operations."[24] One of the most pervasive tropes of late Victorian imperial culture was that of war as sport.[25] This public school coding of the behavior of the governing class emphasized the values of courage, selflessness, team spirit, and forbearance, and promoted an attitude of condescension toward foreigners, women, and the lower classes.[26] This upper-class public schoolboy's view of the world became hegemonic at the end of the century.[27] It was through the repeated use of these modes of writing about colonized peoples and places that difference was constructed and the landscape of imperial power was fashioned.[28]

Writers of popular imperialist fiction reproduce these modes through their handling of stereotypes and plots. Critics such as John Cawelti have characterized popular fiction as formulaic: it follows conventional plots and uses stereotypes and clichés, engaging the reader by manipulating these in novel ways. Cawelti distinguishes the character of such formula fiction from what he calls mimetic fiction. He writes, "The mimetic element in literature confronts us with the world as we know it, while the formulaic element reflects the construction of an ideal world without the disorder, the ambiguity, the uncertainty, and the limitations of the world of our experience."[29] According to Cawelti, mimetic fiction evinces the "more complex and ambiguous analyses of character and motivation" to do justice to the doubts and difficulties of the world as we experience it. By contrast, the formula story presents a simplified and predictable world, the very familiarity of which gives pleasure to the reader. Rather than regard formula fiction as less complex, however, one might look for a different kind of complexity in the experience of reading popular fiction. Homi Bhabha, in his analysis of the colonial stereotype, identifies a complexity in the *process of signification*, a complexity that belies the simplistic character of the stereotype itself.[30] He contends that the stereotype is "a form of knowledge and identification that vacillates between what is always 'in place,' already known, and something that must be anxiously repeated."[31] Bhabha suggests that there is a fetishistic and aggressive aspect to the repetition of the stereotype, which serves to compensate for a lack of knowledge, and of power. Bhabha's analysis of the ambivalence of the colonial stereotype rightly points to the anxiety that runs through colonial discourse.

However, the claim that Bhabha makes for what an understanding of this ambivalence can achieve is questionable. Bhabha aims to grasp "the productive ambivalence of the object of colonial discourse—that 'otherness' which is at once an object of desire and derision, an articulation of difference contained within the fantasy of origin and identity."[32] He goes on to suggest, "What such a reading reveals are the boundaries of colonial discourse and it enables a transgression of these limits from the space of that otherness." That is, the "otherness" produced by colonial discourse, when shown to be ambivalent, undoes colonial discourse itself. Here as elsewhere, Bhabha offers an analysis of colonial power that is predicated on a poststructuralist model of language, and suggests that critical reading presents a challenge to the operation of colonial power. In stressing the anxious moments of colonial power, and understanding these moments vis-à-vis the operation of language, Bhabha does not adequately acknowledge the material determinations that buttress colonial power. The colonial stereotype may be ambivalent, but it nonetheless validates and is backed up by coercive practices—practices of what I would call "police." Police and detection is not merely a theme, then; it is the complement of colonial ambivalence and its anxieties.

THE DETECTIVE AND IMPERIALISM

In fiction of intrigue, imperial domination, premised upon power over and knowledge of the Other, is expressed in a discourse of law and order. The detective and spy are, above all, agents of order in both its legal and cognitive senses. The detective and spy further law and order. They work to uncover solutions to crimes or to expose subversive plots, though, as I will elaborate later, they are often expressly not members of an official police. Running through these stories is a concern with the rule of law: the stories are located squarely within the domain of the legal. At the same time, they exhibit a preoccupation with order in the sense of systematic arrangement. Placed in a world of mysterious causes and effects, the detective unearths facts and puts them in an order of significance to yield a total solution, one that generally takes the form of a reconstruction of a past event. The spy, faced with shifting identities and interests, unmasks personae and uncovers subterfuges, usually to counter imminent threats to British security and dominance. The furtherance of law and order involves, in both instances, a concerted attempt to make sense of—that is, to impose cognitive order upon—a seemingly inexplicable, uncertain, and dangerous world.

Fiction of intrigue suggests that imperial order is only precariously maintained, hence the anxiety that attends imperial domination. Empire appears in fact to produce disorderly entities—in both senses of the word *disorderly*. The in-between, the anomalous, the uncategoriz-able, the awry—what Kristeva calls "abject"—is in these stories often dangerous, both posing a direct threat to law and order, and unsettling socioeconomic, political, and libidinal orders.[33] At times the abject destabilizes European hegemony and European identity itself. The detective's task is to render these unsettling entities into knowable objects. To this end, he delimits characters and events not only by attributing coordinates of time and place to them, but also by determining motives—that is, by probing identities and commitments. His method is eclectic. He employs deduction and conjecture, and makes reference to an ever-expanding imperial archive.[34] He assimilates the imperial world to the metropolis by fixing, categorizing, and imposing a singular meaning upon the former. The spy also allays anxieties concerning imperial identity and hegemony by unmasking imposters and gathering intelligence—information vital to the security of the state. Although, like the detective, he protects law and order, he does so in a more risky way. His knowledge is intimate rather than synthetic—he actually assumes the identity of the Other. Though their methods differ, both the detective and the spy gather intelligence to secure a certain state order. They both render the stuff of the imperial world into objects of knowledge. In so doing, they stave off disorder and stabilize European subjectivity in a reciprocal relation of Otherness.

Detective fiction demonstrates the validity of Enlightenment rationality. It celebrates the ability of the detective to counter ignorance and to redress social infractions through the systematic use of reason and scientific method. This Enlightenment ethos is, however, interwoven with an ideology of romantic adventure.[35] While the Empire must be ordered, it is also a realm in which the ethos of heroism and adventure endure. Here not only elite but also ordinary Englishmen can experience agency and the pleasures of mastery, or so imperial fiction of intrigue would have us believe. In other words, detective and spy fiction are fantasies of imperial order that imaginatively recapture the lost agency and puissance of the Western subject in the well-disciplined metropolis, and that compensate for the insufficiency and ineffectuality of disciplinary power in a rapidly expanding, heterogeneous imperial world.

While they serve the ends of modern governmentality, there is an important respect in which the detective and the spy do not precisely extend disciplinary power to the imperial domain. Disciplinary power, as Foucault understands it, is exercised minutely and invisibly, not through agents, but rather by the rational organization of time and space. Disciplinary power is promulgated by apparatuses rather than by agents, whereas the detective and spy are agents in the full sense of the word. They are not functionaries, cogs in suprahuman machinery that produces quiescent subjects. In detective fiction, a police function is personified; a solitary and singular agent undertakes the task of guaranteeing order.

While power might indeed have become more rationalized at the end of the nineteenth century, the subjects on whom it acts do not necessarily experience their lives and world as rationally ordered. Reflecting on the cultural politics of the detective novel in *The Country and the City*, Raymond Williams argues that in nineteenth-century England, the city increasingly becomes a place where there is an absence of "common feeling."[36] At first, writers depict the city as senseless and chaotic; later it is characterized as predictable in its chaos. The detective is able to make sense of the increasingly bewildering terrain of England, acting as a safeguard against the seeming irrationality of modern industrial society. Through his efforts, identities are established, social relations are rendered transparent, and mysteries are solved.[37] His cultural function is twofold: he validates individual agency; and he renders the world explicable and safe for his late Victorian readers.[38]

While critics have tended to study the culture of imperialism and the culture of late modernity separately, the Sherlock Holmes stories attest to the fact that their discourses overlap. Written between 1886 and 1927, these stories straddle the late Victorian period and the decades of high modernism; they are also products of a culture of an imperialism the most aggressive phase of which spanned the years 1880 and 1914. The solutions put forward in the persona of the detective, and in his method, address problems associated at once with imperialism and with late modern culture.

This was a culture regarded with deep ambivalence by English people of the time. It was perceived on the one hand as a "wasteland," peopled with "hollow men"—faceless monads whose lives lacked meaning and beauty. This pessimism was countered by a celebration of modern life, of machinery and technology, by some. Perceptions of Empire were similarly divided; a deep gloom about Britain's imperial destiny coexisted with a jingoistic celebration of imperial values and imperial might. The wealth generated by Empire gave rise to new social classes; these were the beneficiaries of imperialism. At the same time, the rise of financial imperialism went hand in hand with the decline of a traditional aristocracy. The imperial order of capital had produced another new class, an imperial lumpenproletariat that was locked out of the spoils of Empire, and that is represented in the Sherlock Holmes stories as a threat to law and order in the metropolis. The metropolis had itself become an anonymous mass of faceless workers and the intermittently employed, and in the view of respectable Victorians, criminal "residuum." No longer were people readily placed in a well-knit hierarchy in which the origins, identity, and position of every person were known.

The ambivalent attitudes of late Victorians toward both modernity and imperialism may explain why Sherlock Holmes, the paradigmatic detective, is an ambiguous figure. In numerous ways, he at once embodies the supposed virtues and values of modern European society and represents the opposite of these. He upholds law and order, but distinguishes himself from the official guardians of public safety, the police; he acts independently of them. In so doing, he both endorses the liberal ideal of individual autonomy and affirms the efficacy of state regulation. He is an unmitigated individualist, operating alone but for Watson's clumsy help. He not only functions outside the ranks of the official police, he frequently one-ups them. In this respect, he represents the modern ideal of the exceptional man, who rises above the masses and takes control of destiny. Also, as I have suggested, he refuses the position of a functionary, carving out a residual space for individual agency. His representation with respect to social milieu is equivocal as well. He identifies himself as a professional consultant, and charges fees for his services. Yet he cuts the figure of an aristocrat—he is fond of being on "the hunt," following the scent of a miscreant. And though Holmes is professional and eminently practical, setting little store by knowledge that is not useful to him, he is at the same time something of an artiste—he regards his métier as an art; he is reclusive and moody; he has a taste for cocaine. While he works to expose and demystify the outré, he is himself an exotic figure who bears certain marks of cultural "Otherness."[39]

Sherlock Holmes's method reflects his ambivalent characterization. He stands both inside and outside the knowledge practices of European modernity. His location within the ambit of Enlightenment modernity is evident from the kind of knowledge he seeks, the means by which he pursues knowledge, and the way he disposes of this knowledge. He emphatically seeks only objective and useful knowledge. He maintains a careful emotional detachment toward the people he investigates, and prides himself on his dispassionateness. And he concerns himself solely with those kinds of knowledge that bear directly upon his profession—his view of knowledge is highly practical and instrumental. In his quest for enlightenment, Holmes espouses the procedures of Western science. He uses his exceptional powers of observation and deduction to construct hypotheses, which he then tests against further developments and discoveries. He combines analysis with synthesis, isolating and scrutinizing the significant elements of a puzzle from the outside, and piecing together fragments of knowledge in order to come up with a coherent picture of the whole.

Holmes insists on the effectiveness of scientific deduction. He rejects supernatural explanations out of hand in *The Hound of the Baskervilles*, in "The Adventure of the Sussex Vampire," and in "The Adventure of the Devil's Foot." He exclaims to Watson, "This agency stands flat-footed upon the ground, and there it must remain. The world is big enough for us. No ghosts need apply."[40] In this, Holmes espouses the principles of scientific positivism, and assumes that objects of knowledge are visible and can be examined. He stresses the importance of observation as a prerequisite to deduction, which then involves coming up with a theory that fits the observed facts. Holmes valorizes the notion of cold objectivity: "Detection is, or should be, an exact science and should be treated in the same cold and unemotional manner." He confirms the view that the world is objectively graspable, if studied in the proper way. Furthermore, the detective draws on the tools of modern culture, both in his quest for knowledge and in the management of this knowledge.

The stories make frequent allusions to Holmes's use of modern technology—to telegraphs and trains in particular. This technology is not merely innovative; it is revolutionary in its transforming effects on the space and time of everyday life. Holmes's reach is hugely augmented by this technology. Finally, Sherlock Holmes draws upon official, popular, and personal archives, and the knowledge he produces is recorded and stored in the form of an archive from which it can be readily retrieved and reused.[41] That is, knowledge is not fleeting; it is given a solidity and solemnity. According to Holmes, the ideal detective must possess, in addition to the power of observation and the power of deduction, concrete knowledge. Holmes is himself a storehouse of information, which he "dockets quietly and accurately in his brain." He is the human prototype of the computer, able to store and use the vast accumulation of fact that marks modern modes of governmentality.

Apart from an eclectic knowledge of botany, geology, chemistry, and anatomy, Holmes has an extensive familiarity with sensational literature. He has recourse to older forms, such as the criminal broadsides, in which crimes were made the subjects of narrative. His knowledge encompasses the "high" and the "low"—the popular and the elite. Holmes and Watson collect information; they keep an alphabetized scrapbook of old cases, bits of information, and memorabilia. They have access to official sources of information: the police, with whom he sometimes works; Lloyd's register of ships (in "The Five Orange Pips"); maps and timetables; and newspapers. He has at his disposal a vast imperial archive of encyclopedias, gazetteers, and treatises, such as Eckermann's "Voodooism and the Negroid Religions"—"expert" knowledge about alien places and peoples. In *Orientalism*, Edward Said discusses the significance of such an archive, an accumulated and ordered body of knowledge, in the project of colonial domination. Doyle is able to refer to this vast archive as a supplementary source for Holmes when the detective requires additional knowledge of the imperial world. If Holmes needs a bureaucracy and an archive, these derive their usefulness from the ability of an independent investigator to sift through vast amounts of accumulated knowledge to select what is relevant. Holmes, then, is able to master a complex modern imperial world by carefully observing clues, by piecing them together, and by manipulating a bureaucracy and archive when necessary.

Although Sherlock Holmes is often held up as a paragon of scientific method, his method, according to Carlo Ginzburg, is not that of the physical sciences. In those fields, one makes deductions about particulars on the basis of general principles that have been arrived at by establishing a relation of identity between particulars and suppressing their unique aspects. Ginzburg distinguishes this epistemological mode from what he calls the conjectural or semiotic paradigm, which entails the interpretation of clues or traces. Such knowledge is "born of experience, of the concrete and the individual." In his method, as in his person, Holmes represents the antithesis of what Adorno was later to call a "completely administered world."[42] By interpreting individual clues, which are traces of an event, generally a crime, the detective is able to come up with a unique and "total" solution.[43] This is quite different from saying, "Individuals behave in such and such a fashion; therefore, this one would have behaved thus." Indeed,

Holmes, the most famous detective in literature, dismisses the abstract physical sciences as useless to him. He knows nothing of philosophy and astronomy; he is ignorant of the Copernican theory and of the solar system. Yet he has a vast knowledge of the subjects that pertain to the interpretation of clues—of poisons, of cigar ash, of types of soil. It is this knowledge that bears upon his everyday experience. The detective draws upon his everyday experience of the concrete and the individual, and uses this knowledge to reconstruct a whole from a trace.

Holmes may be likened to what Levi-Strauss calls the bricoleur. Levi-Strauss attempts to explain mythic thinking by referring to a figure of European culture. The bricoleur, instead of imagining a whole, a structure, and then realizing it as an event, works with fragments and bric-a-brac, residual traces from an event, to fashion a new, yet not new, structure. Holmes works in similar fashion with fragments, clues, pieces of evidence to come up with a structure, the solution, which is not really new but rather is a recapitulation of the crime. He gives a traumatic and incomprehensible event meaning by rendering it narratable. By demonstrating that he can single-handedly imbue a seemingly senseless event with meaning by giving it a symbolic structure, Holmes reassures the reader that the contemporary cultural imaginary, characterized by fragmentation and flux, has a deeper, foundational meaning.

In short, while the Sherlock Holmes stories register anxiety about the possible inscrutability and unruliness of Britain's imperial territories, they also present a fictional solution to these perceived problems in the character and method of the detective. Holmes is a guarantor of stability and order. This is reflected in the nature of his career and his position in English society as an intellectual and modern man who endorses and ratifies a conservative social order. Contrary to common perception, he does so not by adhering rigidly to scientific, rational principles but by combining these principles with an instinctive, conjectural style that better equips him to contend with the variegated elements of an expanding imperial world.

UNDERCOVER IN EMPIRE

Like the detective tale, spy fiction has its lineage in the adventure story rather than the domestic novel. It too celebrates the exploits of a young male protagonist on a quest for knowledge in a world of obscurity and danger. The spy sides with the forces of order, as does the detective. However, at stake in this case is not merely the safety of persons and property, but the security of the entire political and social order. Michael Denning argues in his excellent study *Cover Stories* that spy fiction can be read as symptomatic of and as a response to "a social imperialist crisis." Denning claims that imperial romances exhausted themselves, or rather, metamorphosed into spy novels, which were more efficacious "cover stories" for a period of high imperialist capitalism. At the turn of the twentieth century, a period of intense imperial rivalry and global expansion of capital, the spy functioned as a magical figure who adroitly footed national boundaries and rendered an increasingly complex world-historical situation knowable. The spy emerged as an "agent" who could carry the national torch in a period of imperial and capitalist expansion.

Denning's discussion of the emergent spy novel suggests that the imperialist crisis in question is especially related to Germany's rapid rise at the end of the nineteenth century as an economic, industrial, and military power that poses an urgent threat to Britain's safety and imperial hegemony. This threat is personified in spy novels—Germans frequently appear, though often in unrecognizable form, as villains at the center of a nefarious plot. A compelling villain is, as Denning points out, one of the distinguishing aspects of the spy thriller. He writes, "Unlike the adventure where the hero overcomes a series of trials, or the detective story where the question is the revelation of the guilty party, the thriller is based on paranoia and conspiracy: all of these events are part of a pattern which can be traced back to an evil source, a source which must not only be revealed but also be defeated."[44] The plot of the spy story details the heroic protagonist's pursuit and defeat of this villain, and the frustration of the expansionist impulses of a European state, usually Germany. While many turn-of-the-century spy thrillers are set in Europe, the larger terrain of the Empires that are at stake in European contests for hegemony is frequently also visible. This terrain is, in novels such as Kipling's *Kim*, a site of contention and subterfuge. The threats to the British Empire are portrayed as twofold: from European competitors and from recalcitrant natives. This is hardly surprising. Lenin observed in *Imperialism, the Highest Stage of Capitalism* that this was a period when European nations were engaged in a greedy and belligerent push for colonial territories and the raw materials, cheap labor, and markets they promised. At the same time, colonized peoples were actively contesting imperial rule.

The qualities of the spy that enable him to counter imperial threats are his daring, his spontaneity, and his ability to get into the skin of others. Unlike the detective, who retroactively reconstructs events, the spy is in the very middle of them, and has to show enormous pluck in the face of danger. Because the political and physical landscape in which he operates is murky, the spy must make spontaneous decisions. This spontaneity is nerve-wracking, but it also affords the protagonist the fun of improvisation and frees him from the Enlightenment imperative of rational deliberation. At times the protagonist must make the difficult crossing to another identity. This too is risky but gratifying. The spy runs the hazard of discovery, and even of a disorientation of his own identity, but he gains the pleasure of intimately knowing the Other without the barrier of difference.

In Richard Hannay, John Buchan fashions a character who serves as an ideal agent for the British Empire. Typically, Hannay is catapulted into an adventure with only the sketchiest knowledge of a secret plot. All he knows is that the stakes are high, and involve the fate of nations. Hotly pursued and working against time to subvert a nebulous international intrigue, Hannay "exist[s] within a circuit of paranoia and vulnerability."[45] Hannay finds himself in unknown terrain and moves gropingly across it, evading his enemies, and sometimes the police and his friends as well. When he is caught, he uses his ingenuity to stage audacious escapes. In the denouement, he comes face-to-face with the enemy; his pluck and presence of mind save the day—and the country—but only barely.

Hannay's hybrid and flexible identity make him an especially adept agent. He is South African, but of Scottish ancestry, and so his identity bears an angular relationship to the metropolitan center. Yet "perhaps *because* he is a South African, he is a zealous patriot—for Britain," and the same might be said of him as a Scotsman.[46] His ability to straddle the borders of English and colonial identity makes him supple and culturally mobile—like Kipling's Kim, also a prototypical colonial spy. In addition to being part Scots and South African, Hannay knows German, "having put in three years prospecting for copper in German Damaraland."[47] Having returned from South Africa with enough money to support himself, he is able to operate as a free agent who works alongside the British government and serves it but is not employed by it; he is an independent amateur. Even when he later becomes a major in the British Army, he maintains a certain degree of autonomy. His former occupation as a mining engineer in South

Africa has not only earned him financial independence but also has given him a scientific training that proves useful when, for example, he must work with explosives. In South Africa, he has also honed his "veldcraft," that is, skill in reading and navigating across the countryside, and hiding and surviving in it. Hannay is, above all, young, fit, and quick-witted. An ordinary man, he rises to the occasion when the security of Britain and her Empire is placed in his hands.

Hannay uses his talent for impersonation and for decoding ciphers to gather the information he needs and to elude capture. In *The Thirty-Nine Steps*, he explains the principles of impersonation that he has gleaned from his occasional companion and fellow adventurer Peter Pienaar: "If a man could get into perfectly different surroundings from those in which he had first been observed, and—this is the important part—really play up to these surroundings and behave as if he had never been out of them, he would puzzle the cleverest detective on earth."[48] Pienaar scoffs at elaborate disguises, believing instead in what he calls "atmosphere." Hannay does make use of accoutrements to impersonate characters, but more often than not he does little more than exchange clothes; his success as an impersonator lies in his ability to affect the speech and the manner of his subject. Often this means taking on a working-class or rustic persona. Some characters in Buchan's novels also traverse the bounds of nationality and race. In addition to abruptly shifting shapes, Hannay has a talent for decoding ciphers, that is, for penetrating linguistic screens. Both of these abilities give him the ability to be a successful spy in the arena of Empire. In chapter 4, I look more closely at the exploits of Hannay and of the protagonist of Buchan's *Prester John*. In the next chapter, I turn to an obscure but revealing story by Conan Doyle to explore certain specific anxieties of Empire.

TWO

Imperial Intrigue in an English Country House

An imperial scene haunts what is commonly regarded as the first British detective novel, William Wilkie Collins's *The Moonstone*.[1] In this tale of intrigue, characters from India seek a priceless diamond that has been stolen from Tipu Sultan's palace by a rapacious English soldier, John Herncastle, and they threaten the peace of his descendants in their country estate in England. In Collins's novel, the quest for the Moonstone is the subject of "social detection": Collins links the circulation of imperial plunder with acts of corruption and violence within the metropole. What is presented as a family scandal has its antecedents in a shadowy and macabre imperial past.[2] With hints of a national malaise in his polyphonic narrative, Collins casts suspicion on the entirety of imperial culture, even though guilt is individualized in the figure of Godfrey Abelwhite. That Collins refrains from demonizing the Indians in the novel during the post-Mutiny period suggests that he had a much more ambivalent view of imperialism than, for example, his close friend and collaborator Charles Dickens.[3]

Collins's narrative of detection privileges the kind of scientific authority that was integral to knowledge production about the Empire.[4] In *The Moonstone*, however, India remains in the last instance irreducibly other and opaque. As Ian Duncan writes, "India bears... 'the irresistible positivity' of an alien force that breaks in and out of the domestic order, effortlessly eluding a circumscribed agency of detection.... Prehistoric and sublime, Collins's India conforms to a familiar Orientalist fantasy, except that prehistory and sublimity now fulfill their tropological potential of resistance to the colonizing, rationalizing rearrangements of a Western evolutionary history."[5] In short, not only does Collins question the ethics of imperialism by representing the rapaciousness of Englishmen vis-à-vis Indian wealth unfavorably, he imputes to India a difference that thwarts the knowledge practices of the imperial West.

In this chapter, I will examine the ways in which colonial India is fashioned as an object of knowledge and rule in British fiction of intrigue, focusing on a largely unknown story by Arthur Conan Doyle, "The Mystery of Uncle Jeremy's Household." Before turning to Doyle's story, I want to sketch briefly the ways in which *The Moonstone*, which I suggest is one source for Doyle's story, frames British rule as problematic. Doyle's story, which I discuss in greater detail, represents in effect a conservative response to the questions of knowledge and ethics that the far more critical narrative of *The Moonstone* raises.

The illicit theft of Rachel Verinder's "jewel" has frequently been interpreted as a narrative of symbolic defloration. Tamar Heller, building on this reading, argues that the subordination of women that is entailed by the logic of Victorian courtship and marriage is analogous to the loss of sovereignty by the colonized territory.[6] I want to suggest that the courtship plot is not merely analogous to the colonial plot; rather, it extends the critique of imperialism in several important ways. To recapitulate the plot of *The Moonstone* briefly, Rachel Verinder has been bequeathed the accursed gem by her uncle, who had murdered its three Indian guardians and stolen it during the siege of Seringapatam. (British troops stormed Seringapatam in Mysore in 1799, and the ruler Tipu Sultan was defeated and killed in battle.) On the night that the gem is given to her, it is stolen by her cousin and sweetheart Franklin Blake, acting in his sleep while he is under the influence of opium. Blake is propelled by a subconscious desire to protect her and the diamond from a cohort of Indian performers who have been hovering about the estate.

There are two phantasmatic imperial scenes that inform this episode: the rape of Englishwomen by Indians, which was a mainstay of post-Mutiny narratives and which, as Jenny Sharpe argues, assumed mythical proportions in the British imperial imagination, and the rescuing of brown women by white men from brown men, as Gayatri Spivak pithily puts it.[7] Rachel Verinder is the endangered Englishwoman protected by Blake from "the threat of the Indians lurking outside the house"; at the same time, her dark coloring and Punjabi-sounding last name suggest that she doubles as a figure for the Indian woman who is the proper subject of European rescue. Blake's unwitting crime, and his cousin Godfrey Abelwhite's deliberate theft of the diamond, suggest that it is Englishmen and not their Indian counterparts who are likely to behave questionably.

In fact, the story puts the integrity of the English bourgeoisie as a whole into question. As Chris GoGwilt argues, Wilkie Collins (borrowing from a painting by his godfather, Sir David Wilkie, of General Baird discovering the body of Tipu Sultan after the storming of Seringapatam) plots his novel around missing imperial loot, "which he embellishes to sensational effect as the organizing absence around which the question of English respectability takes shape." According to GoGwilt, the scandal of the Moonstone's theft throws into relief an unstable complex of cultural systems that the novel projects onto a world stage.[8] The domestic plot and the fate of the Indian jewel are separately resolved at the end of the novel: Rachel Verinder and Franklin Blake marry, and the three hereditary keepers of the Moonstone kill Godfrey Abelwhite, retrieve the gem, and restore it to the Hindu idol it once adorned. While the imperial and domestic plot are finally teased apart from each other, they have been so closely entwined throughout the novel as to leave the tainted geopolitical determinations of mid-Victorian culture an open secret.

The final scene of the novel is conveyed in a letter by Mr. Murthwaite the explorer, who describes the ritual purification of the three Brahmins before the idol on whose forehead the Moonstone now shines. India, in this narrative, is described in the register of the sacral as a completely "other" scene, inscrutable and impervious to Western rationality. Collins's novel at once employs the rationalizing detective narrative and points to the limits of this narrative in relation to the scene of Empire. Employing the theory that Foucault elaborates in *Discipline and Punish*, D. A. Miller identifies a disciplinary element in the literary economy of the novel, pointing to the ways in which surveillance operates in it.[9] Miller argues in *The Novel and the Police* that the nineteenth-century novel expresses and enacts a cultural process of "discipline," a discipline that operates through 1) surveillance, 2) a regime of the norm, and 3) technologies of the self and sexuality that constitute the subject.[10] Miller proceeds to demonstrate how this discipline is achieved, both in the structuring of the "world" of the novel and in the structure of the narrative. Foucault limits his studies to Europe, and Miller focuses even more narrowly upon the world of the nineteenth-century English novel. In considering whether the rubric of "discipline" is an appropriate one for analyzing imperial anxieties about order, one would have to question both the validity of the model itself, as well as its applicability in an imperial context. Does disciplinary power operate as Foucault describes even in a metropolitan context? What are its temporal and spatial limits beyond this context?

In fact, it is questionable whether discipline as Foucault characterizes it ever really operates in the British Empire. Even if one agrees that in Western, industrialized, democratic, post-Enlightenment societies, the power that produces docile subjects becomes relatively invisible (and this is debatable), certainly in colonized societies imperial power is manifestly and overwhelmingly writ large. David Arnold has examined institutions such as the colonial prison, and other colonial carcerals such as those for the mentally ill, and has concluded that whatever the aims of colonial administrators may have been, these institutions were far from the rationalized, efficient producers of docile bodies that Foucault found in the metropole.[11] In many of the stories of Empire that I examine, disciplinary power fails to operate: either it has broken down, or it has never gained a hold. In line with Arnold's historical conclusions, here one does not have docile, normal bodies that fit smoothly and obligingly into the productive and reproductive economy of the metropolis. Certainly, the disciplinary logic that Miller identifies does not extend to the imperial scene that is the backdrop to *The Moonstone*.

At the beginning of the novel, the frame narrative of the siege of Seringapatam depicts a scene of chaos and carnage in which an Englishman apparently carries out a murder and a theft. The final pages return us to an Indian frame, where even though Murthwaite is an observer of the scene, his presence is accidental and irrelevant to the proceedings. He is merely a witness to the existence of an alien world where time is cyclical and space is sacred: "Yes! After the lapse of eight centuries, the Moonstone looks forth once more, over the walls of the sacred city in which its story once began... So the years pass, and repeat each other; so the same events revolve in the cycles of time." This ending asserts the continued existence of an alternative rationality and temporality.

KNOWING THE DIFFERENT:
"THE MYSTERY OF UNCLE JEREMY'S HOUSEHOLD"

Arthur Conan Doyle reworked elements of *The Moonstone* so as to make the intelligibility of India and her subjects the center of a story, one that is a forerunner of the Sherlock Holmes oeuvre. During January and February of 1887, six months before he launched Sherlock Holmes's career with *A Study in Scarlet*, Doyle published a short story titled "The Mystery of Uncle Jeremy's Household." In this mystery, Doyle draws upon two of the most sensational episodes of Empire: the practice of Thuggee in India and its eradication in the 1830s, and the Indian Mutiny of 1857.[12] Conflating these historically unconnected events, he weaves a narrative of intrigue set on an English country estate, to which Thugs—cult worshippers of the Indian goddess Kali, in whose name they supposedly strangled unsuspecting travelers—have found their way after their dispossession during the Mutiny. At the crux of the plot of "The Mystery of Uncle Jeremy's Household" is the identity of Miss Warrender, an alluring and mysterious woman of Indian origin and mixed blood who has been orphaned in the Mutiny and has traveled to England to work as a governess. Doyle links the turmoil that endangers an English household with the specter of ungovernability in a distant colonial territory.[13] In making the reader privy to the protagonist's investigations, the story exhibits, in a preliminary and incomplete form, the novel ways of plotting—of shaping desire, anxiety, and intention in the narrative—that come to be characteristic of detective fiction in general and Doyle's detective fiction in particular. In "The Mystery of Uncle Jeremy's Household," as in Doyle's later stories, problems of Empire are articulated and worked through within the narrative frame of fiction of intrigue.

In fact, "Uncle Jeremy's Household" bears striking similarities to *The Moonstone* in plot, characters, and generic form. The name "Warrender" resembles the name of Collins's heroine—Rachel Verinder. The latter sounds distinctly Indian (Punjabi), "Warrender" too vaguely Anglo-Indian. Like *The Moonstone*, "Uncle Jeremy's Household" is set in a country house, and again the security of the house appears to be threatened by Indians visiting on a mysterious quasi-religious quest. As in *The Moonstone*, culpability is attributed to a corrupt Englishman, while the Indian characters merely act from a fanatic religious fervor. These Englishmen are, in each story, killed by the Indians, who disappear from the scene. While Doyle's story has an open-endedness and ambiguity that is similar to that of *The Moonstone*, the contours of character and plot not only express but also contain anxieties about the efficacy of imperial rule.

"The Mystery of Uncle Jeremy's Household" appeared in seven weekly installments of the *Boy's Own Paper*, one of the most popular boys' weeklies of its time in England and in the colonies. The paper, which began in 1879 and was published until 1967, spanned the period of the New Imperialism of the late nineteenth and early twentieth centuries, when Britain aggressively expanded her territories, as well as the era of decolonization. The paper served up an eclectic mix of fiction and miscellany in which Empire was a prominent motif. In so doing, *Boy's Own Paper* contributed to a popular knowledge of Empire different from the official knowledge disseminated in scholarly texts, government reports, encyclopedia entries, and the like. In *Propaganda and Empire*, John MacKenzie groups *Boy's Own Paper* with a number of publications for boys that celebrated Britain's imperial hegemony.[14] Primarily ephemera read by boys, they were nonetheless influential in shaping attitudes about Empire. By circulating for popular consumption adventure stories and trivia about England, its Empire, and the wider world, such publications at once entertained their young readers and invited them to be sharers in an imperial community.[15]

This invitation is extended to the readers of "Uncle Jeremy's Household" in the form of a mystery to be solved: strange characters and questionable events have disturbed the calm of a house in Yorkshire. A medical student, Lawrence, who is the narrator of the tale, is invited by his friend John H. Thurston to visit the home of Thurston's Uncle Jeremy, a kindly, eccentric writer of verse who is likely to bequeath his property to his nephew. The other members of the household are two young children adopted by Uncle Jeremy (a third sibling, Ethel, had died two months earlier in mysterious circumstances); their governess, Miss Warrender, the beautiful, moody orphan whose mother was English and whose father was an Indian chieftain; Uncle Jeremy's secretary, Copperthorne, a saturnine young man; an elderly servant; a maid; and a cook. Ostensibly engaged in preparing for his medical examinations, Lawrence becomes engrossed in studying the members of the household and making sense of their peculiar behavior.

Miss Warrender is especially intriguing. She appears to loathe Copperthorne, yet submits meekly to his domineering. Copperthorne, whose attentions to the governess are clearly unwelcome, is extremely jealous of Lawrence, believing him to have won Miss Warrender's favor. The air of mystery about Miss Warrender becomes more pronounced when a robed Indian man appears in the neighboring village of Dunkelthwaite and pays obeisance to her. Soon after, Lawrence overhears a conversation between Copperthorne and Miss Warrender, and the sinister truth is revealed: Miss Warrender is a Thug. We learn that she has already strangled the daughter of a German merchant who had adopted her in Calcutta, and has recently killed her young charge Ethel. The secretary, having surprised her in this act, has gained a hold over her. He subsequently blackmails her into agreeing to strangle Uncle Jeremy, who has made a will in Copperthorne's favor, the following night. Lawrence must act independently, for his friend Thurston has gone to London, and Lawrence has no evidence with which to approach the police. Resolving to intercede, Lawrence follows Copperthorne the next night to a prearranged meeting with Miss Warrender under an oak on the compound. There, to the narrator's horror, the mysterious Indian wayfarer, evidently also a Thug, drops upon the unsuspecting Copperthorne, strangles him, and escapes. Miss Warrender having disappeared, there is little for Lawrence to do but piece the chain of events together.

"The Mystery of Uncle Jeremy's Household" is an ur-text of the Sherlock Holmes oeuvre, revealing anxieties of Empire in Doyle's fictions of intrigue at their very inception. It prefigures these both in the outlines of its characters and in the emergence of a detective function. In this story, the detective is not a fully formed figure, but his lineaments are to be found in the character of Hugh Lawrence, the narrator of the tale. Hugh Lawrence is clearly a forerunner of Sherlock Holmes. Although he does not knowingly investigate a crime, he quickly discerns that social relations are not as transparent as they may seem. Lawrence assumes the role of a detective in seeking to reveal the true relations between characters. In this project, Lawrence is very much a lone agent, acting independently. He does not seek the help of the police; nor does he confide in his friend Thurston, who ridicules his suspicions. He relies instead on his keen powers of observation. He is clearly more perspicacious than the dull Thurston, who is a prototype of Watson. ("John H." is also Watson's first name and middle initial, and Thurston is the name of the man with whom Watson plays billiards at his club.)[16] The two friends in "The Mystery of Uncle Jeremy's Household" share the professions of their more famous analogues, though it is Lawrence who is a medical man and Thurston who is an enthusiastic chemist. Like Holmes, Lawrence professes himself indifferent to women's charms. But while Doyle is clearly sketching the outlines of the characters who would become his most famous creations, he is also depicting imperial motifs and problems that he would incorporate repeatedly in his detective fiction. The plot of "Uncle Jeremy's Household," in which a mystery or a crime in England has roots in the extra-national space of Empire, anticipates those of roughly a dozen Sherlock Holmes stories.

In the Holmes stories, characters like Miss Warrender who return to England from the colonies are suspect for a number of reasons.

Some have ambiguous identities and uncertain loyalties. Others have become renegades and pose a threat to law and order in England. In "Uncle Jeremy's Household," the narrative of Miss Warrender's return to her mother's country signals two sets of cultural anxieties. One pertains to the relation between the colony and the metropolis. In this story, the colonial expatriate has become estranged from the mother country. Miss Warrender is a misfit—she has been displaced from her Indian milieu, yet is out of her element in England. She complains about the poverty of the flora in Dunkelthwaite, saying that she has been accustomed to "something better" in India. Miss Warrender's cultural oddness—manifest in her strange taste in music and decoration—is harmless enough. However, the Anglo-Indian governess's "ungovernability" is more threatening to the peace and security of Uncle Jeremy's household. Miss Warrender has the accoutrements of civilization, but she remains incorrigibly and dangerously "savage."[17] The story obliquely suggests that imperial territories are irrevocably alien and ungovernable—Empire produces unruly hybrid subjects, who present a veneer of civilization, but are impervious to the influence of education.[18]

A second, more submerged set of anxieties about the material effects of colonialism can also be detected in the story. In addition to being a cultural misfit, Miss Warrender is an imperial lumpenproletarian, that is, a socially and economically marginal colonial. The figure of the indigent returned colonial recurs in Doyle's fiction. More often than not, he is not a heroic "Empire boy" who is embraced upon his return with open arms. Rather, he is a poor white: marginal, impoverished, and footloose. This figure is the antithesis of the successful colonial and gives the lie to the fantasy of imperial adventure. His return to England is problematic in different ways in the stories.

In "Uncle Jeremy's Household," the Indian Mutiny of 1857 constitutes the historical background to the figure of the poor white. The English faction has killed Miss Warrender's father during the Mutiny and she has consequently been left destitute. She has eventually found her way to England by way of Germany, in search of employment. The story suggests that Empire gives rise to economic outcasts whose place in India is unsure but who cannot successfully be absorbed into English society. Doyle also points with some anxiety to the phenomenon of transnational migration, here seen not only in the figure of the imported Indian governess but also in the appearance of an exotically clad Indian man out of nowhere, and his continued presence in the environs of Dunkelthwaite. Lawrence appears to have no power over these comings and goings.

A character such as Miss Warrender would have had real-life counterparts in the expatriate colonials who for one reason or another could be found at "the heart of the Empire," to borrow from the title of Antoinette Burton's book on the experience of Indians in late Victorian England. As Burton suggests, "either because they were part of permanent communities with long histories and traditions in the British Isles, or because they were travelers or temporary residents in various metropoles and regions throughout the United Kingdom, a variety of colonial 'Others' circulated at the very heart of the British Empire before the twentieth century."[19] Rozina Visram, in *Ayahs, Lascars and Princes*, discusses the presence of Indians in England. Indian servants engaged for the voyage from India to England were often discharged in England and given no return passage. A lodging house was set up in Hackney specifically for such destitute Ayahs, sheltering as many as eighty at a time.[20]

The character of the Anglo-Indian governess is noteworthy not so much because Miss Warrender's presence in England, if improbable, does have historical antecedents, but because her fanciful representation engages a number of colonial discourses. In several of Doyle's detective stories, characters turn out to have a problematic colonial past. They have returned to the metropolis, but have not been fully reassimilated. Sometimes sinister, sometimes merely unfortunate, these characters bring intrigue and danger to England. There they become pivotal figures in a developing mystery, the solution of which involves the revelation of past events in the colony.

Return from the colonies was utterly unremarkable throughout the Victorian period. Thus the representations of return that one finds in the Sherlock Holmes stories cannot be read as corresponding directly to actual anxieties about the character of returned colonials. Rather, their misadventures symbolize certain apprehensions about the relationship between the colonies and England, and about the nature of colonial culture.

THE MYSTERY OF MISS WARRENDER'S IDENTITY

"The Mystery of Uncle Jeremy's Household" gives more importance to characterizing Miss Warrender's difference than to pinning down her guilt. In this respect, the logic of the story is different from what would come to be the classic detective story, where one has a crime or wrongdoing, and a culprit whose guilt is exposed and who is apprehended and punished. In "Uncle Jeremy's Household," one has neither a full-fledged story of a crime nor a full-fledged story of its investigation, the dual narrative threads that Todorov identifies as typical of classic detective fiction.[21] Although a crime has taken place in Dunkelthwaite, we don't learn of Miss Warrender's ritual killing of her charge until the conclusion, as an addendum to the central problem posed by the story: the question of Miss Warrender's identity. Lawrence asks "who is she" and not "who dunnit."

That the narrative of "Uncle Jeremy's Household" defers the question of guilt, one might argue, follows precisely from a discourse of difference: if Miss Warrender is so very alien, she is not a full member of the ethical community, and hence she is not "guilty" in the full sense of the word. In any case, the mystery that overtly concerns the narrator and the reader is not that of Miss Warrender's identity as a murderess but as an Anglo-Indian woman. Thurston introduces Miss Warrender at the outset as a character inviting illumination. Her very name is unknown. She is called "Warrender" (and the echo of "wanderer" is telling) after her English mother, but we are left to understand that this is a name given to her by her English companions. She herself cites her patronym at one point in the story. The questions perplex the narrative: Who is Miss Warrender? What is her true name? Is she more English or Indian? Is she merely colorful, or is she dangerous? What is her true relation to Copperthorne? What is her relation to her past?

Thurston and Lawrence treat Miss Warrender explicitly as an object of ethnological study as they attempt to answer these questions. When he invites his friend to Dunkelthwaite, John Thurston tells Lawrence, "By the way, I mentioned the brunettish governess to you. I might throw her out as a bait to you if you retain your taste for ethnological studies." At issue in the story's characterization of Miss Warrender is the status of alterity. While they attempt to understand Miss Warrender's strangeness in terms of oppositions that underpin earlier discourses of alterity—oppositions between animal and human, Christian and Barbarian, and reasonable and irrational—the story folds these residual modes of making sense of the Other into an emergent ethnological discourse.[22]

When I use "Other," I do not want to invoke a transcendental discourse of difference, but rather suggest that within the story, difference is reified through the prism of "ethnological studies." Ethnology emerges in nineteenth-century Europe as "the science which treats of races and peoples, and of their relations to one another, their distinctive physical characteristics, etc."[23] E. B. Tyler, credited with establishing British anthropology as a field, began his influential book *Primitive Culture* thus: "Culture or Civilization, taken in its wide ethnographic sense, is that complex whole which includes knowledge, belief, art, morals, law, custom, and any other capabilities and habits acquired by man as a member of society."[24] Tyler insisted that culture develops in a uniform way because of the uniform workings of the human mind, and he thus argued against essential racial differences. But he, like other scholars, saw cultures as distinct, various, and static entities that transcended the flux of politics and history, and that were properly the object of scientific knowledge. In the discourse of ethnography, individuals "naturally" manifest the traits of their cultures. Tyler's views notwithstanding, one finds in nineteenth-century texts the perception that people from the non-Western world do not merely lack civilization, or manifest debased or incomplete versions of it; rather, Europeans perceive other peoples as radically and essentially different during this period. At the level of culture, this shift is indicated by a change from the metropolitan view that culture was universal and could be acquired with more or less success by all, to the perception of absolute cultural difference and the emergence of geopolitics as a way of negotiating this difference.[25]

In their characterizations of cultural difference, Doyle and Tyler draw on the terms of an emergent social science: anthropology. The terms *ethnology, ethnography,* and *anthropology* are worth defining here. The *Oxford English Dictionary* defines *anthropology* as "the science of man, or of mankind, in the widest sense." As such, anthropology would encompass ethnology and ethnography, which an 1878 entry in the *OED* distinguishes in the following way: "Ethnography embraces the descriptive details, and ethnology the rational exposition, of the human aggregates and organizations." Clearly the terms overlap; it is telling that Doyle invokes the discourse of ethnology, however, in that this is more concerned with establishing differential relationships between, as opposed to descriptive accounts of, different groups of people.

Thurston and Lawrence demonstrate the workings of ethnological discourse when they repeatedly attempt to "read" Miss Warrender by noting her habits, tastes, linguistic abilities, and religious beliefs.

They first attempt to ascertain Miss Warrender's identity by speculating about her religion and her language:

> "She must have been quite a woman before she left her tribe," I said. "What view of religion does she take? Does she side with her father or mother?"
>
> "We never press the question," my friend answered. "Between ourselves don't think she's very orthodox. Her mother must have been a good woman, and besides teaching her English, she is a good French scholar, and plays remarkably well."[26]

While the story introduces the theme of miscegenation to pose this question of identity, it posits the two identities, English and Indian, as mutually exclusive. This is in keeping with the ethnological perspective. Though Miss Warrender has one Indian parent and one English parent, she is perceived in an ethnically absolute way—her companions assume she must be either entirely English or entirely Indian, though they are not sure which. That Thurston is inclined to regard the governess as English, like her mother, is betrayed by his faulty syntax: there is a slippage in the subject of the last sentence from mother to daughter. However, his response is ambiguous—he does not clarify what he means by "orthodox," and admits that the question of Miss Warrender's filiation is never pursued directly. Instead, her identity becomes the subject of speculation and interpretation.

When language doesn't suffice as a way of determining her views ("We never press the question"), they look for aural and visual clues to her identity. For example, Lawrence narrates how, on the evening of his arrival, he and Thurston hear the sound of the piano:

> At first the player struck a few isolated notes, as though uncertain how to proceed. Then came a series of clanging chords and jarring discords, until out of the chaos there suddenly swelled a strange barbaric march, with blare of trumpet and crash of symbol. Louder and louder it pealed forth in a gust of wild melody, and then died away once more into the jerky chords which had preceded it....
>
> "She does that every night," my friend remarked; I suppose it is some Indian reminiscence. Picturesque, don't you think so?" (pp. 47–48)

Two aspects of this passage are striking: its Orientalism, both in the register of the "barbaric" and the "picturesque," and its ethnological overtones. The governess's music, described in words that connote a threatening savagery, is clearly taken as a signifier of her character, which is at best "uncertain" and at worst "wild" and "barbaric." In producing such "jarring" and "jerky" sounds, Miss Warrender disturbs the staid tranquility of an English household. At the same time, though Lawrence and Thurston have reservations about Miss Warrender's "strange" and "discordant" character, they use readily available narrative codes of the "exotic" and the "picturesque" to identify it as curious rather than menacing. The passage also implies that Miss Warrender is not merely an idiosyncratic individual, but rather, that she gives voice to a group identity, and a martial one at that: "a few isolated notes" and "a series of clanging chords and jarring discords" give way to a "strange barbaric march." Romantic chaos is transformed into military order—the order of her father and her "barbaric" people. The narrator implicitly characterizes her behavior as a moment of identification with her ethnos or people.

Lawrence studies her habitat with the same ethnological interest that he applies to her music.

> She had a thousand little knick-knacks there which showed that she had come well-laden from her native land. Her Oriental love for bright colours had exhibited itself in an amusing fashion. She had gone down to the market town and bought numerous sheets of pink and blue paper, and these she had pinned in patches over the sombre covering which had lined the walls before. She had some tinsel too, which she had put up in the most conspicuous places. The whole effect was ludicrously tawdry and glaring, and yet there seemed to me to be a touch of pathos in this attempt to reproduce the brilliance of the tropics in the cold English dwelling-house. (pp. 54–55)

Once again the governess's essential "Oriental" nature, signaled by her love for bright colors, irrepressibly surfaces in and transforms her English environs. Miss Warrender's decorations, patches, knickknacks, and bits of tinsel are the stuff of bricolage. They suggest that her subjectivity is fragmentary, temporary, and incompletely transformed to fit her new circumstances. Again, like her uncertain notes, her patchwork decorations betray a hesitancy in her attempts to transform her new home into a familiar and comforting space. Yet rather than represent this process as one of a hybridization and fusion of different elements, born of the contingencies of displacement, Doyle portrays her efforts as a misguided attempt to import a lesser culture, one that is "tinsel": shiny but insubstantial. "Tinsel" suggests a hysterical subjectivity, marked by a surplus of emotion. Miss Warrender is not only "different," she is potentially unstable.

As the narrative proceeds, metaphors from the natural world predominate in descriptions of Miss Warrender. At first Lawrence regards her as a harmless if interesting "specimen," but he soon notes a more sinister aspect to her "oriental" behavior. He has an intimation of her "savage" nature when, in the course of a walk, she suddenly stalks a rabbit and maims it: "For my part I could not blame her much. It was evidently an outbreak of the old predatory instinct of the savage, though with a somewhat incongruous effect in the case of a fashionably dressed young lady on an English high road." While she is graceful and lithe, demurely dressed, and well spoken, she also has "predatory," feral impulses. Lawrence is perturbed by the violence of her act and the contradiction it reveals in her person. On another occasion, she startles Lawrence with a passionate outburst:

> She leaned forward until I seemed to feel the quick pants of her warm breath upon my face.
>
> "Kill Copperthorne," she said. "That is what I should say to him [a hypothetical suitor]. Kill Copperthorne. Then you can come and talk of love to me."
>
> Nothing can describe the intensity of fierceness with which she hissed those words out from between her white teeth.
>
> She looked so venomous as she spoke that I involuntarily shrank away from her. Could this pythoness be the demure young lady who sat every day so primly and quietly at the table of Uncle Jeremy? (p. 59)

The terms "fierceness," "hissed," "venomous," and "pythoness" connote an animality that is disconcerting in a "demure young lady." Miss Warrender's words are framed as an amatory challenge, and Lawrence expresses a sensual awareness of her body—her "quick pants of warm breath" and her "white teeth." The description of Miss Warrender as a dangerous feral creature is typical of characterizations of the villainess in Victorian fiction. Yet the terms and tone used to represent her emphasize not a malignant disposition but a strangeness that stems from her colonial antecedents. Miss Warrender's forthright appeal to Lawrence to kill Copperthorne is the outburst of a cornered creature acting in self-defense and not the deliberate machination of the archetypal villainess. Although he falls back upon the most hackneyed tropes—here, the native as animal—one can see Lawrence grasping for different ways to characterize Miss Warrender's difference in the above passages. While on the one hand Miss Warrender is characterized as wild rather than wily, on the other the description of her as a "venomous," sibilant "pythoness" calls to mind the biblical image of the serpent in the garden of Eden. Like the serpent, Miss Warrender precipitates a fall into knowledge—the knowledge of alterity and difference. Her presence in Uncle Jeremy's household sets off an attempt on the part of the narrator and the other English characters to classify, order, and control her. Her danger lies in her seductiveness; like the snake charmers of Orientalist representations of India, the English characters try to tame and defang her. The figure of the serpent links the theme of sexuality and knowledge. Given an Orientalist frame, the figure foregrounds the question of how the colonizer may know and rule the colonial subject and at the same time contend with her dangerous attraction.

In this regard, the story is like other fiction of intrigue that introduces to the imperial landscape colonial subjects who are "unruly" and must be better understood and educated if they are to be effectively governed. Writers of such fiction place at the center of their stories the project of "knowing" the colonial subject—of grasping her body, mind, and soul with the apparatuses of Western knowledge production—so as to further orderly government. Foucault uses the term "governmentality" to characterize the practices of government in the modern era and the processes of reasoning that accompany these practices.[27] Foucault focuses on modern, liberal European governmentality whereby a complex of knowledges and practices develops at once to produce disciplined and productive individuals and to manage and care for populations. David Scott, looking beyond Europe, argues that in order theoretically to reinvigorate politics in the postcolonial era, it is necessary to better understand colonial governmentality.[28] Scott contends that scholars of colonial cultures have tended to focus on the attitude of colonizers toward the colonized. By focusing on governmentality, he shifts the discussion to how the colonized are subjected to a series of rationalities and practices. He explores "the targets of colonial power (the point or points of power's application; the object or objects it aims at; and the means and instrumentalities it deploys in search of these targets, point and objects) and the field of its operation (the zone that it actively constructs for its functionality)" (p. 25). He asks, "what in each instance is colonial power's *structure* and *project* as it inserts itself into—or more properly, as it *constitutes*—the domain of the colonial?" (p. 31). Drawing on Foucault's insights about the productive nature of power and its shaping of knowledge, Scott proposes to historicize modes of colonial power and specify their relationship to modern power.

The dialogic relationship between knowledge and rule is at the very heart of anthropology, at least as it was when it originated. The discipline as it developed in nineteenth-century Europe was intimately connected to the exercise of colonial rule, as Talal Asad, in his book *Colonial Encounters,* was one of the first scholars to point out.[29] As Peter Pels puts it,

> Anthropology... needs to be conceptualized in terms of governmentality, as an academic offshoot of a set of universalist technologies of domination—a Statistik or "state-craft" at least partly based on ethnography—that developed in a dialectic between colonial and European states. These forms of identification, registration, and discipline emerged in tension and tandem with technologies of self-control that fostered notions of cleanliness, domesticity, ethnicity, and civilization. Anthropology, in negotiating ethnic, civilized, and savage identities, was at the juncture of these technologies of domination and self-control.[30]

In a collection of essays exploring "the practical history of anthropology," Pels and other anthropologists detail the production of knowledge about a whole host of "types" of Indians under the emergent rubric of ethnology in the context of colonial rule in India.[31] They emphasize that "colonial administrations often tribalized and ethnicized a field of fluid and multilayered ethnic interrelations into a mosaic of discrete, static, and singular identities," and oversaw "the legal fixing of social practices."[32] Authors of imperial fiction of intrigue, such as Doyle, Collins, and Kipling, engage explicitly with the field of anthropology and so include in their stories explorers, anthropologists, and ethnographic surveys. The nexus between anthropology and the rationality of government is not merely a theme in their stories; the underlying problem to be "solved" is that of colonial governmentality, that is, of rendering colonized people into objects of knowledge and subjects of domination.[33]

In its representation of the Anglo-Indian governess Miss Warrender, "The Mystery of Uncle Jeremy's Household" foregrounds this concern with how colonial power should be exercised and what its object should be. The etymological link between *governess* and *governmentality* speaks precisely to the continuity between knowledge production, education, and mentalities of government. Like many repatriated colonials in Doyle's stories, Miss Warrender is from the outset presented as an outlandish figure who does not quite fit in.[34] Though she speaks English perfectly and occupies a conventional role as a governess to the children of an English household, she betrays uncontrollable instincts and antipathies that are out of character in a respectable young woman in England.

Characters from the colony—and more specifically, from India—are putative subjects of colonial governmentality, subjects who must be apprehended, domesticated, educated, and administered by colonial regimes. Fiction of intrigue expresses considerable anxiety about the possible ungovernability of colonial subjects. As we have seen, Doyle constitutes the conduct and identity of the colonial subject as a problem to be solved. The narrative form of fiction of intrigue frames this problem of the colonial subject as at the same time a problem of law and order. In fiction of intrigue, epistemological order and political order are restored at one and the same time. Fiction of intrigue, insofar as it naturalizes a process of ordering, operates like governmentality; it veers away from an acknowledgment of politics.

Foucault suggests that what is distinctive about governmental power is its focus on the rational management of populations and its self-representation as a technical exercise rather than one of force. Fiction of intrigue depoliticizes problems of government—it makes the maintenance of law and order a question of administration, not politics. While governmentality pertains to the management of populations, biopolitics addresses their reproduction. The story yokes together these two imperatives. Miss Warrender is doubly marked as transgressive of the codes of salubrious desire: she is the daughter of a cross-racial union; and she unsettles the libidinal economy of Uncle Jeremy's household. Her power derives from her affective qualities—she herself is "ungovernably" passionate, and she stirs up her companions' passions. As Ann Stoler argues in *Race and the Education of Desire*, the discourses of sexuality and race were intimately linked and mutually constitutive in modern, imperial Europe.[35] If colonial governmentality constitutes a rational attempt to shape conduct, then this attempt necessarily involves intimate knowledge of colonial subjects, both rulers and ruled, and the proper education of their desire.

Colonial anthropology emerged during the nineteenth century as a field of discourse about the native subject precisely so that she might be better known and ruled. Doyle alerts the reader to this discourse at an ekphrastic moment when Miss Warrender peruses a book of portraits of Indian characters. Taken from Uncle Jeremy's library, which is "particularly rich in books of this class," such a book had real-life counterparts in the ethnographic surveys that were a burgeoning genre in the nineteenth century.[36] Often written by civil servants of the British government who were directly involved in the administration of its Indian subjects, these texts bring together visual representations and ethnographic "facts" about the peoples of India. One of the most ambitious and well known of these surveys, *Castes and Tribes of Southern India*, was written by Edgar Thurston.[37] That Doyle names his character John Thurston suggests a familiarity with this work. The book on the peoples of India, a collection of labeled types, brings images of natives into an English drawing room, making them at once exotic and familiar. In a similar vein, Lawrence cites the writing of Philip Meadows Taylor, presumably referring to his extremely popular fictional narrative *Confessions of a Thug*, as an authoritative account of the practice and significance of Thuggee, to make his own representation convincing.

These allusions in Doyle's short story to ethnography and to sensational accounts of native customs represent a broad attempt to rationalize colonial difference, by which I mean a discourse of difference produced in the context of colonialism. If, as Foucault notes, in Europe during the nineteenth century difference comes to be understood as deviation from a norm, in the colonies, alongside a norm that only pertains to the Europeans in the colonies, one has a proliferation of difference and an attempt at its ordering. I want to turn to the project that accompanies this mapping of difference: that of administering the colonial subject.

GOVERNING MISS WARRENDER

At stake in the ethnological study of Miss Warrender's identity is the matter of how to exercise colonial power most effectively. As Pels points out (and many others have as well), technologies of domination developed in a dialogic relationship with anthropological ways of imagining difference in the colonial context. "The Mystery of Uncle Jeremy's Household" elaborates Miss Warrender's difference with a glance toward the forms of colonial governmentality that may be appropriate for unruly colonial subjects.

Miss Warrender's role as a governess underscores the story's concern with tutelage—it is her responsibility to impart learning and culture to her charges. As we have seen, Lawrence begins to doubt her fitness for her job when she mixes exotic and frightening Indian stories with her French lessons, and maims a rabbit. If Miss Warrender is an unsuitable governess, it is because she herself lacks a proper education, and the circumstances of her employment do little to provide her with proper training. Nor is another member of the household up to the task of domestic governance. Uncle Jeremy has renounced all responsibility for the management of his home. In the absence of a forceful patriarch, an interloper is able to threaten the integrity of the estate. Lawrence discovers that

> the real master of Dunkelthwaite was not Uncle Jeremy, but Uncle Jeremy's amanuensis.... He managed his money matters and the affairs of the house unquestioned and uncontrolled. He had sense enough, however, to exert his authority so lightly that it galled no one's neck, and therefore excited no opposition. My friend, busy with his distillations and analyses, was never allowed to realize that he was really a nonentity in the establishment.

Uncle Jeremy has relinquished his patriarchal functions entirely to his secretary, while Thurston, Uncle Jeremy's heir, is so preoccupied with the pursuit of scientific knowledge that he neglects to analyze the more worldly matter of domestic relations and fails to perceive any threat to his position. Indeed, Thurston is absent from Dunkelthwaite at the critical moment when Copperthorne plans to make his move. In other words, Copperthorne is able to exert the influence he does because the proper patriarchal figures are overly ready to cede authority and power.

The absence of a legitimate and proper mother who might govern the domestic sphere is equally striking. The only mother who is mentioned at all in the story is Miss Warrender's, and she is a shadowy figure whose fate is never made known. In any case, she is hardly a model of English motherhood; she has married an Indian chieftain and settled in India. In Uncle Jeremy's strange household, Miss Warrender most closely approximates the character of a mother. She is the sole woman in the house after the maid and cook give notice, and she has the care of the children. However, she is a monstrous mother, having killed one of her charges. Rather than being the angel of the hearth who creates a warm and safe shelter from the demands and dangers of the outside world, Miss Warrender threatens the very lives of her surrogate family. She is not the patriarchally oppressed Indian woman characterized in colonial discourse as requiring rescue and protection from Indian men. Instead, she is domineered over by an autocratic Englishman, from whose yoke an Indian man frees her.

Doyle assigns Miss Warrender the capacity to disrupt considerably the domestic relations in Uncle Jeremy's household. A player in a bizarre family plot, her own status within such a household is peculiar and contradictory: she is a princess but a governess; a surrogate mother who has killed the child in her charge; and the unhappy recipient of Copperthorne's attentions, which she is blackmailed into putting up with. The story also emphasizes the problematic desirability of an "Oriental" woman. Thurston is eager to detect a prurient element in Lawrence's interest in the governess, while Lawrence is convinced that Copperthorne is enamored of her. The phrases used to describe Miss Warrender—"stylish-looking brunette," "beautiful litheness of figure," "feline grace"—emphasize her feminine allure.

In short, Miss Warrender is an unruly and dangerous character at the center of the libidinal economy of Uncle Jeremy's household. She is powerful and disturbing because of her affective qualities. She is unable to govern her murderous instincts and passions; she also has an unsettling effect on her companions, who are distracted from their work, if not driven to extreme jealousy. The nature of her identifications and drives suggests that her desires have been improperly channeled. She is a phallic daughter in that she identifies with her father, taking pride in the fact that she is one of the few women to have been inducted into Thuggee. She is literally a femme fatale, engineering the murder of her unsuccessful suitor, Copperthorne. And she is a murderous mother.

The terms in which her depravity is characterized are significant. She does not undertake to strangle Ethel in a deliberate and calculated fashion, but rather is possessed by an irresistible urge to perform a ritual sacrifice. Thus her behavior is not described as a criminal breach of English law, as murder is usually represented in fiction of intrigue, but instead as an irrational submission to another law, the law of her father. Her aversion to Copperthorne is similarly visceral—she urges potential suitors to kill the secretary. Miss Warrender is not the demurely affectionate subject of Victorian domestic fiction—her fervor is for the public (but secret) vocation of Thuggee. The story suggests that

Empire can influence the prototypical family romance in problematic ways, producing aberrant desires and dangerously impelled subjects.

In "The Mystery of Uncle Jeremy's Household," the Indian Mutiny of 1857 forms the historical background to the figure of the poor white. Insurgency was particularly troubling to the imperial imaginary because it led the regime to doubt its own hegemony. The Indian Mutiny is deemed to have far-flung repercussions in this story. Curiously, Doyle telescopes two historically distinct occurrences: Thuggee, which was supposedly suppressed in the 1830s, and the Mutiny of 1857. This narrative yoking together of Thuggee and the Mutiny can be explained by the fact that both loomed large in the popular imagination and hence made obvious subject matter for a sensational story. While the intertwining of a story of Thuggee with a narrative of the Mutiny is, then, not altogether surprising, it is worth considering in some detail because it imparts a curious logic to the story. Doyle gives the Indian Mutiny a crucial place in Miss Warrender's history:

> She is the child of an Indian chieftain, whose wife was an Englishwoman. He was killed in the mutiny, fighting against us, and, his estates being seized by the government, his daughter, then fifteen, was left almost destitute. Some charitable German merchant in Calcutta adopted her, it seems, and brought her over to Europe with him together with his own daughter. The latter died, and then Miss Warrender—as we call her, after her mother—answered uncle's advertisement; and here she is. (p. 43)

> ...Her father was Achmet Genghis Khan, a semi-independent chieftain somewhere in the Central Provinces. He was a bit of a heathen fanatic in spite of his Christian wife, and he became chummy with the Nana, and mixed himself up in the Cawnpore business so Government came down heavily on him. (p. 47)

Thurston explains Miss Warrender's presence in England by reference to one of the most notorious events in the history of British imperialism: the grisly massacre of English women and children at Kanpur. Doyle does not even have to reiterate the details of the "Cawnpore business." He can assume that official knowledge of the Mutiny has been so widely disseminated that this hackneyed allusion conveys in full the much-publicized horror and barbarity of the episode. Invoked again and again in journalistic accounts and in fiction, the Kanpur massacre was an event that came to define the Mutiny in the minds of English people.[38]

Yet while this official knowledge is taken for granted, Miss Warrender's own history is provided as a supplement. The government's reprisals against Achmet Genghis Khan have caused her destitution, and have led to her presence in England. The Mutiny in general, and the Kanpur massacre in particular, serve Doyle as historical clichés that convey Miss Warrender's barbaric "Indianness" to his readers. However, this allusion in a narrative of return to what was undoubtedly a historical trauma is suggestive also as a fictional gloss on, or supplement to, official knowledge of the Mutiny. Miss Warrender's displacement as a consequence of the Mutiny and her problematic "return" to an English household suggests that the conflagration has left a residual anxiety that continues to manifest itself in literature even when the "truth" of the Mutiny, signified by the Kanpur massacre, has been firmly established in historical accounts and documents.

In making Miss Warrender's destitution and return the direct consequence of British reprisals, Doyle implicitly acknowledges the effects of imperial violence. Of course, he sees this violence as justified; the story is far from being a moral indictment of the brutality with which the mutineers were suppressed. Yet Miss Warrender's return suggests that the narrative of "crime and punishment" does not sufficiently describe the Mutiny and its aftermath. In this story, it could be that Miss Warrender is on a mission of revenge, and that as the daughter of an insurgent she carries his banner. Here, as elsewhere, Doyle's fiction is haunted by a narrative as well as by a historical possibility that he implicitly writes against. By introducing the motif of Thuggee to the plot, and discursively yoking it to an historically disconnected occurrence, the Mutiny, Doyle overlays an apparent narrative of subaltern revenge with one of unreasoning zeal. Miss Warrender does not seek to revenge her father's death and her own dispossession. In fact, she explicitly affirms her debt to her English employer and is reluctant to participate in his murder. Rather, her violent propensities can be explained solely in relation to her induction into Thuggee. She is a savage fanatic, driven by uncontrollable and irrational impulses to kill her charges. When identified as a Thug, the princess Achmet Genghis Khan is represented as someone whose position is "beyond the pale," to borrow a colonial metaphor from Ireland. Her condition as a Thug is described as so abject that her later immiseration is portrayed as a rescue from barbarism rather than as a consequence of British imperial policy. The interjection of a discourse of Thuggee into the story serves to screen and displace the possibility that Miss Warrender's actions are a form of political retribution or that they result from economic dispossession. The logic of the narrative simultaneously acknowledges and effaces the possibility that Miss Warrender is both an insurgent and an imperial lumpenproletarian.

One can see both narrative strategies as typical of what I will call fiction of counterinsurgency, after Ranajit Guha.[39] In such writing, the political moment of insurgency as an expression of the insurgent's will is denied. By identifying the mutineering Achmet Genghis Khan as a Thug, Doyle characterizes the mutineers as fanatics:

> The Thugs! I had heard of the wild fanatics of that name who are found in the central part of India, and whose distorted religion represents murder as being the highest and purest of all the gifts which a mortal can offer to the Creator. I remember an account of them which I had read in the works of Colonel Meadows Taylor, of their secrecy, of their organisation, their relentlessness, and the terrible power which their homicidal craze has over every other mental or moral faculty. (p. 71)

Thuggee is imputed to this rebel, whose actions are dictated by a "homicidal craze" rather than a "mental or moral faculty." By describing his acts as those of a murderous fanatic, Doyle denies their political significance. The attributes that might make an insurgent movement formidable—"secrecy, organization, relentlessness"—are attributed to the followers of a "distorted religion," followers who are homicidal fanatics. Misgivings about the motives and meanings of the Mutiny are rhetorically displaced onto Thuggee.

In stories such as "Uncle Jeremy's Household," insurgencies are depicted as moments of political crisis when certain contradictions and tensions of Empire become acute. Such narratives present occasions to investigate these tensions and explore the anxieties about Empire to which they give rise. Early counterinsurgency theory developed at the end of the nineteenth century with the expansion of colonial empires. The narratives I examine are far removed from the treatises that expound such theory, but they do represent insurgency in ways that delegitimize its political aims and render its threats moot. In this way, fictions of counterinsurgency not only express but also allay anxieties of Empire.

DETECTIVE FICTION AND EMPIRE:
"THE MYSTERY OF UNCLE JEREMY'S HOUSEHOLD"

I have so far discussed figures and problems in "The Mystery of Uncle Jeremy's Household" that point to specific anxieties about the governability of subjects of the British Empire. I want to turn briefly to the question of how, as a narrative, the story exemplifies the way fiction of intrigue deals with such anxieties.[40] This story is particularly appropriate for beginning our investigation precisely because it is not at all as well knit as Doyle's later detective stories. In this story one can clearly discern Doyle's attempts to grapple with questions of narrative, plot, and character, questions to which his elegant later stories provide more seamless solutions.

In detective fiction, one has two narratives: the story of a crime or mystery, and that of its solution. Typically, the detective story focuses its narrative upon the latter—it recounts the investigation and solution of a crime. This investigation enables one to reconstruct the former—the mysterious events in question. In the longer, novella-length Sherlock Holmes stories, especially the early ones, *A Study In Scarlet* and *The Sign of Four*, the story of the crime is presented as a separate narrative.[41] This narrative is set outside the detective's milieu, in fact outside England—in Utah, or in India, for example. This awkward structure suggests that the "outré," to borrow from Doyle's lexicon, is literally extraneous and cannot be smoothly incorporated into the world of Doyle's central protagonists. As I have suggested, these stories displace the problematic of guilt onto other English characters—characters who are truly Other cannot be guilty in a profound sense. Events in India are treated in this way in *The Sign of Four*.

At the same time, these stories show an attempt to master the imperial world by knowing it. In the shorter Sherlock Holmes stories, the imperial world also provides material for Holmes's investigations, but the imperial subtext is integrated into and subsumed within the detective narrative. "The Mystery of Uncle Jeremy's Household," for example, has a number of stories and sources: Miss Warrender's tales of India; ethnological accounts of Indian natives; a letter from "a man of encyclopedic knowledge, and particularly well versed in Indian manners and customs." Also, while Lawrence, the prototypical sleuth, is the primary narrator, Doyle points to the existence of a multiplicity of storytellers. John Thurston writes letters to his friend about the members of the household; Uncle Jeremy offers poetic effusions about

Yorkshire; and Miss Warrender enchants her charges with fanciful stories of India. However, these accounts do not stand by themselves, but rather are selected and ordered by Lawrence into a coherent and intelligible explanation for the mysterious events in Uncle Jeremy's household. The "outré" is subjected to the analytical abilities of the sleuth and is subordinated to the logic of the narrative.

Lawrence, a medical student and astute observer, has the role of objective, rational chronicler. This elevation of the role of the dispassionate, perspicacious scientific interlocutor is, of course, a familiar aspect of the Sherlock Holmes stories. It is noteworthy in this discussion, however, because it is one of the ways in which fiction of intrigue manages and allays anxieties of Empire. From the outset, the narrator, Lawrence, is emphatic that he wants not to tell an anecdote, but to offer a written statement of the facts. He insists that though his story is admittedly "strange," it has not been embellished in any way: "I have little more to add to this strange tale of mine. If I have been somewhat long-winded in the telling of it, I feel I owe no apology for that, for I have simply set the successive events down in a plain unvarnished fashion, and the narrative would be incomplete without any one of them." The story has elements of gothic, from the wildness of the terrain and the remoteness of the country house to the odd characters that inhabit it. However, the emphasis on rational explanation for seemingly weird happenings, and the use of letters, reported speech, encyclopedic entries, and documents, give the narrative a prosaic air. Lawrence contends with the alien and outlandish by unearthing and ordering strange happenings into a coherent and lucid account of the facts of the case.

The mystery of Miss Warrender's identity is "solved" when Lawrence chances upon Copperthorne and Miss Warrender and overhears that she is a Thug; at this point he gives her what he deems her "proper" name: "And now I am coming to that part of this statement of mine which describes how I first gained an insight into the relation which existed between those two strange mortals, and learned the terrible truth about Miss Warrender, or the Princess Achmet Genghis, as I would prefer to call her, for assuredly she was the descendant of the fierce fanatical warrior rather than of her gentle mother"(p. 66). In renaming her as he does with the name of her father, Lawrence resolves once and for all the question of her dubious Englishness: the governess is a "fierce fanatical" and dangerous Indian rather than a "gentle" Christian Englishwoman. Lawrence assigns Miss Warrender to her father's ethnos rather than to her mother's: the story firmly repudiates the possibility that she might belong to both. This moment comes before a full account of his discovery, suggesting that ethnological difference must be named before it has any heuristic value. Indeed, the fact that the mystery to be solved is that of difference is what gives the story its peculiar structure, one that Lawrence's statement exemplifies. He announces that he is coming to that part of the statement when the truth was revealed, that is, he describes the progression of his narrative; alludes to how he gained knowledge of the mystery; and then assures us of Miss Warrender's real identity—which is inadvertently disclosed to him. Rather than following the paradigm of the detective story—the story of a crime, told to us as a climax to the story of its investigation—the narrative charts Miss Warrender's ethnological difference, then discloses her identity and the crime that she has committed. One does not have the story of the crime and the story of its solution precisely because it is not guilt but identity that is at stake—one has the exposition of a mystery of identity and the naming of the Other as its solution.

Not only does the narrative bring order to a panoply of odd events and demystify what is alien, it places itself in a group of texts that circulate particular representations of India. Lawrence is able to make sense of the alien and exotic in part because he can refer to a compendium of knowledge about Empire—what one scholar has called an imperial archive.[42] In yet another instance in which popular texts inform Doyle's representation of Indians, the narrator invokes De Quincey's *Confessions of an English Opium Eater* to describe the appearance of an Indian in the village of Dunkelthwaite. "It was certainly a curious sight which met our eyes when we joined the little circle of rustics. It reminded me of the opium-eating Malay whom De Quincey saw in the farmhouse in Scotland. In the center of the circle of homely Yorkshire folk there stood an Oriental wanderer, tall, lithe, and graceful, his linen clothes stained with dust and his brown feet projecting through his rude shoes." Doyle uses the familiar iconography of popular texts to evoke a sense of the exotic. Implicitly, his story is itself part of an imperial archive, in that it too will furnish images and plots of Empire to his young readers. This fictional account supplements such discourses of Empire as are found in official reports, and borrows from those official forms for recording knowledge of Empire. Doyle not only employs a documentary format to subject "outré" incursions from Empire to the rationality of the metropolis, he points to the existence of an entire field of literary representations that structure and regulate metropolitan understandings of Empire.

We see in "The Mystery of Uncle Jeremy's Household" certain elements that recur in Doyle's later stories of intrigue. Sherlock Holmes interprets clues from past events to unearth the truth. While Lawrence is not in this early story identified as a detective, he acts as a self-appointed sleuth in the sense that he discerns a mystery and pieces together bits of information. In the Sherlock Holmes stories, Doyle makes greater use of the naïve friend, Watson, to achieve the tension between crypticness and disclosure that is characteristic of detective fiction. In "The Mystery of Uncle Jeremy's Household," the companion Thurston is a more tangential figure and the reader is more directly interpellated into the position of partner; Lawrence provides the "facts" and suggests that the reader might have solved the mystery before he did. Lawrence observes the real nature of relations in the household, and determines where the balance of power lies. He does this by chancing upon characters and overhearing their conversations. In this respect, he is more like the spy, another type of agent in imperial fiction of intrigue.

Doyle introduces two other themes that appear in the later stories, those of blackmail, and the presence of secret societies. We learn that Copperthorne has been a secret witness to Miss Warrender's ritual murder of Ethel and has used this knowledge to gain what appears to Lawrence to be an inexplicable hold over her. Secret knowledge is the source of a power that skews social relations, and that can be used for illegitimate ends. Secret societies, which appear frequently in the Sherlock Holmes stories, also present a clandestine and often illegal form of association, though in this case a chosen rather than a forced one. In "The Mystery of Uncle Jeremy's Household," the Thugs constitute a secret order with its own rituals and rules. In many of the stories, the secret society functions in lieu of, or in an angular relationship to, a community of class or nation. In this story, the community bound together by Thuggee plays a compensatory role: her fellow Thugs revere Miss Warrender, who has lost status in becoming a governess, as a princess. The practice of blackmail and the activities of secret societies point to the existence of a network of hidden social relations, which it is the task of the detective to discover.

I have argued that fiction of intrigue expresses certain anxieties of Empire and that it contends with these by imposing order, both in a thematic and in a formal sense. Curiously, many of the stories that I examine are in fact open-ended, and do not exhibit orderly or conclusive closure. This is true of "The Mystery of Uncle Jeremy's Household": Lawrence does not succeed in preventing Copperthorne's murder, and Miss Warrender and her fellow Thug both disappear. The latter exigency suggests that, to the extent that the detective work is aimed at the management of anxieties about mobility, especially transnational mobility, the detective fails. And further, although the full story is made known, and poetic justice is served by the murder of Copperthorne, whose nefarious plans rebound upon him, the "wild fanatic" Thugs are not subjected to English law. As I pointed out earlier, Miss Warrender and her companion are not in fact characterized as guilty, for they are subjects of a different law. Guilt is, rather, assigned to an Englishman, Copperthorne, who is prepared to contract the murder of his generous employer and benefactor. This characterization can be read as a reflection on the pitfalls of colonial rule: Copperthorne's excessive power over and despotic behavior toward the governess recalls arguments about imperialism having a detrimental effect on British political culture in promoting an autocratic attitude.[43] Also, the police force is not mobilized to intercede and set things right. Rather, order is pursued outside the apparatuses of the law. In all of these ways, the story eludes any simple logic. The fiction I examine in the following chapters is intriguing precisely because, while it is addressed to imperial anxieties, it does not allay these in any simplistic or formulaic way, but often acknowledges the failure of the metropolis to subject the imperial world to its laws and rationalities.

CONCLUSION

Wilkie Collins's the *The Moonstone* employs a narrative of detection to locate corruption and violence in the rulers of the Empire: John Herncastle and Godfrey Abelwhite are both characters who fail to govern their greed. Collins does not represent any attempt on the part of the British to shape the conduct of the Indian characters, whose practices and beliefs are represented as entirely alien and mysterious. While the novel does not laud colonial "difference," it abjures an imperial attempt to subject Indians to imperial modes of governmentality. "The Mystery of Uncle Jeremy's Household" affords a glimpse in fictional form into the mentalities of colonial government, and the project of fashioning governable subjects. Several of the imperial motifs and problems that Doyle sketches in "The Mystery of Uncle Jeremy's Household" are rehearsed and developed in other imperial narratives. At the center of this mystery is the figure of the returned colonial, a figure that recurs in Doyle's detective fiction. Miss Warrender, an Anglo-Indian governess, has come to England to seek employment, having been left destitute when her father is killed in the Indian Mutiny. Leaving her orphaned and forcing her to seek work as a governess, colonial insurgency has indirectly led to her presence in Uncle Jeremy's household. Miss Warrender is at once a returned colonial, a legatee of colonial insurgency, and a player in a bizarre family plot. This characterization betrays multiple anxieties about race, class, gender, and political hegemony.

The story foregrounds the rationalities of colonial rule—the knowledges and practices whereby subjects of empire are to be suitably fashioned. It suggests that the "rule of colonial difference" operates alongside colonial governmentality; the colonized are constructed as animalistic, amoral, and in various ways inferior; at the same time, they are envisioned as the proper subjects of colonial governmentality who can be refashioned as good subjects of colonial power. In these early stories, we see rudiments of a literary form that would be used to articulate and contain anxieties about colonial governmentality specifically, and, more broadly, the efficacy of Enlightenment rationality. We see a more explicit articulation of a response to anxieties of Empire in the fully developed figures of the detective and the spy, figures that we will examine in the next chapters.

THREE

Sherlock Holmes and "the Cesspool of Empire"

The Return of the Repressed

In Arthur Conan Doyle's detective stories, a striking number of characters who return to England after a sojourn in the colonies have an outlandish aspect. One, a contorted and bilious ex-soldier, owns a pet Indian mongoose. Another has lost a leg to a crocodile in the Ganges and has a poison-toting Andaman Islander in tow. A third keeps a fiendish hound and passes his South American wife off as his sister. A fourth returns from South Africa with a "blanched" face and a furtive manner. Many of these returned colonials are portrayed as menacing, and their presence in England precipitates a crisis, either a crime or a mysterious tragedy. In actual fact, return from the colonies to the metropole was a routine phenomenon. The journey back to England was an integral part of the imperial circuit, and returned colonials were familiar figures on the metropolitan landscape. Why does Doyle depict the phenomenon of return from Empire as so problematic if it was in fact quite commonplace?

Doyle's unusually consistent pattern of representation of the returned colonial reveals certain recurrent anxieties about imperialism.[1] There is a tendency in discussions of imperialism and colonialism to assume that the English were confident wielders of a self-constituting, autonomous imperial power, which they attempted to exercise on colonized peoples. This is to miss the point that imperial power was exercised in a highly conflicted and contested field, literally and metaphorically. One can better apprehend the tactics and strategies of control if one appreciates how threats to a stable hegemony are imagined and where they are located. In other words, if imperial rule produced anxieties about hegemony and identity, these anxieties in turn shaped the way power was exercised. By putting Doyle's stories under a critical lens, one can detect the contours of some of these anxieties and discern the ideological tensions of late nineteenth-century Empire that give rise to them. My aim here is to clarify the cultural significance of the trope of return in these stories by considering not only its literary aspect, but its relation to psychoanalytic theory and to the historical ethnoscape of British colonialism. A symptomatic reading of Doyle's imperial detective stories brings to light considerable cultural unease about the contradictions of colonial capitalism, especially, I will argue, about the emergence of an itinerant, transnational underclass of poor Europeans—the flotsam and jetsam of Empire.

While here I limit myself to the corpus of Doyle's imperial detective fiction, the anxieties detectable in these stories reflect a sense of malaise that tinged the triumphalist New Imperialism of the late Victorian period.[2] In "The Mystery of Uncle Jeremy's Household" we found a story of intrigue pivoting around a returned colonial. In several of Doyle's detective stories, characters turn out to have a problematic colonial past. They have returned to the metropolis, but have not been fully and satisfactorily reassimilated. Sometimes sinister, sometimes merely unfortunate, these characters bring intrigue and danger to England. There they become pivotal figures in a developing mystery, the solution of which involves the revelation of past events in the colony.

That Doyle expresses anxieties about Empire specifically in stories of problematic return can partly be explained by the fact that he was himself a returned colonial, in a sense. In the course of his varied life as a doctor, writer, and public figure, Doyle spent brief, but to him significant, sojourns in Egypt and South Africa. The details of Doyle's own life, his political commitments, and his oeuvre suggest that the imperial subplots in his stories are not merely incidental but rather are indicative of his cast of mind.[3] Doyle's literary career got under way with *A Study in Scarlet*, which he finished in April 1886.[4] The birth of Sherlock Holmes, Doyle's frustration with the binding of his career to that of the detective, his attempt to kill off Holmes, and Holmes's resuscitation are too well known to need recounting here. In addition to the Sherlock Holmes stories, Doyle wrote adventure tales, historical fiction, science fiction, and plays. His fame as a writer made him a public figure. He was an advocate for the spiritualist movement, a campaigner for justice in several cases including those of Oscar Wilde and Roger Casement, and twice a parliamentary candidate for the Conservative Party (he lost both times). Above all, he was a patriot and a champion of Empire.

Doyle's views about Empire were fairly typical for a man of his mold. His belief in the civilizing mission is clear in his comments about Egypt in *Memories and Adventures:*

> Of all the singular experiences of this venerable land, surely this re-building at the hands of a little group of bustling, clear-headed Anglo-Saxons is the most extraordinary. There are Garstin and Wilcox, the great water captains who have coaxed the Nile to right and to left, until the time seems to be coming when none of its waters will ever reach the Mediterranean at all. There is Kitchener, tall and straight, a grim silent soldier with a weal of a Dervish bullet upon his face. There you may see Rogers, who stamped out the cholera, Scott, who reformed the law, Palmer, who relieved the over-taxed fallaheen, Hooker, who extermi-nated the locusts, Wingate, who knows more than any European of the currents of feeling in the Soudan.[5]

Doyle describes the "rebuilding" of Egypt as the single most signifi-cant period in its history. "Clear-headed Anglo-Saxons" are credited with improving the physical geography, the law, the agriculture, the taxation system, and the health of the people. He also believed in the capacity of Empire to inspire loyalties that transcended the local. He viewed Empire as a vast, heterogeneous, global unity. Moreover, Doyle thought that Empire could have a salutary effect on British manhood, countering the perceived degeneracy of turn-of-the-century English culture. Doyle was able to propound these views from the position of public visibility that his literary fame had given him. His friendships with Rudyard Kipling, Rider Haggard, Andrew Lang, and Robert Baden-Powell also reveal something of his commitment to Em-pire, as does his membership in imperial societies such as the Legion of Frontiersmen.

Though Doyle spent very little time in the colonies, his brief so-journs in Egypt and South Africa brought him close to significant conflicts in Britain's imperial career. He traveled to Cairo in late 1895 for his wife's health, and quite by chance found himself near the spot when Lord Kitchener began his campaign to retake Khartoum. Doyle rushed to the front lines in the capacity of honorary journal-ist. Although he had to return to Cairo before fighting began, he alludes in his memoir to a brief meeting with Kitchener: "He asked me to dine in his tent that night, when he discussed the upcoming campaign with great frankness."[6] Doyle's involvement in the Boer

War was more direct, though once again he was a noncombatant. In December 1899, two months after Britain entered into war with the Orange Free State and the Transvaal, Doyle decided to volunteer for service in South Africa. When he was turned down, he went anyway—as a medical officer, in charge of a field hospital that had been hastily established in Bloemfontein by a philanthropist. While he was there, an epidemic of typhoid broke out and he worked around the clock with his meager staff to treat the sick and wounded. Doyle was knighted for his service in South Africa.

On his return to England after three months, Doyle wrote *The Great Boer War*.[7] Contrary to his expectations, the war continued— and he found himself defending the British faction against the charge of atrocities by journalists such as W. T. Stead. In little more than a week, he compiled a book-length "pamphlet" in which he "made a more effective case by marshalling the statements of eye-witnesses, many of them Boers, on the various questions of farm-burnings, outrages, concentration camps, and other contentious subjects."[8] Doyle adopted the empiricism that Sherlock Holmes is so famous for, and made a dispassionate review of the facts of the case. In this way he was able to revive enthusiasm for the war within England.

Doyle's unwavering support for the war is, however, belied by his fictional account of a soldier's combat in and return from the Boer War, "The Adventure of the Blanched Soldier." Written more than two decades later, this story registers misgivings about the Boer War that are glossed over in Doyle's history. Sherlock Holmes is approached by James Dodd, whom the detective quickly identifies as a veteran of the Boer War, to Dodd's amazement. Dodd is puzzled by the disappearance of his comrade in arms, Godfrey Emsworth. According to his family, Godfrey has embarked on a voyage to recover his health after being shot near Pretoria. Not satisfied with this explanation of Godfrey's silence, Dodd travels to the Emsworth estate, wangles an invitation to stay overnight, and in the course of his visit actually catches a glimpse of Godfrey, whom he describes to Holmes as strangely altered: "There was something shocking about the man, Mr. Holmes. It wasn't merely that ghastly face glimmering as white as cheese in the darkness. It was more subtle than that—something slinking, something furtive, something guilty—something very unlike the frank, manly lad that I had known. It left a feeling of horror in my mind."[9] Doyle uses the code of horror to describe the soldier who has returned from Africa: Godfrey's appearance is at once dreadful and unintelligible. His whiteness is that of cheese, of fish bellies—it is revolting, abject. His demeanor is no longer "manly" but skulking, suggesting that he has a guilty secret. Something has happened to Godfrey Emsworth, something so horrible that his butler believes he'd be better off dead.

Correctly surmising the reason for Godfrey's confinement, Sherlock Holmes forces the family's hand. He and Dodd are finally able to obtain an account of his misadventure outside Pretoria from Godfrey, who describes how, wounded and faint, he stumbled into a house and collapsed on an unmade bed, only to wake up to what appeared to be a nightmare:

> It was morning when I wakened, and it seemed to me that instead of coming out into a world of sanity I had emerged into some extraordinary nightmare. The African sun flooded through the big curtainless windows, and every detail of the great, bare, whitewashed dormitory stood out hard and clear. In front of me was standing a small, dwarf-like man with a huge, bulbous head, who was jabbering excitedly in Dutch, waving two horrible hands which looked to me like brown sponges. Behind him stood a group of people who seemed to be intensely amused by the situation, but a chill came over me as I looked at them. Not one of them was a normal human being. Every one was twisted or swollen or disfigured in some strange way. The laughter of these strange monstrosities was a dreadful thing to hear.[10]

The scene is at once horrible and unintelligible. The passage describes a world turned upside down—Godfrey's borrowed bed is more dangerous than the battlefield; conscious experience is more disturbingly unreal than a nightmare. The hospital is starkly precise, illuminated by a relentless African sun. Yet, though the room is flooded with light, Godfrey can make no sense of the grotesque figures that meet his eyes. He is unable to clarify matters because the people in the ward are unintelligible—they speak Dutch. The overtones of paranoia in his description grow stronger as he focuses on the people surrounding him. By the end of the paragraph they are described as "strange monstrosities" whose laughter inspires dread. Finally, an element of aggression enters the scene; the man with the sponge-like hands attacks Godfrey, drawing fresh blood from his wound. This character is singled out as particularly degenerate; he utters wild beast cries as he drags Godfrey from bed. Emsworth learns that he is in a Boer leper hospital that had been temporarily evacuated in the face of the British advance. The field of imperial battle, far from being one of glory, turns into a scene of horror.

This description of a ward of leprosy patients may be read literally to identify fears of physical degeneration and disease in the colony, but the representation of Boers as diseased can also be understood metaphorically, in the light of political relations between the Boers and the English. The English missionaries of the mid nineteenth century construed the Boers as "no more than half-savages: they led degenerate, unrefined lives, lacked a true European 'spirit of improvement,' and showed their 'monstrous' character by treating blacks as prey to be hunted."[11] The Boers were perceived as an entire nation of "poor whites," a lumpenproletariat of Empire who hindered its civilizing course. By contrast, the British saw themselves as engaged in a mission of improvement, to be realized through the spread of Christianity and commerce. In 1900, in *The Great Boer War*, Doyle echoed this colonial distinction when he described the Boers as "brave, honest farmers, but standing unconsciously for medievalism and corruption, even as our rough-tongued Tommies stood for civilization, progress, and equal rights for all men."[12] The Boers are pictured in this passage as hapless victims, but as degenerate nonetheless.

At the same time, the description of the "extraordinary nightmare" to which Emsworth wakes perhaps recapitulates some of the horror of Doyle's own experience in Langman's hospital treating the casualties of war and disease. The fact that in this story an Englishman returns from the Boer War with a "guilty" and "slinking" demeanor can be interpreted as an implicit admission on Doyle's part that the conduct of the British was not altogether "manly," to use a favorite word of his. The "nightmare" of the concentration camps in which Boer women and children were rounded up after the burning of Boers' farms by the British was, perhaps, not entirely dispelled by Doyle's efforts at rationalization. In "The Adventure of the Blanched Soldier," Emsworth had, it turns out, imagined a case of pseudo-leprosy into being, and a famous dermatologist "solves" his case. Doyle returned from the Boer War to fame and a knighthood, rather than to the travails that Doyle ascribes to his fictional returned colonials. However, a close reading of "The Adventure of the Blanched Soldier" suggests that his own return was perhaps not as free of trauma as it appeared, and that it spurred a return to the scene of the Boer War in the medium of fiction.

Doyle's preoccupation with the fate of the returned colonial in his detective stories stemmed not only from a traumatic personal experience but also from broader cultural anxieties about Empire. Doyle's early story "The Case of the 'Gloria Scott,'" about the return of characters from Australia, exhibits a number of the elements that resurface in other Sherlock Holmes stories. At the same time, it is important to note that the history and nature of British imperialism varied, and that narratives of return have different cultural contexts. The idea of return from Australia, to take the case in point, is particularly fraught because of its penal history. Doyle, in a reconstruction of the detective's life, gives particular significance to the case of the *Gloria Scott* by making it the beginning point of Sherlock Holmes's career of sleuthing. Holmes brings the episode to Watson's attention as especially worthy of study "because it was the first in which [he] was ever engaged."[13]

In this story, Holmes visits his college friend Victor Trevor at the country house of Trevor's father. One afternoon, Holmes exercises his as-yet-uncelebrated detective talents idly upon the person of Justice Trevor. Justice Trevor is a highly respected country gentleman whose character appears to be unassailable, yet Holmes's revelations cause the justice to keel over with shock and fear. Trevor is evidently hiding something, for he begins to regard Holmes with unease after this incident. The sudden arrival of Hudson, an itinerant sailor, who makes claims upon the justice's hospitality, confirms Holmes's suspicion that there is more to Trevor's affairs than meets the eye. In this instance, however, Holmes has *not* been called upon as a detective, and as an overly perspicacious visitor his presence becomes unwelcome, so he returns to London. However, he is summoned a few weeks later by Victor Trevor, who recounts how Hudson has shattered his father's peace of mind, eventually causing him to have a fatal stroke. In a deathbed letter to his son, Justice Trevor reveals the details of his past, the traces of which Holmes has inadvertently detected. Holmes learns that the venerable country judge had in his youth been a transported convict and imperial gold hunter, and had been traced and blackmailed by a witness of his past misadventures.

It is important to note that there are two instances of return from Empire in this story. While one Englishman returns with a colonial fortune and makes a home for himself as a country gentleman, a second comes back to England an indigent and itinerant ne'er-do-well. This asymmetrical twinning of the figure of the returned colonial can be found in a number of the Sherlock Holmes stories: in *The Sign of Four*, "The Boscombe Valley Mystery," "The Crooked Man," "The Blanched Soldier," and *The Hound of the Baskervilles*. In these stories, Doyle depicts the return of colonials in a double or ambivalent way: some colonials are marginal, physically ravaged characters who threaten the peace, while others are their respectable counterparts who attain middle-class or even gentry status by virtue of their colonial wealth. Closer scrutiny of the two different but complementary types of returned colonial suggests the ideological significance of this pattern of representation.

RESPECTABLE COLONIALS

In his posthumous confession in "The Case of the 'Gloria Scott,'" Trevor rehearses the roundabout route by which he is transformed from a clerk at a London bank, to a transported convict, to a respectable gentleman in rural England. Having left England in the most inauspicious of circumstances, that is, as a criminal sentenced to transportation for embezzling money, Trevor benefits from a shipboard mutiny that permits him to escape the *Gloria Scott,* the transport ship on which he is imprisoned. The survivors of the *Gloria Scott* are able in effect to erase their pasts, and to fabricate entirely new identities; they successfully pass themselves off as survivors of a wrecked passenger ship and make their way to Australia as free men.

The story imaginatively weaves together the two events that determined Australia's colonization and settlement: the penal transportation that played a key role in the initial occupation, and the gold rush that spurred large-scale immigration. For the hopefuls who have gathered together for the single-minded pursuit of gold, familial antecedents and social position are unimportant—the anonymity of the crowd and the wealth of the land offer Trevor the chance to re-create himself. Indeed, Doyle reproduces the mythology of the colony as Arcady, implying that Trevor's enrichment follows inevitably from his arrival at the gold mines: "We prospered, we traveled, we came back as rich colonials to England, and we bought country estates."[14] Doyle suggests that it is precisely because Australia is a frontier society in which fortunes may be made by anyone, whatever their past, that Trevor is able to effect a successful rehabilitation and return.

A sojourn in the colonies could in fact be a means of acquiring fame and wealth. Robert Clive's rise from a position as a lowly clerk in the East India Company to that of twice governor of Bengal and one of the richest men in England is a particularly spectacular instance of social and economic ascent through colonial service. In his account of Clive's life, Percival Spear writes, "It was legitimate to make money out of public events and in the course of public activity."[15] With his victory at Plassey in 1757, Clive laid the foundations of the British Empire in India. For the East India Company, he won the title to the revenue of Bengal and Bihar, and an exemption from duties on both company and private trade. For himself, Clive procured a large private fortune. Edmund Burke wrote of Clive's assets, "It is supposed that the General can realize 1,200,000 pounds in cash, bills and jewels; that his lady has a casket of jewels which are estimated at least at 200,000 pounds. So that he may with propriety be said to be the richest subject in the three kingdoms."[16] He also obtained after Plassey an estate or jagir worth an annual income of thirty thousand pounds a year. Clive's critics faulted him for paving the way to the wholesale plunder of Bengal. He later found himself enmeshed in wrangles in the East India Company and in Parliament over his policies, but he was able to acquire numerous estates and lived in style in England as a "nabob."

Arrivistes such as Clive may have been looked down upon somewhat, but they were also embraced by English society. As Benjamin Disraeli put it, "A colonist finds a nugget, or he fleeces a thousand flocks. He makes a fortune, he returns to England, he buys an estate, he becomes a magistrate, he represents Majesty, he becomes High Sheriff; he has a magnificent house near Hyde Park; he goes to Court, to levies, to drawing-rooms.... Our colonists are English, they come, they go, they are careful to make fortunes, to invest their money in England; their interests in this country are immense, ramified, complicated...they look forward to returning when they leave England, they do return—in short, they are Englishmen."[17] Disraeli reiterates the claim that returned colonists are indeed English, as if to quash any hint to the contrary. Their "investment" is both emotional and financial, in that they look forward to returning and to climbing up the social ladder with their newly acquired wealth. So, what makes them English is not any essential quality, but rather their "interest" in reassimilating into and affirming the structures and values, not to mention the economy, of England.

Trevor is just the type of worthy English colonist whom Disraeli idealizes. With his newly acquired wealth, Trevor is able not only to return to England, but also to recuperate a version of the pastoral ideal in England itself. The story presents a backward-looking model of social mobility, in which precapitalist wealth wrested from Empire is able to sustain an older social order. Sherlock Holmes recounts his visit to his friend's home: "Old Trevor was evidently a man of some

wealth and consideration, a J.P., and a landed proprietor. Donnithor-
pe is a little hamlet just to the north of Langmere, in the country of the
Broads. The house was an old-fashioned, widespread, oak-beamed
brick building, with a fine lime-lined avenue leading up to it. There
was excellent wild-duck shooting in the fens, remarkably good fish-
ing, a small but select library, taken over, as I understood, from a former occupant, and a tolerable cook, so that he would be a fastidious
man who could not put in a pleasant month there."[18] Doyle writes in
what Raymond Williams calls the "elegiac, neo-pastoral mode," and
describes in a stylized manner a gracious way of country life associated with a mythic Old England. Trevor's acquisition of a country
estate and the style of life that it supports is a sign of his complete assimilation into a traditional order.

The story at the same time suggests that social position can be
bought—even by a former City clerk and transported convict—with
the help of money from Empire. In fact, the old order is no longer an
"entailed inheritance," to borrow Edmund Burke's famous phrase—it
is sustained from without. Furthermore, representations of the City
and the English countryside are themselves metonymically related to
discourses of Empire. Tom Nairn has argued that after an initially rapid takeoff, industrialization in Britain slowed, and during the crucial
last decades of the nineteenth century Britain did not undertake a program of industrial restructuring and development, but rather fell back
on a conservative mode of financial imperialism, centralized in the
City.[19] In "The 'Gloria Scott'" (and in Doyle's stories in general), there
is a singular absence of any direct reference to industrial wealth—we
have London banking houses and merchants, and returned colonials
who establish themselves on country estates. Doyle seems to acquiesce
in the view that Empire, more than industry, is vital to Britain's power
and prosperity; in this story, at least, Empire provides the discursive
framework for understanding social transformations. Returns from
Empire, both financial and individual, become crucial to developments in the nation.[20]

Doyle presents as part of the logic of return not only assimilation
into but also a revival of the milieu of the rural gentry. This revival is
psychological as well as material. He inserts into his ideal portrait of
England the figure of the "natural man." Holmes says of Trevor, "He
was a man of little culture, but with a considerable amount of rude
strength, both physically and mentally. He knew hardly any books,
but he had traveled far, had seen much of the world, and had remem-

bered all that he had learned."[21] This idealized image of the imperialist is drawn in the language of neopastoral. The metropole is cultured but corrupt, refined but cloyed—the colonial has his learning not from books, but from immediate experience, and he is able to bring a "rude" and rejuvenating wisdom to England.

Trevor exemplifies the virtues of the respectable colonial. He has acquired wealth abroad; he returns to England and invests this wealth in land; he lives by and reproduces the traditional style of life of the English gentry; and his "rude strength" and his experiences abroad enable him to reinvigorate the milieu to which he returns. Doyle sketches similarly favorable profiles of respectable and desirable colonials in other detective stories. In "The Crooked Man," Sherlock Holmes is called on to investigate the apparent murder of Colonel Barclay, who has had a distinguished military career, made in different parts of the British Empire, and has returned to England a much venerated and liked soldier. In a second story of imperial battle, "The Adventure of the Blanched Soldier," James Dodd, a veteran of the Boer War who has returned successfully to civilian life in England, calls upon Sherlock Holmes to trace the whereabouts of a fellow combatant. Holmes's famous companion Watson is himself a wounded veteran of the Afghan War and has returned to England after a medical tour of duty. In yet another story of colonial return and intrigue, *The Hound of the Baskervilles*, heirs to the Baskerville estate return from abroad to restore the languishing family seat with a colonial fortune, and extend their beneficence to the surrounding countryside.

Doyle portrays these characters as desirable because of their wealth, experience, and character. They exercise each of these not in a revolutionary way, but to resuscitate a traditional order dominated by landed gentry. What haunts this imaginary social landscape is the shadow of an unregenerate aristocracy that has failed to live up to the responsibilities of hegemony. In stories such as "The 'Gloria Scott'" and *The Hound of the Baskervilles*, genteel colonials are implicitly defined in contradistinction to degenerate aristocrats. The respectable colonial is, in Doyle's scheme, an intermediary character. He is a bearer of traditional values and an agent of an inherited order, like the aristocracy, but he is not portrayed as profligate in the way the aristocracy frequently is in English writing of the nineteenth century. He is, in a sense, the double of the degenerate aristocrat.

IMPERIAL LUMPENPROLETARIANS

The respectable colonial has another undesirable double: the imperial lumpenproletarian. While Empire provides opportunities for enrichment, and colonial wealth enables repatriates, even convicts and outlaws, to represent themselves as English country gentlemen, Empire produces its own lumpenproletariat, who might return to plague the metropole. In Doyle's stories of return, the past ineluctably catches up with reformed colonials when their less successful fellows return to torment them in their homes. Hudson, in "The Case of the 'Gloria Scott,'" is precisely such a character. In Doyle's Australian stories, these figures, demonized as they are, implicitly confirm that the Empire that was touted as the poor man's Arcady has its own down and out. Hudson represents a class of colonial that causes particular anxiety to the imperial government—the "poor whites" who have been excluded from the spoils of Empire, and have come back for their share of the loot. The itinerant sailor tries to capitalize on his damning knowledge of how rich colonials have made their money to get some part of it.

As the sole surviving crew member of the *Gloria Scott*, Hudson is in a position to blackmail Trevor. In Doyle's account, the imperial lumpenproletarian is not satisfied simply with extortion—he covets the place of the successful colonial. Doyle codes Hudson's course of blackmail as a series of transgressions of the social and domestic order. Hudson torments Trevor by requiring the judge to give him a "position"—first as a gardener, and then as a butler—and then refusing to "know his place." As he climbs up the stairs of domestic service, and establishes his domain over more and more of the house, he becomes increasingly insolent. His crowning act of insubordination is to commandeer the judge's boat and best gun and go on shooting trips, challenging the core of the English country gentleman's privilege. Hudson finally causes Trevor to have a stroke by threatening to expose him. The imperial vagabond is the nemesis of the successful repatriated colonial, destroying the latter's life in England.

In Doyle's detective stories of Empire, such characters are often cast as perpetrators of crimes or suspects in investigations within England.[22] These characters covet the riches that have been denied them or have slipped through their fingers. In "The Boscombe Valley Mystery," a relatively poor witness to a bushranger's lawless career in Australia exploits his knowledge to live off the wealthy colonial, following him to Britain. In "The Crooked Man," a former soldier who has been betrayed by his rival in love into the hands of the Indian mutineers of 1857 returns eventually to England as his rival's nemesis. The protagonist of *The Sign of Four* is also a displaced and impoverished imperial soldier, Jonathan Small, who returns from India in pursuit of the Englishman who has defrauded him of his loot. In *The Hound of the Baskervilles*, a poor and illegitimate relative of the heir to the Baskerville fortune returns from South America and looks for a chance to do away with his wealthy kin. In all of these instances, while one colonial prospers, another experiences a decline in his fortunes.

The fictional representation of such poor, discontented characters must be understood against the historical backdrop of colonial social and economic formations. Colonial regimes, by invoking the discourses of racism (and with slightly different inflections, patriotism and nationalism), held out to Europeans the promise of a society of two classes, the colonizers and the colonized, and differences within these classes were construed as far less significant than differences between them. Yet the ideology of colonialism was belied by the actual organization of colonial society, characterized by differential access to wealth and power. The class differences within the colony were no less extreme than those of bourgeois European society; along with its English "nabobs," colonial European society produced its contingent of paupers, vagrants, orphans, prostitutes, insane, and criminals.[23] Had a social investigator conducted a survey of this population similar to Henry Mayhew's study *London Labour and the London Poor*, the findings would have been analogous.[24] These so-called "poor whites" struggled to subsist by whatever means they had, sometimes falling into poverty when they were discharged from jobs in the army, the railways, on ships, and the like. Like Mayhew's "nomads" who traversed London, they often wandered from country to country. This class was an imperial lumpenproletariat, an underclass found throughout the colonial world, including Australia, India, and Africa.[25] Historians of colonial societies have studied these marginal groups, pointing out that they bore witness to a social stratification by class in colonial societies that was at odds with imperial ideology.[26] Existing on the borders, such colonials threatened the integrity of the colonial category of superior European.

In India, the East India Company, during the period of its monopoly, severely limited access to the colony, keeping the numbers of those not in its own employment or that of the British Army small. One reason for this may have been a desire to maintain its own commercial and political grip, but another certainly was the fear that an influx of poor whites would decrease racial prestige and authority.[27] After the replacement of Company rule by that of the Crown, this policy was no longer adhered to, and especially with the growth of a market for European labor in the railways, construction, communication, and textile industries, more and more "poor whites" came to India, numbering, by the end of the century, as much as half the European population.[28] These Europeans would sometimes slide into extreme poverty.

The status and comportment of this colonial underclass was particularly troubling to colonial regimes, which saw the racial superiority of Europeans as a key justification for, and instrument of, imperial rule. One British official in India complained in 1867, "The sight of Europeans in the lowest depths of degradation brought on by drinking and profligacy must tend to degrade our race in the eyes of all who see them, and must go far to weaken our prestige amongst a nation avowedly ruled by the respect and fear in which they hold their conquerors."[29] This observer locates colonial power in the field of vision: it is the spectacle that these Europeans present to natives that proves to undo the homogeneous category of superior European. Not only did the spectacle of these degraded and degrading colonials threaten to discredit the mythology of European racial supremacy, but their ambiguous appearance also confused the boundary between European and native identity. The "poor white" was an abject subject, threatening to disrupt the distinctions that organized colonial identity and colonial rule. One European described a "European loafer" to the Madras Vagrancy Committee in 1867: "He was dressed more like a Native than a European, he had a red fez cap on his head, and native slippers on his feet."[30] Such cross-dressed figures were perceived as scandalous because in "going native," they revealed European identity to be a fragile construction.

As the number of destitute Europeans increased, so did the repressive measures taken by the government: these outcasts of empire were repatriated, institutionalized in orphanages and workhouses, and incarcerated. Significantly, poor Europeans in India were singled out as subjects of the Vagrancy Acts of 1869, 1871, and 1874; no such legislation applied to destitute Indians. Poor Anglo-Indians, that is, people of English and Indian ancestry, were also socially and politically stigmatized, especially when they became vagrants. It was not the fact of vagrancy itself but that of European vagrancy and the consequent loss of imperial face that was seen as detrimental to imperial rule. Located on the boundaries and margins of Empire, such colonials threatened "the illusion of a homogeneous white race, affluent, powerful, impeccable, aloof."[31] By institutionalizing and repatriating European vagrants, orphans, insane, and criminals, the imperial regime attempted to maintain that illusion.

While the presence of poor whites embarrassed the imperial regime, they were also regarded as a desirable buffer against native insurrection, especially after the Indian Mutiny. The poor whites could fill out the numbers of Europeans in the colony; they could also do the "dirty work" of Empire, acting as immediate supervisors of the natives, and as intermediaries between them and the colonial elite. It was from such useful positions that they slid into destitution and vagrancy. Poor Englishmen appear in other fiction of Empire— Kipling's stories are replete with these figures, from Daniel Dravott and Peachum in "The Man Who Would Be King," to Kim O'Hara's father in *Kim*.[32]

One finds in the writing of Doyle, and certainly in Kipling, considerable sympathy for such down-and-out Europeans. Even in the accounts of British administrators, one can occasionally detect an awareness that poor whites were not simply backsliding or inherently degenerate, but were, rather, casualties of the vagaries of colonial capitalism and colonial administration. One British official observed in a memorandum that poor whites were like the effluvium emitted from factory chimneys.[33] At the same time, although they threatened to weaken the construct of "superior European," they also enjoyed a certain license by virtue of their position on the borders of colonial society, as members of a ruling race but degenerate class. Kipling accordingly celebrates Kim's marginal mobility, one that enables him to gather intelligence.

Yet the allegiances of this group to the colonial elite were questionable. Of all the classes in the colony, it was the least wedded to the status quo of colonial capitalism.[34] Racial ideology militated against alliances between the colonized and poorer Europeans in the colonies; yet economic divisions possibly introduced an element of precariousness to the hegemony of the imperial regime over poor whites.[35] So, while poor whites may have been useful to colonial society, they had to be properly interpellated by imperial ideology, as well as suitably disciplined and regulated.[36] The representational terrain of popular fiction becomes a place in which to articulate this problem. In the Sherlock Holmes stories, the poor white "idlers and loungers of Empire" have become a social menace and must be appropriately dealt with.

Sherlock Holmes and "the Cesspool of Empire"

"UNHOMELY" COLONIALS

Doyle's "idlers and loungers of Empire" frequently bear the marks of their outcast status on their bodies. In imperial fiction, European bodies are often represented in a dual way. On the one hand, the body of the male adventurer can be indomitable. It triumphs over hunger, thirst, disease, injury, and exhaustion. Yet imperial fiction is also replete with bodies that are unstable and fragile—bodies that change color, that shrink, that bleed and bend and break. In several stories by Doyle, the bodies of Europeans in Empire change in undesirable ways. Representations of the European body as consummately powerful yet tremulously frail can be understood in relation to the contrary nature of corporeal experience in the colony. On the one hand, the European body was invested with symbols of the power of a ruling race—in the body's coloring, shape, and vestments. In the colonies, as in Europe, the elite large and strong masculine body became the focus of public rituals of social power, whether on parade or on a hunt. Writers celebrated the imperial body in narratives of extension, traversal, and endurance. However, Europeans were acutely aware of the weakness and vulnerability of their bodies. Influenced by the theories of degeneration that were popular in the late Victorian period, English people believed that imperial location had harmful effects upon European bodies, passions, and intellects.[37] In the colonies, strange and debilitating diseases were an everyday fact of life. Writers of colonial fiction would have us believe that dangerous beasts—scorpions, snakes, tigers, and rogue elephants—also menaced Europeans. Evisceration, emaciation, and exhaustion loomed as constant threats.

Yet this debility cannot be understood entirely as a condition of imperial experience—it has a class dimension. It is especially the down-and-out colonials to whom I have referred whose bodies are disfigured or disturbing in some way. Jonathan Small has a wooden leg; Henry Wood has a contorted frame; Godfrey Emsworth of "The Adventure of the Blanched Soldier" has a "ghastly face glimmering as white as cheese in the darkness"; Stapleton's visage bears an uncanny resemblance to that of a notoriously venal ancestor, Hugo Baskerville. Such "irregular" imperial bodies are not unique to Doyle's fiction: in Kipling's imperial stories, one finds bodies that are burnt, decapitated, amputated, and bloated and discolored with disease. Of course, one cannot generalize about all imperial fiction of the period, but other characters are similarly marked by their sojourns in Empire: Conrad's

Marlow returns to England weakened by illness, and compelled to recount his misadventures. Why are certain returned colonials marked in a bodily way? What do these deformities signify?

While the psychoanalytic concepts of the "uncanny" and the "abject" may too strongly connote fear and horror to characterize Doyle's doubling of well-to-do and down-at-heel returned colonials, these concepts nevertheless suggest why the characters seem anomalous and disturbing, and the concepts enable us to probe the political unconscious of his stories. Freud discusses the phenomenon of the uncanny in a number of ways, offering several accounts of its nature and basis. He points out that the etymology of "unheimlich" or "unhomely"—translated as "uncanny"—reveals that it is associated with two sets of ideas: what is agreeable and familiar; and what is kept out of sight and hidden. From this he concludes that "this uncanny is in reality nothing new or alien, but something which is familiar and old-established in the mind and which has become alienated from it only through the process of repression."[38] Freud also links the uncanny to the "double":

> Thus we have characters who are to be considered identical because they look alike. This relation is accentuated by mental processes leaping from one of these characters to another—by what we should call telepathy—so that the one possesses knowledge, feelings and experience in common with the other. Or it is marked by the fact that the subject identifies himself with someone else, so that he is in doubt as to which his self is, or substitutes the extraneous self for his own. In other words, there is a doubling, dividing and interchanging of the self. And finally there is the constant recurrence of the same thing—the repetition of the same features or character-traits or vicissitudes, of the same crimes, or even the same names through several consecutive generations.[39]

According to Freud, the double is originally a safeguard against the destruction of the ego, but takes on an uncanny quality after a person's passage beyond the stage of primary narcissism. When this stage has been surmounted, the "double reverses its aspect. From having been an assurance of immortality, it becomes the uncanny harbinger of death." Freud explains the uncanny in terms of a problematic relationship of the individual subject to his or her past.

Applying Freud's analysis of the "uncanny" to understand the tension between imperial experience and national location requires a shift in one's frame of reference from the individual self to a collective cultural formation. The patterns of doubling and return that I have pointed to in Doyle's detective stories of Empire suggest that the Englishman who has returned from the colonies is represented as "unhomely" not only in an individual sense but in relation to the nation. Though still a part of the nation, he has become alienated from the culture of the mother country. His return to England is disturbing because it forces an engagement with a self that has become estranged from its native matrix.

Not only is the returned colonial "unhomely," he is frequently abject in his destitution and disfigurement. Julia Kristeva argues in *Powers of Horror* that there are certain experiences that undo the very modalities of subjective experience. She calls these experiences instances of abjection, citing among them food loathing, the revulsion produced by a corpse, the horror of an open, pus-filled wound, and disgust of feces. The abject—"what disturbs identity, system, order. What does not respect borders, positions, rules. The in-between, the ambiguous, the composite"—tends to draw the self "to the place where meaning collapses."[40] In this, the abject is unlike the object, which stabilizes the subject in a reciprocal relationship of otherness. At times Kristeva suggests that the abject has a social character—it exposes the fragility of the law—but for the most part her analysis concerns the terrain of the individual psyche. She invokes ostensibly timeless, universal experiences of the body to elaborate the notion of abjection. Moreover, Kristeva appears to assume a bodily experience that is anterior to, indeed antithetical to, a symbolic order. While she eloquently conveys the psychic quality of abjection, she pays little attention to the social matrices in which abjection occurs. Mary Douglas, by contrast, focuses on the *social* marking of certain entities as disturbingly anomalous and ambiguous.[41] The ravaged bodies of returned colonials are reminders to the national body that it is not whole and robust, but is instead divided and damaged. Of course, the nation is not a self but a cultural and political formation—a continually reasserted fiction of natural community. The colonials who return disturb the psychic and social orderliness of late Empire and trouble the consciousness of the nation.

The doubling and return of colonials—some abject, some not—is, then, a trope that expresses a number of underlying cultural anxieties. It suggests that the colonials who return to England have become estranged from their native country. It also suggests that an episode or experience—a historical trauma—that has been repressed has come back to trouble the present; the return of disfigured and violent colonials points to a troubled political unconscious, upon which the original and repeated violence of colonization—a violence largely directed at natives, and left out of celebratory accounts of the civilizing mission—has left its traces.[42]

This violence is symbolically displaced onto the bodies of poor whites. In "The 'Gloria Scott,'" the aboriginal inhabitants of Australia are erased from the imperial scene. Native Africans are similarly elided in "The Adventure of the Blanched Soldier," which is set in South Africa. Such repeated elisions suggest that Doyle allows no space for the native inhabitants in his imaginary representations of settlement colonies and little more room in those of other colonies. Yet in the maimed and sometimes racially degenerate European characters who inhabit his stories, Doyle presents hybrid figures of the poor whites and the natives who have been agents and subjects of colonial violence. The insistent presence of these abject bodies suggests that though the imperial subject has become a pariah, he haunts metropolitan society, like Conrad's "secret sharer."

The physical irregularity of the returned colonials in Doyle's stories points to the alienating effects of colonial service. In several instances, the bodies of characters from the colonies are wounded, bearing the marks of battle or some other form of violence. Dr. Watson, who becomes Sherlock Holmes's friend and assistant, is the first returned colonial with a wounded body to appear in the Sherlock Holmes stories. A number of other characters—such as Jonathan Small in *The Sign of Four*, Henry Wood in "The Crooked Man," Godfrey Emsworth in "The Adventure of the Blanched Soldier"—are, like Watson, soldiers, suggesting that the male warriors of Empire are especially vulnerable to misadventures. At the very beginning of *A Study in Scarlet*, Watson recounts his service in the Second Afghan War at Maiwand, where he was struck in the shoulder by a bullet. Doyle writes against the grain of fiction of imperial romance, portraying India not as a field of glorious adventure, but as a dangerous and deadly place. During his recovery, Watson contracts enteric fever.

> For months my life was despaired of, and when I came to myself and became convalescent, I was so weak and emaciated that a medical board determined that not a day should be lost in sending me back to England. I was despatched, accordingly, in the troopship Orontes, and landed a month later on Portsmouth jetty, with my health irretrievably

ruined...I had neither kith nor kin in England.... Under such circumstances I naturally gravitated to London, that great cesspool into which all the loungers and idlers of Empire are irresistibly drained.[43]

In this brief passage, Doyle provides a thumbnail sketch of an unfortunate colonial. Watson is wounded, unemployed, and footloose.[44] Furthermore, Doyle makes a metaphorical link between the human waste of Empire—the imperial lumpenproletariat—and the social pool into which it drains: the imperial city. In describing London as a "cesspool," Doyle imputes an abject condition to the heart of Empire. This is a strikingly different image of London from the one we find in, for example, *The Heart of Darkness*, where Marlowe regards with awe the majestic expanse of the great city, upon returning from the "heart of darkness"—though he too finds darkness in a European city. In Doyle's view, if the colony is unhealthy, as the wounding and infection of Englishmen would suggest, so is the imperial metropolis, and it is in part made so by the presence of imperial lumpenproletarians. The health and wholeness of Empire are implicitly staked upon Watson's successful rehabilitation.

The nature of Watson's profession also suggests that health and bodily integrity are a preoccupation in the stories. As a doctor, he can restore wounded bodies. Also, his own wound heals, an indication that he can reintegrate into English society. Watson is a median figure, a potential lumpenproletarian who becomes a respectable former colonial—he regains his health, and takes on a curative role in the society he rejoins. Although at risk of becoming one of the legion of "loungers and idlers of Empire," he is in fact rehabilitated and reabsorbed into the bourgeoisie after his return to England. He is not abject, precisely because he is able to blend into a middle-class milieu. In comparison with the other "loungers and idlers of Empire" in the stories, Watson's body has been normalized. In fact, the text betrays a certain anxiety even about Watson's improvement. His wound gives him lingering pains, suggesting that his recovery has not been complete, and that traces of his ordeal in India remain. More curiously, Watson's wound wanders. In *The Sign of Four*, it is his shoulder that is wounded; in another story, he has a leg wound. This slippage leads one to conjecture that Watson's body has an incongruous status. His residual pains are a reminder that some imperial adventures can adversely and indelibly mark the bodies of Englishmen, and that return to English society in the full sense is uncertain and difficult.

These returned colonials have another curious aspect: they are racially coded as "Other." The "crooked man," Henry Wood, is quite brown from exposure to the tropical sun and he speaks an unintelligible language. Jonathan Small, with the wooden leg, has an inseparable companion, Tonga, who is described as a homicidal savage. Godfrey Emsworth, the "Blanched Soldier," possesses skin of an unnatural "cheese-like whiteness." These descriptions betray a preoccupation not only with health and disease, but with skin color, arguably the most salient of racial markers in the late nineteenth century. The "poor whites" in Doyle's stories are themselves of questionable whiteness. Doyle, by representing these characters as he does, symbolically affiliates imperial lumpenproletarians with non-Europeans. In Doyle's fictions of return, the very "whiteness" of Englishmen who occupy the lowest rungs of imperial society becomes doubtful.

COLONIAL DISCONTENTS

The recurrent images of damaged and distorted bodies and the presence of doubles in Doyle's detective stories suggest a concern about the vulnerability of Englishmen in the colonies, and their troublesome and outcast nature upon their return. While the concepts of the "abject" and the "uncanny" help characterize the disturbing aspect of returned colonials in these stories, a solely psychoanalytic account cannot adequately illuminate the troubling social and economic dimensions of this aspect of imperial experience. The appearance of both prosperous and impoverished colonials is not merely coincidental—the relation between the two is one of complementarity. While Empire produces wealthy colonials, it also produces large numbers of impecunious, displaced "poor whites." This doubling of colonials and the divergence of colonial fortunes points to the inequality engendered by colonial capitalism.

By and large, studies of late nineteenth and early twentieth-century imperial and metropolitan cultures rotate on two axes. While some examine class, concentrating on disparities between groups within England, others stress the importance of Empire, underscoring differences between European colonizers and "natives," and exploring how structures and discourses of imperial rule shaped metropolitan culture. In fact, social and economic stratification traversed imperial formations and cannot be neatly traced along racial or cultural lines, as between Europeans and "natives."

This complex social and economic stratification is an underlying source of anxiety in Doyle's imperial stories. His characters have not merely become estranged from the culture and the consciousness of the nation—they have become economically dispossessed. They lack steady and lucrative employment, often because the bodily damage they have suffered in Empire has made them unfit for conventional work. In *The Sign of Four*, Jonathan Small, for example, loses his position in the Indian army after a crocodile bites off his leg. He is able to find work as an overseer on a plantation, but this job ends with the outbreak of the Mutiny. His subsequent participation in the Four's murderous plot marks him as a criminal and outlaw. When he returns to England, he earns his livelihood by exhibiting his companion, an aboriginal Andaman Islander, at fairs. Henry Wood, in "The Crooked Man," is tortured and crippled so severely during the Mutiny that he balks at the prospect of returning to his regiment and his betrothed. After his eventual escape from the mutineers and then from a hill tribe that has enslaved him, he too makes a living as a wandering performer with his pet mongoose in tow. Godfrey Emsworth appears to have contracted leprosy while serving in the Anglo-Boer War, and consequently becomes a complete recluse, opting for a secret seclusion rather than state-sanctioned incarceration. The bodies of all of these returned colonials have become undisciplined both with respect to the norms of legality and to the imperatives of labor. Contrary to the ideology of imperialism, which holds that everyone gets rich in Empire, these indigent and rootless colonials who return to England are social and economic outcasts.

In sum, the category of "colonial subject" is ambiguous in that it can include both Europeans and native inhabitants of the colonies. This conflation obscures the profound differences between the colonizers and the colonized, but it allows for other ways of understanding colonial experience. While the discursive distinction between the "ruling race" and the ruled was prominent, it is worth examining the ways in which class and occupation cut across and complicated it. Colonial capitalism and government not only disrupted indigenous social structures and impoverished natives; they also produced European vagrants and paupers—a group I have called imperial lumpenproletarians. Lumpenproletarians appear frequently in the landscape charted by imperial fiction of the late nineteenth and early twentieth century. Sometimes, they are allied with native inhabitants.

The narratives of return in a number of detective stories by Doyle express another set of anxieties—ones that pertain to a historical trauma, frequently an insurgency or other violent occurrence in the colony such as the Indian Mutiny or Thuggee. In these narratives of return, the historical trauma in question is a significant episode in the history of British imperialism and colonization, such as the Anglo-Boer War or transportation to Australia, that has officially been resolved in a seemingly conclusive way. In Doyle's detective stories, one has excerpts from official narratives of these events—encyclopedia entries, letters from experts, references from books. These official narratives claim to establish the "truth" of the event in question and relegate it to a historical past that has been closed. In the detective stories, however, a residual element of the traumatic episode, an element impossible to assimilate, reappears in the person of returned colonials, whose past histories connect them in some way to these events. The detective narrative then has to manage the supplement or the unresolved residue of historical trauma. In this sense, Conan Doyle's stories are energized by the contradictions of Empire. At the same time, they explicitly affirm British civilization and imperial ideals, and steer clear of overt social critique.

FOUR

The Fiction of Counterinsurgency

In fiction of intrigue, native cabals and conspiracies against imperial rule rumble upon the horizon. Scholars have pointed to the cultural and political importance given in Britain to the Indian Mutiny of 1857, the New Zealand Wars of the 1860s, the Jamaican rebellion of 1865, the Mahdi uprising of the 1880s, the Fenian uprisings of the same period, the Anglo-Boer War, and other challenges to British imperial rule. The late nineteenth century also saw the rise of competition between imperial powers. It is hardly remarkable, then, that insurgencies and imperial rivalries should be depicted in fiction of intrigue.

One can well read Kipling's 1901 classic boy's adventure tale *Kim* as a novel about imperial competition, insurgency, and espionage: an Indian ruler has been recruited by the Russians in the "Great Game"—the imperial rivalry between Britain and Russia that forms the backdrop to the novel—and Kim is employed as an intelligence gatherer in a secret mission to thwart the Russians' plans. Erskine Childers's *The Riddle of the Sands*, commonly recognized as the first full-fledged spy novel, and a bestseller when it was published in 1903, is about two young men's discovery of a German plot to invade its rival Britain by submarine. In these novels the nature of the threat posed to Britain is obvious. Fictional representations of insurgency are worth examining closely, however, because in expressing misgivings about the efficacy of Empire they often reveal interesting anomalies in the politics of British imperialism. Colonial insurgency is significant to the plot of Doyle's *The Sign of Four* and "The Crooked Man," both of which relate the misfortunes of British soldiers caught up in the events of the Indian Mutiny. Insurgency is also the central problematic of two of John Buchan's extremely popular fictions of intrigue, *Prester John* and

Greenmantle. In this chapter, I explore how these stories cover over imperial contradictions using strategies of representation and narrative resolution that void the act of insurgency of its political content. In this respect, these fictions of imperial intrigue are literary analogues of what Ranajit Guha calls the prose of counterinsurgency.

In "The Prose of Counter-Insurgency," Guha argues that accounts of peasant insurgency, whether by contemporary administrators, later British historians, or nationalist historians, fail to represent the peasant "as an entity whose will and reason constituted the praxis called rebellion."[1] In primary, contemporaneous accounts, writers use metaphors that characterize peasant insurgency as a natural, spontaneous phenomenon. In later, secondary accounts, British historians portray insurgents as irrational and atavistic. Some historians are critical of the local administration and sympathetic to the rebels, but even these make sense of events "in terms of a code of pacification." Their rhetorical thrust is to portray the rebellion as a reflexive protest caused by the inadequacies and improprieties of a particular colonial administration—these historians do not take the step of criticizing colonial rule per se. By contrast, tertiary historical writing about peasant insurgency is sympathetic to the rebels and does challenge the effectiveness and legitimacy of colonial administration.

However, even this kind of historiography, usually nationalist or Marxist in its perspective, fails to do justice to the peasant's agency. Guha writes,

> The purpose of such tertiary discourse is quite clearly to try and retrieve the history of insurgency from that continuum which is designed to assimilate every jacquerie to 'England's Work in India' and arrange it along the alternative axis of a protracted campaign for freedom and socialism. However, as with colonialist historiography this, too, amounts to an act of appropriation which excludes the rebel as the conscious subject of his own history and incorporates the latter as only a contingent element in another history with another subject.[2]

In other words, tertiary writing, like primary and secondary prose of insurgency, erases the colonial peasant's agency as a self-conscious political actor. Of course, it would be naïve to suggest that the peasant insurgent's actions could be fully recovered or truly represented in some putatively authentic way, and Guha readily acknowledges this.[3] Nevertheless, as Guha suggests, historical distortions can be more or less severe, and the production of historical knowledge can serve better or worse political ends.

Fiction of intrigue employs narrative codes that similarly deny or distort the political impulse of the rebel's acts. In historical prose, the meaning of insurgency is driven by the rhetorical manipulation of causes: spontaneous forces, fanatic impulses, or revolutionary energies supposedly move the peasant. Fiction may make similar claims, but it has the latitude to interweave other narrative threads with accounts of insurgency so as to color its significance. Doyle's and Buchan's fictions of counterinsurgency, for example, do this by inscribing revolt within a narrative of crime, or alternatively, of fanatic messianism. In so doing, these stories not only diminish the political import of insurgency but also assert the need for, and rhetorically enact the gathering of, knowledge and the pursuit of order and control. While Doyle and Buchan share a preoccupation with acquiring knowledge and maintaining order, an examination of their tales reveals that they treat the theme of insurgency in different ways. These differences follow in part from generic elements of detective and spy fiction.

DETECTION AND INSURGENCY

On May 9, 1857, eighty-five sepoys of the Third Native Cavalry in Meerut, India, were dismissed, sentenced to ten years' imprisonment, and fettered, for refusing to use cartridges greased with pig and cow fat. The ends of the cartridges had to be bitten off before they were loaded; because Muslims regarded the pig as profane while Hindus regarded the cow as sacred, the religious sensibilities of both groups were deeply offended. On May 10, comrades released the imprisoned sepoys and killed their officers. The revolt spread to Delhi, and then all over northern and central India. Grievances against the British had been brewing among the native elite and middle classes, the army, and the peasantry; parts of these groups also joined in the insurrection.

The Indian Mutiny was an event of particular significance in the colonial imagination. It marked a turning point in English attitudes toward India in particular, and toward colonial rule in general. Until the events of 1857–1858, Englishmen had governed India with a firm belief in the ameliorative role of British rule. The violent rejection of British hegemony shook the imperial government's confidence in its own ability to administer India, and in the Indians' capacity for "improvement." After the 1857 Mutiny, India came increasingly to be represented as an irrevocably degenerate space, mired in superstition and ignorance.[4] The significance of the Mutiny in the Victorian culture of Empire can be discerned from its impact on writing in the latter half of the nineteenth century. The Mutiny spawned a large number of personal accounts, histories, novels, poetry, and plays. In fact, writing on the Mutiny constitutes an entire subgenre of imperial fiction by virtue of its quantity and its characteristics. It is almost uniformly Orientalist in Said's sense of the word, subscribing to binary oppositions between degenerate, violent, irrational, and altogether blighted Indians on one hand, and enlightened, rational, culturally advanced Englishmen on the other.[5] *The Sign of Four* and "The Crooked Man" can be situated within this genre of writing, sharing as they do its fundamental tropes.

These stories represent insurgency only tangentially. In both, the Indian Mutiny serves as a backdrop to a crime. The Mutiny is significant in each story not so much because it marks a moment of crisis for the imperial regime, but because it is the origin of a mystery that the detective is later called upon to solve. The brief account of insurgency is subordinated to the narrative of this mystery. Insurgency may appear to be incidental to the plot of each mystery, but in fact this very subordination can be read as part of a code of counterinsurgency. The breakdown of hegemony marked by insurgency brings to the fore certain contradictions in the makeup of imperial regimes. As a close reading of Doyle's stories shows, these contradictions are suppressed when a narrative of insurgency is overlaid by one of crime.

The Sign of Four

In the previous chapter, I alluded to *The Sign of Four* as a narrative of colonial doubling and return. Jonathan Small goes to India as a soldier, experiences a series of misadventures, and returns to England as a fugitive from the law, on a mission of revenge against another colonial who has swindled him and his Indian comrades. *The Sign of Four* evinces a code of counterinsurgency in obvious ways. At one point, caught in the turmoil of the Mutiny, Small flees the plantation on which he has worked and joins the English garrison in the Agra fort. Small repeatedly characterizes the rebels as an amorphous, irrational mob:

> Suddenly, without a note of warning, the great mutiny broke upon us. One month India lay as still and peaceful, to all appearance, as Surrey or

Kent; the next there were two hundred thousand black devils let loose, and the country was a perfect hell.... From where I stood I could see hundreds of the black fiends, with their red coats still on their backs, dancing and howling round the burning house.... The beating of drums, the rattling of tom-toms, and the yells and howls of the rebels, drunk with opium and with bang, were enough to remind us all night of our dangerous neighbours across the stream.[6]

Doyle's cliché-filled characterization of the rebels as drugged, frenzied fiends who emit yells and howls and beat drums rather than speak is typical of Mutiny fiction. This type of writing represents the mutineers as atavistic renegades rather than as political malcontents.

The terms in which Small's fall into criminality is described mark the story as counterinsurgent fiction in more interesting ways. Stationed at a remote part of the fort during the Mutiny, Small finds himself at the mercy of the three Punjabi soldiers in his charge. They press him to join with them, whereupon he avers his loyalty to the British faction. Upon pain of death, Small enters into a conspiracy with the three Indian subalterns to murder the envoy of a native prince and steal the prince's treasure. While Small readily colludes in a murderous plot for personal gain, he adamantly refuses to participate in an act of political betrayal, and insists upon the safety of the fort. Doyle writes against the implicit possibility that the four soldiers will reject the hegemony of the British. Whereas the mutineers have been personally affronted by the introduction of the greased cartridges and have translated this outrage into an occasion for a violent political revolt, the Four engage in a private betrayal but nonetheless assert and demonstrate their fidelity to the Raj.

The soldier Abdullah Khan's argument that he is merely asking Small to fulfill his purpose in India and become rich suggests not merely that the Empire is a vehicle for piracy, but also that the British soldier might in fact have sound economic reasons for making a compact with the Indian subalterns.[7] Small is a "poor white," impoverished, rootless, and insignificant, as his name suggests. His sorry state belies the promise of Empire—plentiful wealth for all. The soldier invokes this promise when he invites Small to "be rich." As an imperial lumpenproletarian, Small shares the class position and interests of similarly indigent natives, as opposed to those of wealthier segments of the British regime. It is only by joining forces with the Indian soldiers that Small is able to "get rich." The story acknowledges the possibility of a "poor white" making common cause with Indians, but blunts the edge of this possibility by representing the subalterns as cohorts not in an insurgency but in a criminal conspiracy.

The story insists on the private, intimate nature of the pact between Small and his Indian companions. Abdullah Khan swears a religious and filial oath of sincerity, and expects Small to do the same. After they kill the merchant Achmet and bury the treasure, Small makes a map of where it is stowed and puts the sign of the four on it. The sign of four, from which the story derives its title, symbolizes a unity and commitment that supersedes the ties of nation and race: "we had sworn that we should each always act for all, so that none might take advantage. That is an oath that I can put my hand to my heart and swear that I have never broken." The clandestine fellowship of the four is repeated in a number of Doyle's stories, in which secret societies provide an alternative mode of community to those of class and nation. In *The Sign of Four*, the association of the four soldiers is emphatically characterized as a secret fraternity and not as a political organization. *The Sign of Four* also promotes a code of counterinsurgency by discounting the possibility that the hegemony of the Raj may be shaken under political pressure. While the story raises the prospect that disaffected and impoverished English and Indian soldiers—imperial lumpenproletarians—may unite to advance their interests, Doyle rhetorically skirts that troubling possibility by framing their dealings within a narrative of crime and detection rather than one of insurgency and political containment.

Doyle is hardly unique in representing the down-at-heel and disenfranchised of Empire as politically volatile outcasts. The imperial lumpenproletarian, both "poor white" and native, had also been represented in English imaginative writing in the figure of the pirate. On the margins of the project of "civilized" imperial enrichment, the pirate was an ambiguous character, both villainous outlaw and heroic adventurer. Robert Louis Stevenson's *Treasure Island*, written five years before *The Sign of Four*, had portrayed this ambiguity, pointing to the particular inconstancy of Long John Silver's loyalties, and the general instability of the imperial regime.

In a brilliant reading of *Treasure Island* as imperial fiction, Diana Loxley argues that the text is unusual because it throws into relief the inherent instability of imperial formations: "The problem of order and instability is represented by the threat of lawlessness and criminality internal to the system of European cultural identification, that is, issuing from within its own ranks as opposed to a racial, territorial or cultural otherness from outside."[8] The treasure hunters on the Hispaniola are the miniature of an imperial regime: buccaneers, ordinary hands, a commanding elite, and a member of the gentry, who are united hierarchically in a common project. However, this articulation of interests is far from stable; a segment of the crew challenges the hierarchy, crossing the bounds of law, and identifying themselves as "gentlemen of fortune." An open contest for power ensues, in which individuals keep changing camps, and camps keep changing leaders and locations, destabilizing the very terms of imperial politics. Though the novel achieves closure with a final restitution of order—the Squire bows to the superior professional instincts of the Captain; the degenerate buccaneers are purged from the enterprise; the heroic qualities of the "empire boy" Jim Hawkins are recognized; the treasure is recovered; and the troublingly ambiguous figure of Long John Silver disappears from the scene—the text foregrounds the fact that disparate interests and groups are articulated in imperial formations, rendering them unstable, and liable to implode.

This instability is evident in stories of insurgency. The first Mutiny story to be written in England, "The Perils of Certain English Prisoners," by Charles Dickens and Wilkie Collins, at once registers the putative instability of imperial hegemony and masks it by describing the adventures of the English "empire boy" hero in manicheanly racist terms.[9] Though the story is set on an island off the Mosquito Coast of Central America, it clearly takes as a point of departure the events of the Indian Mutiny.[10] Gill Davis is part of a contingent of marines sent to Silver-Store, a "very small English colony" where silver mined in Honduras is stored before being shipped to Jamaica; the marines expect to give chase to a gang of pirates that has harassed English cruisers along the coast. In addition to the sailors, soldiers, and English colonists, the island hosts an indigenous population of "Sambos ... half-negro and half-Indian." When Davis voices his visceral suspicion of the natives, he is assured that they are perfectly trustworthy: "We are all very kind to them, and they are very grateful to us." This relationship of fond patronage is exposed as a fiction when the natives betray the Englishmen to the pirates. Once again, the pirates are clearly the erstwhile lumpen of Empire, both European and native: "There were Malays among them, Dutch, Maltese, Greeks, Sambos, Negroes, and Convict Englishmen from the West India Islands; among the last, him with the one eye and the patch across the nose."[11] Men of diverse nations and races are united in a common project: fortune hunting outside the bounds of "legitimate" colonial enrichment. The scene of piracy proves that interest rather than identity is the ground of mobilization, at least at the margins of Empire.

The story is somewhat different from *The Sign of Four* in that the newly rich lumpen are already situated beyond the pale of "civil" society; the argument of the story is that this is where the natives must properly be located. The story further does the ideological work of tracing Davis's interpellation into the position of subservient yet loyal "poor white."[12] Though, upon his arrival at Silver-Store, Davis begrudges the colonists their easy life and Captain Carton the status that permits him to woo the maid Marion Maryon of the colony, when he discovers the natives' treachery he devotes himself to the defense and then the liberation of the colonists. Collins and Dickens's story uses the motif of native insurrection to elaborate a solution to the problem of poor white resentment: the story draws lines of affiliation in starkly racist terms, glossing over the contradictions within European imperial formations.[13] Doyle's fiction is more complex in that it acknowledges the possibility of solidarity between poor whites and natives, but again, it voids this putative solidarity of political content by coding it as criminal.

Assessing the role of a native lumpenproletariat in the struggle for liberation from colonial rule, Frantz Fanon was to stress the inherent instability of this group.[14] Because it is the most dispossessed, the native lumpenproletariat has the least interest in compromise. Free of the restraints of traditional society, it is ready to erupt at any moment, but because the class lacks organization and leadership, it is readily swayed or bought. The character of the European lumpenproletariat must be distinguished from that of the native colonial lumpenproletariat: imperial ideology and imperial privilege, which they benefit from, exert a degree of hegemony over the former group. Yet, situated in the interstices of empire, poor whites could change from a passive, perhaps mildly recalcitrant group to rebels and outlaws. While poor whites were necessary and useful to the colonial regime, the potential volatility of this class was cause for anxiety about destitute Europeans.[15] Doyle, Stevenson, and Dickens and Collins all hint at this instability in their stories.

Doyle, himself of Anglo-Irish descent, exploits this paradox in one of his short stories, "The Green Flag."[16] The geographical and historical details provided in the story suggest that it is based on a famous imperial battle of 1885 in which an advance guard of General Charles Gordon's troops fought Mahdists at Abu Klea, near Khartoum.[17] The fact that Conan Doyle was visiting Egypt ten years later in 1895 at the time that Lord Kitchener had received orders to attack the Mahdi and retake Sudan, and in fact rushed to the front lines as a war correspondent to glean first-hand knowledge of the battle, suggests that Conan Doyle was familiar with the history of the Mahdi in Sudan.[18] From 1881, Egyptian authorities faced a challenge by Mohammad Ahmed, a messianic holy man who had built up a large following in his mission to purify Islam. As Egyptian control in the Sudan crumbled, General Gordon was called in to supervise a withdrawal. Contravening orders, he prepared to defend Khartoum and resist the Mahdi. In the ensuing engagement, Dervishes, as the Mahdi Mohammad Ahmed's followers were called, penetrated one side of a square, wreaking havoc upon British troops. Ultimately, the square re-formed after men from an unengaged side fired into the melee, but the casualties were high. In an intriguing rewriting of the incident, Doyle weaves a story of Irish disaffection and rebellion into the plot. His fictional account betrays a concern about the political cohesiveness of imperial regimes, especially under the pressure of insurgency.

"The Green Flag" begins with an account of Dennis Conolly's recruitment in Ireland into the British Army, upon the shooting of his twin brother by the constabulary. As Doyle explains, "The countryside had become too hot for him; and, as the seventy-five shillings were wanting which might have carried him to America, he took the only way handy of getting himself out of the way. Seldom has Her Majesty had a less promising recruit, for his hot Celtic blood seethed with hatred against Britain and all things British."[19] C Company of the Royal Mallows, Conolly's regiment, contains a particularly large number of similarly disposed Irish recruits, but their officers are confident that they will make stalwart British soldiers. Doyle, while he refers to the appropriation of these Irishmen's lands and their impoverishment at the hands of the British, hastens to add that there were outrages and grievances on both sides.[20] In any case, conscription is presented as a pragmatic way to divert energy from insurgency in Ireland. While it is not clearly stated, there is even an implication that the militant resentment of the Irish can be harnessed for the purposes of Empire.

This theory is put to the test in the Sudan. Even as the British troops prepare for battle, disaffection is evident in C Company, and Conolly appears to be the instigator of the trouble. When the side of the military square on which they are positioned is attacked and begins to give, the men hold back instead of responding vigorously. Their angry captain admonishes them:

> "What is it then?" he cried, looking round from one fierce mutinous face to another. "Are you Irishmen? Are you soldiers? What are you here for but to fight for your country?"
>
> "England is no country of ours," cried several.
>
> "You are not fighting for England. You are fighting for Ireland, and for the Empire of which it is a part."
>
> "A black curse on the Impire!" shouted Private McQuire, throwing down his rifle. "'Twas the Impire that backed the man that druv me onto the roadside. May me hand stiffen before I draw thrigger for it."
>
> "What's the Impire to us, Captain Foley, and what's the Widdy to us ayther?" cried a voice.
>
> "Let the constabulary foight for her."
>
> "Ay, be God, they'd be better imployed than pullin' a poor man's thatch about his ears."
>
> "Or shootin' his brother, as they did mine."
>
> "It was the Impire laid my groanin' mother by the wayside. Her son will rot before he upholds it, and ye can put that in the charge-sheet in the next coort-martial."[21]

Doyle foregrounds the paradoxical nature of the relationship between Ireland and England, adversarial countries yet members of the same Empire. What is in dispute in this discussion is Ireland's standing vis-à-vis Empire. Captain Foley tries to appeal to his subalterns' national pride, challenging them as Irishmen and as soldiers, but cannot convince them that identification with their nation—Ireland—signifies a commitment to Empire. They, on the contrary, aver that it is the Empire that has left them and their families destitute, or even dead. They stoutly reject the view that they have any obligation to Empire. In fact, they explicitly assail the violent tactics of the constabulary. They are very clear that the violence that underpins imperialism is directed against them. The members of C Company refuse to obey their officer's orders and instead crowd around Private Conolly. Even though the square is caving in rapidly, the Irish are clearly unwilling to make a stand against the Arabs. However, at the moment of attack, as the Arabs surge towards the company, Conolly experiences a reversal of feeling. "Their yells, their bounds, their crouching, darting figures, the horrid energy of their spear-thrusts, made them look like a blast of fiends from the pit. And were these the Allies of Ireland? Were these the men who were to strike for her against her enemies? Conolly's soul rose up in loathing at the thought."[22] The characterization of Ireland as feminine and the Arabs as spear-toting "fiends" mobilizes a certain gender discourse to argue against an alliance between the two groups. Doyle appeals to a crudely racist logic of difference to assert that a political association between Arabs and Irish is untenable. He does not refute the plausibility of such an alliance—no process of deliberation is imputed to Conolly. Rather, Doyle employs caricature to argue for a spontaneous realignment of the Irish with the English.

What is curious about this story is that Doyle does not dismiss or dispute the Fenians' nationalist aspirations.[23] He readily acknowledges the political differences and tensions between the Irish and the English, and implicitly reinforces a sense of cultural difference in his portrayal of the Irish subalterns: he writes their dialogue in dialect, whereas he uses standard English for the rest of the story. Though this sense of political and cultural difference is maintained, the implicit argument of the story is that this difference can be accommodated, and even exploited, by the imperial regime. Conolly subsequently rallies his rebellious compatriots, who at first ignore his call to reform, by invoking their patriotism. It is ultimately the very emblem of revolt, a "rebel ensign," that becomes a symbolic rallying point for the Irish contingent on the imperial battlefield. The green flag has a double value: it at once betokens the insurgency and the unity both of Empire and of nation. Doyle sums up the moral of the story: "For Irish regiments have before now been disaffected, and have at a distance looked upon the foe as though he might, in truth, be the friend; but when they have been put face on to him, and when their officers have dashed to the front with a wave and a halloo, those rebel hearts have softened and their gallant Celtic blood has boiled with the mad joy of fight, until the slower Britons have marveled that they ever could have doubted the loyalty of their Irish comrades."[24] The story suggests that while Irish republicanism is dangerous for Britain, it also inspires a selfless heroism that can be made to work for Empire.

I have discussed this story at some length because it vividly illustrates one of the political contradictions of Empire: the peculiar status of the Irish as both subjects and agents of imperial rule.[25] This contradiction raises the specter of revolt within imperial ranks. In "The Green Flag," Doyle portrays the moment of insurgency as on the one hand a threat to Empire, but also as a flashpoint when imperial sentiments coalesce and solidify.[26] Clearly, the question of whether the Empire had the power not only to overcome opposition, but also to command the allegiance of heterogeneous and dispersed groups of people, especially in periods of crisis, was one that concerned Doyle. He took it up in *The Great Boer War*, his immensely popular contemporary account of another imperial contest. The Boer War of 1899–1902 had a profound impact on Britain's self-conception as an imperial nation.[27] Doyle, who was decorated for his service in the Boer War, presented it as a test of the very cohesion of the Empire:

> Men had emptied their glasses to it in time of peace. Was it a meaningless pouring of wine, or were they ready to pour their hearts' blood also in time of war? Had we really founded a series of disconnected nations, with no common sentiment or interest, or was the empire an organic whole, as ready to thrill with one emotion or to harden into one resolve as are the several States of the Union? That was the question at issue, and much of the future history of the world was at stake upon the answer.[28]

For Doyle, the Boer War forced the question of whether the imagining of community was limited to the form of the nation, or whether a second-order imagining was efficacious, one that would bind nations into a larger totality, the "organic whole" of Empire. The very existence of Empire, for which the blood of its soldiers was a metonym, was staked upon the war.

At the end of *The Great Boer War* (written before the end of the war), Doyle answers the question he has posed in the affirmative.

> The only difference in the point of view of the Briton from Britain and the Briton from the ends of the earth was that the latter with energy of youth was more whole-souled in the Imperial cause. Who has seen that army and can forget it—its spirit, its picturesqueness—above all, what it stands for in the future history of the world? Cowboys from the vast plains of the North-West, gentlemen who ride hard with the Quorn or the Belvoir, gillies from the Sutherland deer forests, bushmen from the back blocks of Australia, exquisites of the Raleigh Club or the Bachelor's, hard men from Ontario, dandy sportsmen from India and Ceylon, the horsemen of New Zealand, the wiry South African irregulars—these are the reserves whose existence was chronicled in no blue-book, and whose appearance came as a shock to the pedant soldiers of the Continent who had sneered so long at our little army.... On

the plains of Africa, in common danger and in common privation, the blood brotherhood of the Empire was sealed.[29]

Here Doyle emphasizes the diversity of the British Army, and uses esoteric and allusive language to paint its myriad colors. The description of the conscripts is composed of a series of oppositions phrased with regard to places, classes, occupations, and styles of masculinity. Gentlemen of the Quorn and Belvoir, that is, huntsmen from Leicestershire, are opposed to gillies or attendants to sportsmen in the Scottish Highlands; bushmen in Australia are distinguished from "exquisites" who attend elegant London clubs; hard men are contrasted with dandy sportsmen. In stressing the heterogeneous character of the British Army, Doyle implicitly raises the question of what unites such a multifarious group of men together under a common banner.

Doyle invokes multiple connotations of "blood" to explore this question. At the beginning of the book, he wonders whether a pledge made with wine can be realized in blood in the event of war. His metaphor brings to mind the symbolism of the Eucharist, but also the image of blood sacrifice. His conclusion is that Empire is a viable "blood brotherhood." In making this claim, Doyle invokes the familial connotations of blood: imperial ties are congenitally strong. Yet he realizes that neither religion nor the myth of a common ancestry actually unites the different men of Empire. The model of unity he proposes is, rather, that of masculine fraternity, brought into being through a common experience of hardship. This model is different from a nationalist one of community based on a shared past, culture, language, religion, or race.[30] The nature of imperial ties is more flexible and inclusive than the nationalist model would allow for, or so Doyle would have it. War, in his account, tests these ties, but also serves as a catalyst in their consolidation.

Crooked Men

"The Crooked Man," published in July 1893 in the *Strand Magazine,* employs a similar code of counterinsurgency, but reveals different apprehensions about imperial hegemony. Like *The Sign of Four,* the story is a locked-room mystery. Once again an enigmatic death is linked indirectly to events that have taken place during the Indian Mutiny. The story once more shows advancement in the arena of Empire to be somehow tainted: it occurs at the expense of a colonial servant who is abandoned to a life of shiftless poverty. In this, as in the stories discussed in the last chapter, the marginal, vagrant, poor ex-colonial returns as the nemesis of another colonial who has become rich and successful. The repetition of this pattern of representation indicates, as I argued earlier, unease about the possible displacement and vagrancy caused by imperialism. Doyle also contends with the possibility that Irish subalterns might be disloyal to Empire on the battlefield.

The story begins with a visit by Holmes to Watson late one night. The detective recounts his present case to his friend and comrade with the request that Watson accompany him to the scene of a death. Sherlock Holmes has been called in to investigate the apparent murder of Colonel Barclay, commander of the Royal Munsters, one of the most famous Irish regiments in the British Army. Barclay is found dead on the floor of a locked room in his villa at Aldershot, with his unconscious wife beside him. On detecting the traces of a third man in the room, Holmes tracks down the intruder, Henry Wood, and learns the full story. Barclay and Wood, stationed in India thirty years before, had competed for the hand of Nancy Devoy, the daughter of a sergeant in the regiment. At the height of the Indian Mutiny, when the regiment was waiting for relief, Barclay betrayed Wood into the hands of the mutineers, and married Nancy. This deception never becomes a matter of public knowledge, but when the now scarred and deformed Henry Wood returns to England years later and has a chance encounter with his former fiancée, it becomes the subject of a violent quarrel between Nancy Barclay and her husband. In bursts Henry Wood, "the bare sight of [whom] is like a bullet through [Barclay's] guilty heart." Barclay falls over dead, Nancy faints, Henry Wood flees, and the scene appears to be that of a murder. However, Sherlock Holmes uncovers the truth, and does so in a discreet way, so that no one's reputation is marred. When the doctor rules that Barclay has died of a heart attack, the official police conclude that the case is quite unremarkable. It is only Watson's readers who learn the solution to the mystery.

If one turns to page twenty-eight of the volume of the *Strand Magazine* in which the story was first published, one finds Sidney Paget's illustration of Wood's encounter with Mrs. Barclay. Below the drawing is the caption, "It's Nancy!" Two women face an approaching man, who has paused in mid-step and looks up with staring eyes at one of the women. We cannot see her expression—we are presented with a three-quarter profile of her from behind—but her companion's wide-eyed gaze bespeaks alarm. The man is bent over, carries a cane, and has a box strapped to his back. His nondescript, ill-fitting clothes contrast with the smart apparel of the women. The most curious element of his dress is a turban wound around his head, but for which he would appear to be an ordinary tinker. The turban clearly gives him an Oriental aspect. Doyle's text makes no mention of a turban, but Paget's pictorial interpretation of the character is licensed by descriptions of the crooked man as swarthy, prone to speak in a strange tongue, and the owner of a strange animal—a mongoose, we later learn.

Henry Wood's abject, quasi-Oriental appearance is explained in part by his experiences in India, which he recounts to Holmes and Watson. Abducted by the rebels during the Mutiny, Wood is repeatedly tortured—his body is physically made crooked. He is later enslaved, escapes, and wanders the country, living by conjuring tricks. The story portrays more graphically than any other of Doyle's detective stories the predicament of "poor whites" in the colony. When he returns to England, the itinerant Irishman's back is bent, his face is "crinkled and puckered like a withered apple," and his eyes are bilious. Colonial experience has culturally and physically marked Henry Wood: in his appearance and habits he is represented as having "gone native."

While "The Crooked Man" evinces some of the concerns about the degradation of "poor whites" that I have noted earlier, there is a specificity to the representation of an Irish soldier in these terms that derives from the anomalous position of the Irish in British imperial formations. Ireland had been the longest subjugated of Britain's colonies. At the end of the nineteenth century, the Irish were actively engaged in both insurgent and peaceful agitation for their liberty. At the same time, Irish soldiers were valued agents of imperial rule. This contradiction became explosively manifest in political developments of the late nineteenth and early twentieth century.

The subterranean logic of "The Crooked Man" becomes clearer when the story is read against the backdrop of this Irish-Indian connection. The title of "The Crooked Man" stresses the possibility of corruption—of crookedness—in the colony. There are two "crooked men" in the story: degeneration is split into narratives of moral depravity and physical deformity. At the height of the Mutiny, a moment when imperial hegemony is threatened, the Irish soldier Barclay compacts with an Indian servant to betray his comrade into the hands of the rebels. This betrayal is emphatically a private one, engendered by romantic rivalry. His "crookedness" is personal and secret. In his public life, Barclay's conduct is evidently impeccable—he proceeds to become a highly decorated soldier, and eventually, colonel of his regiment. Henry Wood, by contrast, is outwardly made crooked and becomes an outcast. As Paget's illustration suggests, he appears to "go native." Yet Wood remains committed to the imperial center, acknowledging England (and not Ireland) as his home: "For years I've been dreaming of the bright green fields and the hedges of England." Though he is bent from the waist, he remains upright in his commitment and character. At the time Doyle wrote, the Irish were divided in their support of the British. In depicting the "crookedness" of two soldiers from an Irish regiment, the story suggests that Irishmen may be deceitful. Moreover, this fiction of intrigue places the two narratives of crookedness in the context of the Indian Mutiny. In so doing, it at once hints at and writes against the possibility that Irish soldiers may act in solidarity with Indian insurgents against British rule.

"The Crooked Man" betrays a further anxiety about the Irish: their otherness is difficult to discern. Though now considered "white," the Irish were nonetheless discursively coded as racially Other in nineteenth-century England.[31] The story's emphasis on Wood's physical deformity betrays an anxiety racially to mark the Irishman, to render difference visible. As Paget's illustration confirms, the body of Henry Wood is coded as criminal—he bears a strong resemblance to the rebels depicted waiting in an ambush—and Oriental. Barclay, too, is other than he appears. He returns to England, where, although he rises through the ranks to become colonel of the regiment and enjoys a happy marriage, he is plagued by spells of depression, and is chronically afraid of being left alone in the dark. Also, the "dashing, jovial old soldier" is "capable of occasional violence and vindictiveness"— that is, though to all appearances he is a model Irish soldier, he has "some singular traits" that suggest that he is not who he seems.

Barclay is finally physically marked with horror when he sees the man whose torture and disfigurement he has caused: "There was one thing in the case which had made the deepest impression both on the servants and the police. This was the contortion of the colonel's face. It had set, according to their account, into the most dreadful expression of fear and horror which a human countenance is capable of assuming." Until then invisible, his (Irish) capability for deceit at last abjectly marks his face. Praised as model soldiers, the Irish are nonetheless subaltern, potentially disaffected partners in the imperial enterprise. As in *The Sign of Four*, Doyle adopts a counterinsurgent code, employing a narrative of crime to counter the logic of insurgency. One

Irishman may be personally dishonest and the other may be abjectly crippled, but neither threatens to undermine British hegemony. The imperial regime, of which Doyle is again tacitly a part, exercises the discursive power of coding challenges to its hegemony as "crime" and consequently delegitimizes them.

Doyle's rewriting of political conflict as crime is arguably in keeping with the power/knowledge relations of modernity. In his book *Toward A New Common Sense: Law, Science and Politics in the Paradigmatic Transition*, Boaventura de Sousa Santos presents a critique of the epistemologies of modernity.[32] He suggests that political power in fact accrued from and fed into the production of scientific knowledge, which was given greater significance and authority than the seemingly more contingent domain of politics. Pointing, as numerous scholars have done, to the privileging in modernity of scientific rationality and its fetishism of efficacy and efficiency, Santos argues that the scientific management of society was underpinned by law. In rewriting social conflict as crime, Doyle engages in such a normative invocation of law. Furthermore, it is no coincidence that Doyle employs the particular strategies of counterinsurgent fiction in conjunction with a valorization of scientific rationality. Imperial conflict is depoliticized in being coded as crime; and "crime" is not, in his stories, a complex social phenomenon but rather a problem that can be "solved" by the application of rational scientific methods.

Santos limits his discussion to Europe. Speaking of an epistemological colonialism that inheres in modernity, a colonialism "which is no less than the incapacity to relate to the other but by transforming the other into an object," Santos fails to consider more literally the induction into modernity of the non-Western world through the violent practices of colonialism. Here the processes of scientific and juridical depoliticization to which Santos alludes are far less evident than in Europe. However, his remarks about the yoking in European modernity of scientific and legal discourses are strikingly germane to Doyle's detective fiction. While these stories do not illustrate the means by which colonial modernity is established in the non-Western world, they do present fantasies of how disorder, and often a disorder that originates in the imperial world, is countered by the forces of science and law.[33]

Detective fiction concludes by bringing hermeneutic and juridical order to an unquiet and dangerous world. Puzzles and unsolved identities are resolved, blame is assigned, and peace is reestablished. In some of his stories of return, Doyle makes the coupling of good and bad returns from Empire palatable by superimposing a juridical and ethical narrative of crime and detection upon a social and economic narrative of unequal fortunes. Moreover, the outcast colonial generally deserves his ill fortune because he is a reprobate. This is the logic of stories such as *The Hound of the Baskervilles* and *The Sign of Four*. When the outcast is discovered and the story of his crime is told, the cosmos in which he is placed is rid of uncertainty and the community cleansed of guilt. W. H. Auden, in an essay on detective fiction, "The Guilty Vicarage," argues that the criminal expiates the sins of all. "In the [detective story] it is certain that a crime has been committed and, temporarily, uncertain to whom the guilt should be attached; as soon as this is known, the innocence of everyone else is certain."[34] The assigning of guilt purifies the community as a whole. To take this argument in a secular direction, in fiction of imperial intrigue this individuation of criminal culpability is also a way of displacing social and political problems—the "sins of all." Christopher Clausen comments, "As Holmes' critical observations apply only to individuals, so his vocation, the solution of individual crimes, merely restores the social balance that each crime has upset. It never brings that balance into question, for the causes of disorder, where they involve more than individual motives, are not his concern."[35] This bracketing of causes in favor of effects is, according to Jon Thompson, the fundamental logic of empiricism that drove the imperial project.[36]

However, in many instances, Doyle does not offer ideologically and psychologically tidy resolutions. Guilt is often not neatly assigned to the hapless imperial malingerer. These lumpen are never valorized (Doyle would hardly go that far), but sometimes their grievances are presented as just. In "The Crooked Man," for example, Henry Wood is in no way culpable for his misfortunes. Although Colonel Barclay is ultimately exposed, and justly suffers a stroke, Wood is not rehabilitated. While Doyle distinguishes between the respectable and unprepossessing colonial, and marks the latter as abject, he does not impose any neat moral schema upon this pattern of depicting colonials. Often, the seemingly successful and respectable colonials are corrupt—as in *The Sign of Four* and *The Crooked Man*. In "The Case of the 'Gloria Scott'" and "The Boscombe Valley Mystery," it is the law-abiding colonial and not the former outlaw who is characterized as a villainous tormentor and blackmailer. Nor is there always a conclusive ending to the stories. In "The 'Gloria Scott,'" Hudson disappears at the end of the story. Sherlock Holmes speculates that Beddoes, a supposed victim of Hudson's course of blackmail, has done away with Hudson, but we do not know this for certain. Thus Doyle's detective stories are more ambiguous than would first appear to be the case. Criminality and guilt are the substance of detective cosmology, yet these are often shown to be insufficiently clear-cut. The open-endedness of the stories suggests that the ideological and ethical contradictions they raise are not fully resolved.

To focus in Doyle's detective stories on the discontents of Empire is to read these stories against the grain, for Doyle emphatically does not indict colonial capitalism and administration. When he acknowledges their existence at all, he characterizes the native inhabitants of the colonies as corrupt and savage. In his view, the influence of English culture is unquestionably civilizing. When English characters experience a moral and physical decline in the colonies, they become more and more like the ostensibly unregenerate natives. The shadowy figures of English colonials who have fallen through the cracks of the imperial economy and society haunt his stories. Their return to England and embroilment in misadventures or crimes suggests that something is rotten in the state of Empire. While imperial rhetoric celebrates the ideal of a prosperous and superior ruling race, imperial economies produce impoverished and ailing colonials, abject characters who can be neither assimilated nor entirely separated from the metropole. One might go as far as to argue that in failing to effect complete closure, assign blame unequivocally, and purge the entire community of guilt, Doyle, wittingly or not, expresses the antinomies of late Victorian imperialism.

EMPIRE AND THE SPY

The spy novel emerged on the scene of popular British fiction at the end of the nineteenth century, when imperial rivalry between European powers was at it peak. Erskine Childers's *The Riddle of the Sands*, which, as I have noted, is widely regarded as the first modern spy novel, dramatizes two Englishmen's discovery while on a yachting holiday in the Frisian Islands of a secret German plot to invade England. While this novel is about the growing hostility between imperial powers rather than about colonial insurgency, Childers was himself pursued by the British for his participation in the Irish Republican struggle, and was executed in 1922 for treason when he was caught with a small pistol given to him by Michael Collins.

In the last chapter we explored the ambiguous position of the Irish vis-à-vis the British Empire. In 1901, Kipling fashioned in the character of Kim a colonial spy of Irish origins whose fluidity of identity is exploited by the British in India, to foil a plot by a native ruler who is pressed to assist the Russians in "the Great Game"—the rivalry between the British and the Czarist empires for control in Central Asia. The spy novel, at its inception, was linked to anxieties about imperial rivalry as well as colonial insurgency . In this section, I examine how John Buchan's novels *Prester John* and *Greenmantle* depict insurgencies in the making. In *Prester John*, the protagonist discovers and preempts an incipient native rebellion in southern Africa. A pan-Islamic uprising, yoked to a German expansionist plot, threatens in *Greenmantle*. Like Doyle's stories of colonial insurgency, these novels suggest that the British Empire is indeed politically vulnerable even as they delineate the triumph of the imperium. And like the detective stories, these spy novels can be viewed as counterinsurgent fiction in that they rhetorically disavow the efficacy of anticolonial insurgencies. However, these fictions of espionage represent and respond to the threat of insurgency in ways that differ from detective fiction.

A brief review of John Buchan's life and career provides a personal and political context for his fiction.[37] Like Doyle, Buchan was born in Scotland and spent his youth there. His literary skill at describing landscapes was perhaps a consequence of his great love for the Scottish countryside. Although his family was not wealthy, Buchan was able to obtain an education in letters at the University of Glasgow and then at Brasenose College, Oxford, by means of scholarships and his earnings from his writing. After obtaining a first in Greats (classics) at Oxford, Buchan joined the bar. He spent two years in South Africa as an aide to the high commissioner, Lord Milner, after the Boer War. Back in London, Buchan pursued varied and overlapping careers as a writer, publisher, politician, propagandist, and at one point director of intelligence at the newly founded Department of Information (later made a ministry). His last post was that of governor-general of Canada, from 1935 to 1940.

Buchan is a particularly interesting figure because, again like Doyle, he not only embodied the ideals of imperial service in his public life, but also expressed his views about Empire in his essays, historical writing, and fiction. In her study *John Buchan and the Idea of Empire*, Juanita Kruse traces Buchan's enthusiasm for Empire to a childhood verve for marauding outdoors and reading adventure stories and historical romances; to a youth spent at Oxford where he found in his set of accomplished and worldly-wise friends the lack of a commitment to anything larger than themselves; and most of all, to his years as a secretary to Milner in South Africa, where "the Empire seemed to Buchan more than ever to offer the ideal opportunity for a young Briton to widen his horizons and to stretch himself to his full potential."[38] Buchan saw in the project of imperialism not only the opportunity to bring civilization to subject peoples, whom he thought childlike and backward; he saw in imperialism the chance to give a worthy purpose to young men in England.

While he is an unquestioning champion of British imperialism, and undoubtedly racist in his representation of Africans, Buchan refrains from the celebration of extreme and gratuitous violence that is characteristic of other writers of imperial adventure fiction such as G. A. Henty and Rider Haggard.[39] Buchan's heroes are by comparison judicious and moderate in their dealings with Africans. This is not to say that Buchan was any less convinced of the desirability of British rule over the "subject races." Although he did not trumpet his racism quite as loudly as did his peers, he classed peoples according to their supposed capabilities, and did not hesitate to seek to exploit these for the benefit of Great Britain and her territories.[40] For example, he believed that Africans were culturally unsuited to work the mines of South Africa, and hence he recommended that indentured Chinese laborers be brought to do so at the will and convenience of the British administration.[41] He believed that colonized peoples should be allowed to "develop" culturally and politically, but under benevolent British supervision.

Buchan's imperial rhetoric is more restrained than that of other writers, in part because he wrote after the expansionist period of Victorian imperialism, when the object was no longer the conquest but the defense and administration of territory.[42] A shift in the tone of imperial fiction can be detected in other novels, too, such as *Kim,* where the boyish spirit of the protagonist, seen in his exuberant pleasure in exploring India and mingling with her peoples, is harnessed and refashioned for the purposes of the "Great Game"—intelligence gathering intended to forestall a Russian challenge. In such fiction, the lawlessness and aggressiveness of the buccaneer are less desirable than the dedication and dependability of the subaltern. The hero of *Prester John* observes that he would have made a poor general, adding, "But I think I would have done well in a subaltern command, for I had a great notion of carrying out orders, and a certain zest in the mere act of obedience."[43] Although Buchan's heroes occasionally strike out on their own, they embrace their roles as reliable imperial servants. Such was Buchan's own commitment to Empire.

Prester John, written in 1909, was the first of Buchan's novels to be a popular success. Buchan drew upon his years of experience with Milner in South Africa after the Boer War to write a story that conveys a vivid sense of the African veld. Like novels by Stevenson and Haggard, *Prester John* belongs to the genre of the adventure story for boys. Young David Crawfurd sets off for South Africa as an employee of a trading company. On the way, he catches a glimpse of an enigmatic African minister, John Laputa, whom he has encountered earlier in suspicious circumstances as a child in Scotland. The minister appears to have a mysterious connection with Henriques, a shifty-looking Jewish Portuguese passenger (Buchan's notorious anti-Semitism is evident here), and also with Blaauwildebeestefontein, Crawfurd's destination. In Blaauwildebeestefontein, Crawfurd catches wind of a number of suspicious goings-on: these include an illegal trade in diamonds, the rumored existence of a devil in the nearby Rooirands, his own ongoing surveillance by his African neighbors, and messages being transmitted by native drums. His inference that a native rebellion is about to break out is confirmed by a disguised English intelligence agent, Captain Arcoll, who has been on Laputa's trail for many months.[44] Laputa, it appears, claims descent from the legendary Prester John, a "remote Christian priest-king," whose fetish, a collar of rubies, he supposedly possesses.[45] Laputa proposes to unite all Africans and lead them in a rebellion against their European oppressors. Crawfurd, by dint of his pluck and resourcefulness, foils his efforts. At the end of the novel, he finds he is "the little reef on which a great vessel has foundered," to use Laputa's dying words. He saves his country and returns to England with a fortune in gold and diamonds.

David Crawfurd encounters the African minister Laputa for the first time in Crawfurd's native Scottish town of Kirkcaple when he is a young boy. *Prester John* begins with an incident in Scotland before moving into the space of Empire, and so raises the question of how to interpret the Scottish backdrop to the novel. I suggested earlier that in Doyle's stories "The Green Flag" and "The Crooked Man," the Irish subtext reveals anxiety about the commitment of Irish soldiers to Empire. Buchan, by contrast, expresses profound confidence in the imperial allegiances of Scotsmen. His confidence can be explained in historical terms, and also in relation to his own experience and beliefs. Historically, Scotland represented the Union that worked whereas

Ireland represented the Union that did not, at least at the time when Buchan wrote. Himself Scots, Buchan had been able to straddle the two cultures and achieve considerable success in British governmental service. In his view, an attachment to home and nation was not inimical to a commitment to the British Empire. In fact, early in his career, he espoused an ideal of imperial federation that accommodated strong local patriotism. Both Doyle and John Buchan, then, implicitly acknowledge the heterogeneity of "Britishness." In their writing, Empire becomes an arena in which the viability of Britishness and of imperial hegemony is demonstrated. Doyle, in interweaving narratives of private crimes by Europeans with ones of political insurgency by natives, elides anxieties about the political allegiances of the Irish and of poor whites. John Buchan emphasizes the daring and dedication of his Scots hero David Crawfurd in his service to the British Empire.

A passage early in *Prester John* exemplifies several aspects of John Buchan's writing. Crawfurd and his two companions spy on the imposing Laputa by moonlight as he performs a mysterious ritual on the beach. Crawfurd recalls,

> I remember looking back and seeing the solemn, frowning faces of the cliffs, and feeling somehow shut in with this unknown being in a strange union. What kind of errand had brought this interloper into our territory? For a wonder I was less afraid than curious. I wanted to get to the heart of the matter, and to discover what the man was up to with his fire and his circles. (p. 12)

Buchan introduces a crucial theme that runs through the novel: the desirability as well as difficulty of knowing the Other. On the one hand, Crawfurd regards Laputa as an intruder who has penetrated the boys' secret hideout. Crawfurd expresses displeasure at the violation of their territory. He also balks at a forced intimacy with Laputa; he is "shut in with this unknown being." Interwoven with this discomfort, verging on claustrophobia, is an impulse to know and understand this stranger more profoundly—"to get to the heart of the matter." His "strange union" with Laputa is both problematic and compelling.[46]

The mixture of fascination and suspicion evident in this passage is the structure of feeling that motivates surveillance. While not expressly a spy novel like Buchan's later books, *Prester John* frequently dramatizes the clandestine observation of characters, as it does at this moment. Crawfurd and his friends spy on the minister's un-Christian worship and learn that the minister is not all that he appears to be in public. In Buchan's novels, characters frequently observe others in secret and are themselves objects of surveillance. In separate studies of the nineteenth-century novel, D. A. Miller and Mark Seltzer remark upon the literary incidence of surveillance. Miller's project is to study the "policing function" in literature and to determine how "the novel—as a set of representational techniques—systematically participate[s] in a general economy of policing power," while Seltzer considers the "ways in which the novel, as a form and as an institution, reinscribes and supplements social mechanisms of policing and regulation."[47] Looking at different sets of works, both critics argue that the trope of surveillance exemplifies the ways in which power acts invisibly to further social control. Undoubtedly, surveillance and the other modes of operation of disciplinary power are crucial to the constitution of the liberal European subject. The status of surveillance in imperial culture is somewhat different—power is not exercised in Empire in invisible and dispersed ways to instantiate a "free" subject. The foregrounding of spying can be better explained with regard to problems of knowledge and of identity to which I will return shortly.

Buchan's heroes are drawn into intrigues not only out of a reasoned commitment to the forces of imperial order, but also out of an insatiable, incorrigible curiosity, one subtly different from that of the detective. Sherlock Holmes, when presented with a mystery, also strives "to get to the heart of the matter." His will to know, however, is exercised in a systematic and masterful fashion, and involves the careful observation and reconstruction of traces. Buchan's heroes, by contrast, are often impulsive and foolhardy in their pursuit of knowledge. Rather than retreat unobtrusively, and reconnoiter, Crawfurd is inclined upon his first encounter to approach Laputa and puzzle over his doings. Because they are impelled by curiosity, Buchan's protagonists act spontaneously and follow erratic and risky courses of action.

The passage quoted above hints at another recurring preoccupation in Buchan's tales: the fascination of the ritual and cabalistic. Crawfurd observes Laputa in the middle of a strange pagan ceremony. Such scenes of fetishism and ritual worship recur in the novel. This fascination with non-Christian spiritualism is also found in *Greenmantle*, where the occult intrudes upon the everyday. In Buchan's novels, a sense of mystery derives not only from a transgression of legality but also from a departure from Western religious rationalities. While he exploits the spiritual practices of other cultures to impart a sense of the uncanny and the mysterious to his scenes, he also posits these practices as marks of otherness and indeed backwardness.

The passage also reflects Buchan's skill at describing landscape. One is given little sense of Crawfurd's companions, or even of Laputa, whereas the terrain is described vividly, in anthropomorphic terms. This is no less typical of Buchan's accounts of the South African veld than of those of his native Scotland. In this respect, his writing is markedly different from that of Conrad, who renders with enormous skill the psychological complexity of characters; it is different also from the imperial fiction of Kipling, who excels in colorful sketches of incidents. Buchan's stories engage the reader in no small part because of his vivid depictions of the land that his protagonists traverse. While his characters are by and large psychologically flat and the quandaries in which they find themselves somewhat predictable, Buchan infuses his accounts of terrain with a vitality and mystery that keeps the reader turning the page. Buchan's skill at vivifying Crawfurd's experiences of the land is not merely noteworthy as a matter of literary ability; the ideological significance of the hero's intimate engagement with the land, and the reader's pleasure in this experience, are worth querying. In an introduction to *Kim*, Edward Said suggests that Kipling's descriptions of Kim's knowledge of and pleasure in the Indian terrain he traverses support an ontological claim to the land.[48] A like argument can be made about Buchan, whose fiction expresses a heightened awareness of landscape, and a marked investment in knowing, crossing, penetrating, and securing imperial space. At the same time, in his fiction the landscape, and more broadly, nature, has an integrity and autonomy that eludes full rationalization and full knowledge. In Doyle's detective fiction, by contrast, the physical world can be fully known if it is properly subjected to the rigors of scientific method, that is, observation, analysis, and rational deduction. While Buchan's novels demonstrate a will to know the terrain of the colony, they also evince a romantic element in their emphasis on its inscrutability and mystery.

Laputa's enigmatic behavior on the Kirkcaple shore is explained when years later Crawfurd travels to South Africa and discovers the preacher to be the prime mover in an incipient insurgency. At first, the prospect of rebellion is raised purely in hypothetical terms. Crawfurd listens to the arguments of a schoolteacher and neighbor in Blaauwildebeestefontein:

> Mr. Wardlaw thought we were underrating the capacity of the native.... It was not his intelligence which he thought we underrated, but

his dangerousness. His reasons, shortly, were these: There were five or six of them to every white man; they were all, roughly speaking, of the same stock, with the same tribal beliefs; they had only just ceased being a warrior race, with a powerful military discipline; and, most important, they lived round the rim of the high-veld plateau, and if they combined could cut off the white man from the sea.... It would be a second and bloodier Indian Mutiny. (p. 53)

The teacher invokes racist ideas, ethnography, geography, and historical precedent to argue the plausibility of a dangerous uprising. His reference to the Indian Mutiny is particularly resonant, conjuring up the specter of insurrection and carnage. Wardlaw's companions are inclined to construe his remarks as alarmist. It is not until Captain Arcoll, whose business it is "to act as chief Intelligence officer among the natives," arrives on the scene and shares his findings about John Laputa that the full extent of the danger of insurgency becomes clear.

Buchan's depiction of insurgency was undoubtedly influenced by accounts of the numerous rebellions by Africans against European domination. Tim Couzens enumerates several historical episodes of resistance that resonate strongly with Buchan's fictional account: the rebellions of Makgatho and Mphefu of the Venda tribe from the 1850s through the 1890s; the Ndebele-Shona uprising of 1896–1897; the opposition of Magoeba in 1895 in the Wood Bush area; the refusal to pay taxes in 1894 of Malapoch and his people, who took refuge in caves but were attacked by the Europeans with dynamite; and the Bambatha rebellion of 1906, among others. Buchan's service in South Africa under Milner would have left him with some familiarity with these episodes. A knowledge of these insurgencies, Couzens argues, was supplemented by the idea of Ethiopianism, with which Buchan would again have been familiar.[49] While the conditions for insurgency prevail in a general way in *Prester John,* it is the galvanizing leadership of Laputa in the cause of Ethiopianism that makes insurgency a real threat.

The African minister is the most intriguing and powerful character in *Prester John.* Crawfurd repeatedly describes Laputa as commanding in figure and visage, well spoken, well educated, disciplined, and determined. He predicates his historical mission, the emancipation of his people, upon the claim that he is an incarnation of Prester John, a legendary Christian ruler of Abyssinia in the fifteenth century who conquered a vast territory that extended to southern Africa. Arcoll has discovered after "days in the best libraries in Europe over it," that subsequent tribes who have advanced to the south of Africa have invoked the spirit of Prester John as a beneficent force.[50] He explains, "[The Zulus] brought with them the story of Prester John, but by this time it had ceased to be a historical memory, and had become a religious cult" (p. 72). Crucial to this cult is a fetish that has descended from Prester John. Reverend Laputa has draped himself in the mantle of this mythical figure, and has yoked together a discourse of political emancipation and one of religious deliverance to instigate an insurgency. Arcoll recounts, "Presently I found that he preached more than the gospel. His word was 'Africa for the Africans,' and his chief point was that the natives had had a great empire in the past, and might have a great empire again" (p. 73). Although his ambition may be exorbitant, his sense of his historical mission is impressive and moving. Crawfurd, who later manages to slip into a secret gathering of the rebels in the cave of the Rooirand, recounts Laputa's speech to his followers.

> He pictured the heroic age of his nation, when every man was a warrior and hunter, and rich kraals stood in the spots now desecrated by the white man, and cattle wandered on a thousand hills. Then he told tales of white infamy, lands snatched from their rightful possessors, unjust laws which forced the Ethiopian to the bondage of a despised caste, the finger of scorn everywhere, and the mocking word. If it be the part of an orator to rouse the passion of his hearers, Laputa was the greatest on earth. "What have you gained from the white man?" he cried. "A bastard civilization which has sapped your manhood; a false religion which would rivet on you the chains of the slave. Ye, the old masters of the land, are now the servants of the oppressor. And yet the oppressors are few, and the fear of you is in their hearts. They feast in their great cities, but they see the writing on the wall, and their eyes are anxiously turning lest the enemy be at their gates." I cannot hope in my prosaic words to reproduce that amazing discourse. Phrases which the hearer had heard at mission schools now suddenly appeared, not as the white man's learning, but as God's message to His own. (p. 105)

Laputa urges his companions to rebel by invoking a heroic past, and by describing the subsequent era of European hegemony as a period of tyranny and exploitation that must be ended. This political exhortation is given added potency by an infusion of messianic language. In this passage, Buchan presents the insurgent's arguments in an even-handed manner, giving them credibility. So eloquent and persuasive is the minister that Crawfurd himself is almost swayed. Laputa is depicted as a charismatic leader who justly seeks the deliverance of his people.

While Buchan portrays Laputa as, in Guha's words, "an entity whose will and reason constitute[s] the praxis called rebellion" and gives some credence to the point of view of the insurgent, he also introduces to the narrative elements that mark it as fiction of counterinsurgency. In naming him after the imaginary nation of Swift's *Gulliver's Travels*, Buchan directs a measure of ridicule at the African preacher and his schemes.[51] Laputa, Gulliver's first stop on his third voyage, is the name of an island in the air. Its inhabitants are so lost in abstract speculation that they must be periodically roused to attend to the world about them by especially employed "flappers." Swift satirizes an excessive preoccupation with abstract science, mathematics, and musical theory at the cost of more practical ethical concerns. By implication, the African John Laputa is an overreaching builder of castles in the air. His ritual of fires and circles on the Kirkcaple shore refers to the occult but also to geometry gone mad. His mission to liberate his people is depicted as unrealistic and misguided.

Buchan further discredits Laputa's political aspirations by describing his recourse to ritual and fetishism, and by characterizing his religion as a distorted and degenerate Christianity. Arcoll tells of Laputa's reversion:

> At full moon when the black cock was blooded the Reverend John forgot his Christianity. He was back four centuries among the Mazimba sweeping down on the Zambesi. He told them, and they believed him, that he was the Umkulunkulu, the incarnated spirit of Prester John. He told them that he was there to lead the African race to conquest and Empire. Ay, and he told them more: for he has, or says he has, the Great Snake itself, the necklet of Prester John. (p. 75)

In this account, Laputa's claims are set against the backdrop of a moonlit animal sacrifice. The temporality of the passage is one of regression: the minister takes his followers back in time. The phrase "he told them, and they believed him" suggests an element of chicanery on the part of Laputa and gullibility on that of his listeners; the rhetorical effect of "he has, or says he has" is similar. And finally, Laputa's political mission is described in a brief, simple sentence, depleting the mission of the glory and historical persuasiveness that is communicated by Laputa's reported speech in the passage above.

Ranajit Guha suggests that in prose of counterinsurgency, political uprisings are often characterized as motivated by unreflective fanaticism. In Buchan's novel, the Africans' religious practices are described as atavistic and irrational. Arcoll here suggests that the Reverend willfully sets aside his Christianity, but in fact he employs a distorted version of Christian discourse. Laputa appropriates the religious rhetoric that has been disseminated by missionary schools to urge rebellion. One can detect a similar anxiety about the colonial corruption of Christianity in Joyce Cary's novel *The African Witch*, in which a native self-appointed preacher uses a perverted Christian rhetoric to urge a crowd to decapitate a German missionary.[52] If, as Chinua Achebe suggests in *Things Fall Apart*, Christianity is generally allied with colonial government, it can also be turned against the colonial regime. In *Prester John*, a syncretic Christianity takes on a dangerous aspect, lending Laputa's incendiary language added resonance.

Buchan's portrait of Laputa and of his headquarters in the Rooirand is markedly romantic. In *Prester John*, nature has an autonomous status and integrity. Whereas in detective novels, nature can be rationalized, here nature cannot be fully known. The cave in the Rooirand is represented as a sublime natural formation. There is a parallel between this view of nature and of Laputa's character—the romanticism of Laputa is suggested by his return to nature in death. While Buchan portrays Laputa as a great leader, he also distinguishes Laputa from his fellow Africans as racially exceptional: "He had none of the squat and preposterous negro lineaments, but a hawk nose like an Arab, dark flashing eyes, and a cruel and resolute mouth." His followers are variously characterized as cowardly, boastful, and given to a "strange, twisted reasoning" (p. 198). In a conversation with Laputa about the feasibility of a rebellion, Crawfurd demurs, "Where are the patriots in your following? They are all red Kaffirs crying for blood and plunder. Supposing you were Oliver Cromwell you could make nothing out of such a crew" (p. 151). Laputa answers, "They are my people." The minister is a tragic figure—he recognizes his people's failings, but undertakes to lead them to freedom. When its remarkable leader dies, the insurgency collapses.

If Buchan rhetorically discredits political rebellion by casting it as a fanatical uprising led by a megalomaniac, his characters Crawfurd and Arcoll literally foil Laputa's plans by spying out the insurgency that is brewing in the hinterland. *Prester John* is not obviously a spy novel, as are Buchan's more famous later books, *The Thirty-Nine*

Steps and *Greenmantle*. Spying and surveillance, however, play a large part in the various characters' activities. Crawfurd first spies on Laputa on the Kirkcaple shore, where he discovers that the minister is not all he seems. This suspicion is confirmed when years later he happens upon Laputa talking to Henriques and overhears their conversation. At first, these instances of secret observation are fortuitous. As the story develops, characters engage in espionage and intelligence gathering in a more concerted way.

The African insurgents use surveillance and "native telepathy" to organize themselves and to deter anyone who might interfere. In Blaauwildebeestefontein, Crawfurd discovers that he is being watched: "For I now became aware that I was being subjected to constant espionage.... Wherever I went—on the road, on the meadows of the plateau, or on the rugged sides of the Berg—it was the same. I had silent followers, who betrayed themselves now and then by the crackling of a branch, and eyes were always looking at me which I could not see" (p. 37). Later, Crawfurd realizes on a walk along the Berg that he is being monitored to preempt him from traveling to one of the towns to tell what he knows. The surveillance he describes is systematic and constant, the work of a large and well-organized group of people. Laputa's followers are able to use a native form of communication, drumming, to coordinate their activities. Wardlaw points out, "They can send news over a thousand miles as quick as the telegraph, and we have no means of tapping the wires" (p. 54). The Africans' effective way of clandestinely gathering and transmitting intelligence also makes them dangerous.

Captain Arcoll also resorts to espionage to gather information about the incipient insurgency. When Crawfurd first meets him, he is convincingly disguised as an old Kaffir, as the Africans are called. His ability to pass as an African has enabled him to penetrate the inner circles of the tribal organization. He tells Crawfurd, "I have sat in tribal councils and been sworn a blood brother, and I have used the secret password to get knowledge in odd places. It was a dangerous game, and, as I have said, I had my adventures, but I came safe out of it—with my knowledge" (p. 75). Arcoll gains intimate knowledge of his adversaries by participating in rites of consanguinity, and by using secret code words. Crawfurd, too, on one occasion enters the headquarters of the conspirators by using a secret watchword, and participates in Laputa's ritual ordination as king. He is thus able to learn about the rebellion firsthand. Arcoll and Crawfurd operate from within the camp of the enemy because they require immediate and personal knowledge of their antagonists to thwart them.

Arcoll's and Crawfurd's experiences undercover suggest that spy fiction represents the task of knowing the Other in ways quite different from detective fiction. I suggested earlier that the detective pieces together fragments of knowledge from a position of exteriority to solve a crime. While Arcoll and Crawfurd do this sort of detective work, they also cross the boundaries of culture in their quest for knowledge, and go as far as to assume the identity of the Other. This act of passing as another entails the risk not merely of being unmasked, but of destabilizing the self. When Crawfurd listens to Laputa in the cave of the Rooirand, he is so enthralled that he loses a sense of his own allegiances:

> By rights, I suppose, my blood should have been boiling at this treason. I am ashamed to confess that it did nothing of the sort. My mind was mesmerized by this amazing man. I could not refrain from shouting with the rest. Indeed I was a convert, if there can be conversion when the emotions are dominant and there is no assent from the brain. I had a mad desire to be of Laputa's party. (p. 136)

Crawfurd is able to gain firsthand knowledge of Laputa's doings, but from such an intimate perspective that he identifies with Laputa. As the other men move forward to take the oath, Crawfurd awaits his turn, impelled by the force of Laputa's personality. Ironically, it is only when Henriques shouts, "By God, a spy!" and Crawfurd is gripped and faints that the spell is broken. In detective fiction, the identification of a miscreant is the purpose of an investigation. While this may prove difficult, identity itself is not problematized. In spy fiction, the doubleness of identity makes identity itself a problem, and leads at times to a crisis.

Greenmantle, written during World War I, brings together the themes of espionage and insurgency in such a way as to throw into relief more sharply than *Prester John* the precariousness of identity. The novel is loosely based on an episode that Buchan describes in his history of World War I: "under German direction an attempt was made to preach a Holy War throughout the Moslem provinces. It was represented that the German Emperor was a convert to Islam, and presently the Khalif would order a Jehad against the infidel.... The Mohammedan world was believed to be a powder magazine waiting for the spark."[53] Buchan takes up the possibility of a pan-Islamic jihad and weaves around it a story of espionage and counterinsurgency. Hannay, the protagonist of his earlier novel *The Thirty-Nine Steps*, is recruited by Sir Walter Bullivant of the Foreign Office to uncover the origins of an Islamic war of liberation in the East, against the backdrop of Germany's alliance with Turkey. Bullivant suggests that Germany's imperial ambitions hinge upon the success of this movement. Consequently, Hannay's mission to preempt this insurgency is crucial to the thwarting of German expansion. Provided with three enigmatic clues, "kasredin," "cancer," and "v. i.," Hannay and his comrades disperse with a plan to meet in Constantinople two months later. Hannay and Pienaar go to Germany undercover as Boer soldiers, Blenkiron travels as an American sympathizer of the Germans, and Sandy Arbuthnot disappears eastward. After a series of adventures the group meets as planned in Constantinople, where they pool their findings. They conclude that a German woman, Hilda von Einem, is the brain behind a German plan to exploit the fervor of the faithful for a newly arisen saint, Greenmantle, who is dying of cancer. Von Einem hopes to rally his followers in Erzerum against the Russians. She involves Sandy—who has taken on the character of a Turkish gypsy—in her scheme, and proposes that he assume the role of Greenmantle. The dénouement takes place at the German front where Pienaar smuggles a stolen map of the German defenses to the Allies. Hannay, Sandy, and von Einem meet on a mountaintop, where Sandy rebuffs the German woman's offer to discuss terms. Shortly afterward, she is killed by a shell. The Allies overpower the Germans with the aid of the map, and Hannay and his friends emerge as heroes.

Buchan's account of the stirring jihad is, like his depiction of insurgency in *Prester John,* ambivalent. He represents Islam, and Greenmantle its new prophet, as austere and dignified. "The West knows nothing of the Oriental. It pictures him as lapped in color and idleness and luxury and gorgeous dreams. But it is all wrong. The Kaf he yearns for is an austere thing. It is the austerity of the East that is its beauty and its terror.... Well, Greenmantle is the prophet of this great simplicity. He speaks straight to the heart of Islam, and it's an honorable message."[54] Buchan rejects Western stereotypes of Oriental decadence, replacing these with images of purification and revitalization. Sandy himself is enthralled by this vision. "It's the humanity of one part of the human race. It isn't ours, it isn't as good as ours, but it's jolly good all the same. There are times when it grips me so hard that I'm inclined to forswear the gods of my fathers" (p. 183). While one might object to the implications of this argument—that fundamentalism is all right for them—it does show a certain respect on Buchan's part for Islam. Once again Buchan presents an intimate knowledge of the point of view of the antagonist as a desirable end. His characters do not merely accept the insurgents' beliefs but rather find them compelling.

The religious uprising is pernicious not in itself, then, but because the Germans are able to manipulate it for their imperial ends. "But for our sins it's been twisted into part of that damned German propaganda. His unworldliness has been used for a cunning political move, and his creed of space and simplicity for the furtherance of the last word in human degeneracy" (p. 183). While Greenmantle's mission is to regenerate a cloyed society, the Germans' aim is to reduce it to its crudest elements. Hannay has divined as much and has praised the German ideal to win the German mastermind Hilda von Einem's trust: "Germany, in spite of her blunders and her grossness, stood forth as the scourge of cant. She had the courage to cut through the bonds of humbug and to laugh at the fetishes of the herd" (p. 179). Buchan draws a likeness between the Islamic revivalists and the German imperialists, but claims that the former are simply adherents of a different creed, whereas the latter have totalitarian ambitions that will obliterate difference.

Buchan's portrayal of Stumm and Hilda von Einem, the two most important German characters, suggests that the German ideal is a false one. Stumm is not only a brute but has a streak of effeminacy, betrayed in the opulence of his private room: "It was the room of a man who had a passion for frippery, who had a taste for soft, delicate things." This luxury is at odds with the austerity of his public chambers, and with the ideal of simplicity that the Germans hold. If Stumm is not properly masculine, Hilda von Einem lacks feminine sympathy. Sandy protests, "Woman!...Does a woman drag a man through the nether-pit? She's a she-devil" (p. 179). While ordinary Germans, such as Gaudian the engineer and the peasant woman who shelters Hannay when he is on the run in Bavaria, are depicted as good-hearted folk, the leaders Stumm and von Einem are represented as having abnormal gender identities and by implication grotesque political ambitions.

Hannay and his friends thwart these ambitions by entering not only the territories, but also the hearts and minds of their adversaries. Hannay applauds this capacity for crossing the boundaries of culture and identity in Sandy Arbuthnot: "We call ourselves insular, but the truth is that we are the only race on earth that can produce men capable of getting under the skin of remote peoples. Perhaps the Scots are better than the English, but we're all a thousand percent better than anybody else" (p. 223).[55] The character of Sandy Arbuthnot may have been loosely patterned on T. E. Lawrence, but was more clearly modeled upon Buchan's friend Aubrey Herbert.[56] The reference to the Scottish is intriguing, and suggests that Buchan viewed them as especially adventurous travelers and hence valuable servants of Empire. Hannay's own nationality is ambiguous—we learn in *The Thirty-Nine Steps* that he has just returned from South Africa, but has a Scottish background. By counting himself in the "we" whom he lauds, Hannay posits an inclusive and malleable notion of Britishness. Variously disguised as a Boer soldier, a German postman, and an American adventurer, Hannay exploits this ability for impersonation to elude Germans and to gain their trust. Sandy Arbuthnot is so convincing in his role as head of the Companions of the Rosy Hours, a band of Turkish gypsies, that he takes even Hannay in. Sandy is more than an impersonator—he's a longtime member of the company, and blood brother of the boss. Again, Buchan's protagonists are so effective in large part because they shed their own personas and embrace other identities.

Buchan's heroes take pleasure in espionage. Their adventures require them to act spontaneously, impulsively, and bravely. Early in *Greenmantle,* Hannay and Peter Pienaar are taken by Stumm to a prisoners' camp, where an English prisoner of war recognizes Hannay, his former major. Hannay must think on his feet, and he stages an upset of cards, taking advantage of the confusion to get a message across to the prisoner. This example is typical of the moments of unexpected danger and near undoing of his cover that recur in the spy's adventures. Hannay's bravado is often foolhardy. In the middle of a rooftop escape from Stumm in Erzerum, Hannay hangs back and enters Stumm's room upon an impulse. When Crawfurd escapes from his captors in *Prester John,* he rides toward Laputa's headquarters instead of attempting to rejoin Arcoll. Unlike the detective, who deliberates and acts cautiously, the spy relishes the unpredictable.

This penchant for spontaneity and for the pleasure of unconstrained action is allowed free play in the colony. John Cawelti points out that Buchan's characterization of Sandy Arbuthnot encapsulates "the lure of the exotic, the dream of casting off the burden of identity like a suit of old clothes and letting oneself be swallowed up in the mysterious spiritual worlds of alien peoples, the desire to escape from the dull routines of civilized life into a more primitive and daring world, the search for a crusade to deepen and intensify the sense of life, to get away from the orderly and civilized patterns of the Cotswolds which seem so constructive."[57] Buchan's heroes are committed to the defense of "civilization," but relish the opportunity to conduct this defense on terrain where they are released, if only temporarily, from the dull orderliness of everyday metropolitan life. The attractions of "going primitive" are expressed by a number of writers of this period.[58] In Buchan, this characteristically modern sentiment—expressed for instance by Freud, Gauguin, and Conrad—is yoked to the imperatives of Empire's defense.[59]

Accordingly, this spontaneity is tightly controlled, and when the risk of "passing" to counter an insurgency is acknowledged, it is as a psychological danger rather than a political one. We saw that insurgency was a moment when the identity of the imperial servant—that is, his identification with the colonial regime—was implicitly called into question. In *Prester John* and *Greenmantle,* the protagonist's identity is once again put under strain. Intimate knowledge of the Other entails a risk of excessive identification—of going over to the other side. When they penetrate to the core of the enemy camp, Buchan's heroes are at risk not only of being exposed, but also of being enthralled. The strain of keeping up an alias tells on their nerves, and Hannay feels on several occasions that he has reached the limit of his endurance. However, his political allegiances do not for an instant come into question. In fact, the spy's spontaneity mirrors that of the insurgent, but in anodyne form. The former is coded as play, with its connotations of ebullience and daring, at a risk of psychological exhaustion. The spontaneity of the insurgent—an expressly political impulse—is represented in fiction of counterinsurgency as the spontaneity of regressive lunacy. Recall Laputa's antics on the Kirkcaple shore under the full moon.

With the pleasures of spying come certain dangers. Buchan's characters frequently express fear and similarly unmanly feelings. For example, Crawfurd admits, "I was horribly afraid, not only of unknown death, but of my impotence to play any manly part. I was alone, knowing too much and yet too little, and there was no chance of help under the broad sky" (p. 61). One might take the view that this readiness to admit weakness is a peculiarity of Buchan's heroes, but it is a quality that also reflects on the character of the spy. His fluid identity goes hand in hand with a less rigid masculinity. The model of subjectivity prescribed for the male protagonist is different from that found in Conan Doyle's detective fiction, in which Holmes is extremely rational and fearless. Buchan is the more modern and complex writer, celebrating the qualities of the "clubland hero," but at the same time voicing more fully the hero's vulnerability when pitted against modern forces of disorder. Robin Winks summarizes important elements of Buchan's thought: "We have from him at the very least two convictions that are less simple than they seem: that the amateur, thrown into the right circumstances, can react with imagination and courage in equal measure, to beat the professionals at their own game, and that there is a permanence to violence and crime beneath the surface of the civilized, with which those who live in society must learn to deal."[60] In their struggles against threats to civilization, Buchan's heroes come out on top, but only just, and only for the moment.

In sum, Doyle and Buchan both express anxieties about political insurgencies in their stories, but they treat insurgency in markedly different ways. In Doyle's detective fiction, a narrative of an insurgency is displaced by or rewritten as one of a crime, which the detective solves by rationally piecing together bits of knowledge. In Buchan's novels, the enterprise of the spy is much more risky. He goes into enemy territory and assumes an identity that will give him access to the very heart and mind of the rebel. From this position of intimacy, and with the help of luck and intuition, he seeks to foil the insurgent's plans. In so doing, he tarries so closely with the position of the Other that he risks a crisis of identity. The detective, by contrast, is dispassionate and aloof, observing and making sense of events in a detached, controlled way. While their methods are different, the detective and the spy both demonstrate their mastery over the dangers of Empire and give pleasure to a large and enthusiastic public. They bespeak a confidence in Empire that would be challenged in the postcolonial era.

FIVE

Intermezzo

*Postcolonial Modernity
and the Fiction of Intrigue*

From the vantage point of the present, the world that formed the backdrop to the fiction I have discussed so far seems in some ways un-recognizable, yet in other ways strangely familiar. In the early twenti-eth century, the imperial territories—colonies, dominions, and protec-torates—of France, Britain, Belgium, the Netherlands, Portugal, and Spain included much of Africa, South Asia, Southeast Asia, Australia, Canada, the Middle East, and the Caribbean. By 1980, European rule in these areas had virtually ended. This rapid and extensive decoloni-zation can be understood in terms of the rise of nationalism, changes in international relationships, and a questioning of priorities in the imperial metropoles. Colonialism created the structural and ideologi-cal conditions for nationalist movements, many of which gained mass support. These anticolonial movements were frequently spearheaded by charismatic leaders and powerful political parties—Gandhi, Nehru and the Indian National Congress, Nasser in Egypt, Nkrumah in the Gold Coast, which became Ghana, Senghor in Senegal, Kenyatta and the Mau Mau in Nigeria, the FLN in Algeria, Sukarno in Indonesia—that were key in precipitating decolonization.

The United States and the Soviet Union, which emerged as super-powers after the World War II, by and large opposed European impe-rialism. The creation of the United Nations in 1945, and its recogni-tion of the right of colonized territories to self-determination, also put pressure on the imperial powers to decolonize. In the metropolitan centers, the colonies came to be seen as a drain on financial resources that might otherwise be used by an emerging welfare state. The actual process of decolonization, even when independence was supposedly achieved peacefully, was often violent, and it was overwhelmingly the so-called "natives" who bore the brunt of this carnage. For instance, in India, the decision of the British abruptly to partition the country before they departed meant that organic communities where people of different religions had coexisted relatively peacefully were torn apart: over one million people died during the partition riots.

Many argue that decolonization is itself incomplete: Ngugi, for example, points to the persistent cultural hegemony of the West and calls for a decolonizing of the mind. The term *neocolonialism* refers to the continued financial and economic hegemony of the former colonial powers over the decolonized territories. Indeed, one might argue with reference to the Israeli occupation of the West Bank and the U.S. occupation of Iraq that decolonization in its fundamental geopolitical sense has far from ended and that the forms of an older mode of colonial occupation persist.[1]

In the late 1940s tensions escalated between the United States and Soviet Union as Stalin installed communist regimes in Eastern Europe and President Truman articulated his doctrine of containment. The newly independent countries of Africa and Asia came under tremendous pressure to align themselves with either the United States or the Soviets, who proposed to provide these client states with economic, military, and diplomatic backing. In 1955, leaders from a group of twenty-nine independent African and Asian nations who jointly represented almost half of the world's population met in Bandung, Indonesia, at what came to be called the Bandung Conference. There they declared their commitment to promote cultural, economic, and technical cooperation among themselves, and to oppose colonialism and neocolonialism, both by the West and the Soviet Union. The Bandung Conference laid the ground for the nonaligned movement, which was established in 1961. The nonaligned nations identified themselves as a "Third World" in contrast to capitalist ("First World") and socialist ("Second World") countries. The term, coined by the French demographer Alfred Sauvy after Emmanuel-Joseph Sieyès (who identified a "Third Estate" during the French Revolution), recognized the exploited but revolutionary status of decolonized countries.

Since the end of the Cold War—strikingly marked by the fall of the Berlin Wall in 1989, the dissolution of the Soviet Union in 1991, and the collapse of communist governments in Eastern Europe in the same years—a new pattern of geopolitical, economic, and cultural alignments has emerged. The United States has asserted its supremacy as a superpower, European nations have formed an economic union that has absorbed countries of the former Soviet Bloc, Japan and the East

Asian "economic tigers" have established their economic power, and China and India are at the forefront of rapid capitalist development and economic growth. Current theorists of globalization have tried to make sense of the new world order, characterized by the emergence not only of powerful financial institutions such as the International Monetary Fund and the World Bank, but also new forms of governance.

The nations of the Third World face new challenges in this postcolonial landscape. Originally meant to designate a nonaligned geopolitical stance, "third world" has come to signify the poor and underdeveloped nations of the world. These nations contend with the challenges of corruption, economic development, religious and ethnic conflict, and neocolonial forms of domination in the context of a global capitalism that imposes its own forms of governmentality or rationalities of rule. These geopolitical developments of the latter half of the twentieth century have left their mark on literature as well as on criticism and humanistic studies in general.

MODERNITY AND ENLIGHTENMENT RATIONALITY IN SOUTH ASIA

Before analyzing how South Asian novels use and refashion the generic conventions of fiction of intrigue to address these developments, I briefly want to consider several of the theoretical issues that the novels raise. The first of these is the relationship of South Asians to Western modernity and Enlightenment rationality. I have suggested in earlier chapters that the cultural and literary solution that Sherlock Holmes represents to problems of Empire pivots on his role as a champion of Enlightenment rationality. However, the status of that principle in the postcolonial world is ambiguous. On the one hand, it underpins the practices of police, and of the state more broadly speaking. On the other hand, it is the ground for the influential Nehruvian postcolonial vision of progress and development. To what extent is Enlightenment rationality affirmed, and to what extent is it challenged? In what ways is it oppressive, in what ways enabling?

The novels also address a second, related issue: the rationality of the postcolonial state in South Asia. In colonial fiction, Enlightenment rationality is embraced by the detective to maintain law and order and to uphold the political order of the colonial state. To what extent is the same rationality carried over to the postcolonial state? Novels of intrigue often present a critical view of the state's rationalities in South Asia and raise questions about the lineage and character of the postcolonial state.

And third, the fact that the state and civil society are being radically transformed in postcolonial South Asia with the advent of globalization raises questions for postcolonial novelists about how to understand and represent new relations of domination. Contemporary writers give narrative expression to the lineaments of the New Empire as these are taking shape, and literary scholars have sought to interpret and map the paths that imaginative writing takes in a postcolonial world.

Postcolonial literary studies emerged as a field of inquiry some twenty years ago, out of the growing awareness that metropolitan writing provided an ideological buttress for the forces of imperialism. Critics also turned their attention to the fact that the experience of European colonization and its aftermath had strongly marked cultural production—indeed, all of social and cultural life—in South Asia, Africa, the Caribbean, Canada, and Australia. For example, Dilip Gaonkar introduced a recent volume of *Public Culture* devoted to a consideration of "Alternative Modernities" by announcing, "Born in and of the West some centuries ago under relatively specific sociohistorical conditions, modernity is now everywhere. It has arrived not suddenly but slowly, bit by bit, over the longue durée—awakened by contact; transported through commerce; administered by empires, bearing global inscriptions; propelled by nationalism, and now increasingly steered by global migration and capital."[2] Gaonkar went on to suggest that Western modernity is not simply imported by or imposed upon the rest of the world, but undergoes what he calls in Darwinian fashion "creative adaptation." Varied in its contours and uneven in its effects, postcolonial modernity is shaped by people's efforts to create out of a mélange of cultural forms, and under the pressure of myriad historical, economic, and political forces, identities and lives that bear witness to their inventiveness.

The view that colonial societies had been violently propelled into a trajectory of modernization, for worse and for better, was voiced as early as in 1853 by Karl Marx. In "The Future Results of the British Rule in India," he famously assessed the modernizing effects of British rule on India as both destructive of traditional social forms and potentially regenerative in the long run.[3] While Marx noted that "England was actuated by the vilest interests" in introducing administrative and technological innovations, and characterized the effects of British rule as "sickening...to human feeling," he also described the transformation of India in celebratory tones.[4] England had propelled India into modernity, albeit violently. In the same passage quoted above, Marx assessed the processes and effects of modernity favorably. The reorganization of the army and of land revenue had made India stronger and more dynamic. Inventions such as the telegraph, steamship, and railroads had rescued the land from isolation and stagnation. The press and educational institutions had contributed to the emergence of a new class of Indians who were scientific in their outlook, and were better equipped to rule. The processes of modernity had caused India, a place once remote and fantastic, to be "annexed" to the West. Marx suggested that the kinds of transformations induced by colonialism, brutal as they were, had jolted India out of social and economic stasis and fostered the conditions for revolution by breaking down traditional social structures and paving the way for a greater development of productive forces. Today we can see that India had indeed been "annexed to the Western world"—not only had it been conquered and ruled by the British, but it had also been incorporated into a trajectory of modernity defined by the European Enlightenment.

This belief that India's destiny has inevitably been determined by the world historical forces of capitalism, of which Empire was the violent but necessary agent, has been implicitly embraced by modern Indians of different political stripes, weaned as we were on the ideologies of development and progress. Gandhi explicitly rejected this historicist understanding of India's desired future in "Hind Swaraj," where he argued that the "civilization" championed by the British was a disease, and that India's future lay in the regeneration of village life and in the spiritual development of her people.[5] Yet it was Nehru's vision of an India on the path of industrialization and technological progress—an India governed by reason and free from superstition and the crushing weight of material poverty—that has largely shaped the national imaginary in India.[6] Nehru gave a privileged place to Enlightenment rationality in his conception of what it meant to be modern.

Enlightenment thought has, of course, had its critics in the West.[7] An exhaustive account of the philosophical critique of the Enlightenment is beyond the scope of this book, but the work of Adorno and Horkheimer is particularly notable. In *Dialectic of Enlightenment*, they contend that man's will to subjugate nature, a sine qua non of modernity, comes to take as its object man himself, leading to the depredations of fascism.[8] Adorno and Horkheimer argue that a logic of domination inheres in Enlightenment modes of knowledge. "In thought, men distance themselves from nature in order thus imaginatively to present it to themselves—but only in order to determine how it is to be dominated."[9] According to Adorno and Horkheimer, the path of Enlightenment comes full circle: seeking to free themselves from the realm of necessity, men impose an oppressive necessity—the subordination of object to subject—in the realm of thought itself. It is this aspect of Enlightenment—the logic of domination inherent in its modalities—that contemporary critics of postcolonial culture have subjected to critique. In *Orientalism*, the single most influential text of postcolonial studies, Edward Said criticizes the historicism of European thinkers, that is, their failure to, as Robert Young puts it, "analyze plural objects as such rather than offering forms of integrated understanding that simply comprehend them within totalizing schemas." Young examines the ways in which colonial discourse analysis enables the "questioning of Western knowledge's categories and assumptions."[10] He builds on the claim of Adorno and Horkheimer and of poststructuralist critics such as Jacques Derrida that a logic of domination inheres in the very modes of Enlightenment knowledge. Philosophers of the Frankfurt School proposed to purge Enlightenment reason of an instrumental rationality. Poststructuralists, on the other hand, focus "not so much upon the continued presence of irrationality, for irrationality after all is simply reason's own excluded but necessary negative other, but rather on the possibility of other logics being imbricated within reason which might serve to undo its own tendency to domination."[11] Poststructuralists suggest that Enlightenment rationality involves a doing of violence to the Other. Young, who focuses on the writing of history, contends that Marxists are culpable of a certain historicism, that is, an assumption of a single trajectory of history with a universal subject and an assimilation of the Other, an assumption that poststructuralist critics, and especially postcolonial poststructuralist critics, are much more wary of.

This question of the ambiguous and highly charged status of Enlightenment rationalism in postcolonial countries such as India is a vexed one. In "Radical Histories and Question of Enlightenment Rationalism: Some Recent Critiques of Subaltern Studies," Dipesh Chakrabarty points to the problematic effects of Enlightenment rationalism on colonial historiography.[12] He suggests that Marxists have been limited by their trenchant dismissal of the force of religion; that the actualization of modernity in India involved a colonizing violence; and that a departure from this path of not only material but also epistemological violence requires a respectful openness to the Other, the subaltern. Yet elsewhere, Chakrabarty claims that he does not call for a wholesale rejection of Marxism because it has given rise to critical narratives of imperialism that "are part of our origin myths." He suggests rather that "a postcolonial reading of Marx would have to ask if his categories can be made to speak to what we have learnt from the philosophers of 'difference' about 'responsibility' to the plurality of the world." He points to the implicit departure from Marxist historiography that one sees in the work of the Subaltern Studies group, and suggests that the reasons for this departure are precisely those that the poststructuralist critics offer—the need not to have totalizing, universal narratives, and to respect difference, alterity, and particularity. However, at the same time Chakrabarty emphasizes that those who inhabit colonial modernity cannot simply jettison Enlightenment rationality, for it has formed them for better and for worse.[13]

Enlightenment rationality has indelibly marked nationalism, which was the defining political experience of twentieth-century India. Partha Chatterjee argues that nationalism is in fact derived from Enlightenment rationality. Chatterjee questions the assumptions of liberal and conservative theorists of nationalism, both of whom are implicitly rationalists; he also challenges the premises of cultural relativists. He argues that liberal theorists of nationalism take the view that it is a positive phenomenon, the correlate of Enlightenment thought, and "good" and "bad" nationalisms differ merely in their degree of adherence to a liberal political program. They suggest that irrational and regressive elements are vestiges of the past, and once impediments to their progress are removed, non-European nations can approximate the institutions and ethos of Western ones. Conservative theorists of nationalism argue that non-European peoples are incapable of acquiring the values of Enlightenment. Cultural relativists claim that there is no cross-culturally valid standard of rationality.

All three kinds of critics are hindered by assumptions about Western Enlightenment rationality. Liberal and conservative theorists of nationalism hold this rationality as a universal standard by which they gauge the efficacy of non-Western nationalisms. Cultural relativists attribute Enlightenment rationality wholly, exclusively, essentially, and categorically to Western cultures, and disavow or deny the possibility of cross-cultural discourse. The cultural essentialism of both schools is, according to Chatterjee, the corollary of the post-Enlightenment outlook. Furthermore, this cultural essentialism assumes a view of rationality that validates an imperial logic of domination:

> It is indeed a post-Enlightenment view of the world in which the idea of rational knowledge assumes a very definite form. The sciences of nature

become the paradigm of all rational knowledge. And the principal characteristic of these sciences as they are now conceived is their relation to an entirely new idea of man's control over nature—a progressive and ceaseless process of the appropriation of nature to serve human "interests." By extension, a notion of "interests" also enters into the conception of the new sciences of society. The rational knowledge of human society comes to be organized around concepts such as wealth, productive efficiency, progress, etc., all of which are defined in terms of the promotion of some social "interests." Yet interests in society are necessarily diverse; indeed, they are stratified in terms of the relations of power. Consequently, the subject-object relation between man and nature that is central to the new conception of the sciences of nature is now subtly transferred, through the "rational" conception of society, to relations between man and man. The sciences of society become the knowledge of the Self and of the Other. Construed in terms of rationality, it necessarily also becomes a means to the power of the Self over the Other. In short, knowledge becomes the means to the domination of the world.[14]

Chatterjee's argument strongly echoes the claim made by Adorno and Horkheimer that the logic of domination that drives man's will to subjugate nature comes to take as its object man itself. In his analysis, Chatterjee extends the reach of this dialectic of Enlightenment, seeing in it the epistemological underpinnings of colonialism. The rationality of colonial culture is inherently one of domination. This rationality does not only drive the will to dominate the colonial world; rather, once European assertions of ethnic privilege and moral privilege have been contravened, rationality becomes the principle upon which Western privilege stands.

Chakrabarty's call to "provincialize Europe" marks an attempt to displace the West from this epistemological position of privilege within India. Chakrabarty acknowledges the powerful influence of Western thought on Indians' self-conception, but points to its limitations: "European thought…is both indispensable and inadequate in helping us to think through the various life practices that constitute the political and the historical in India."[15] Chakrabarty is especially cautionary of the historicist lens through which not only European philosophers but also the generations of Indians who have embraced the universalism of Enlightenment thought see India.[16] In the following chapters, I trace the ways in which writers use the genre of intrigue to dramatize the mixed fortunes of modernity in postcolonial South Asia, and show how it is embraced, creatively adapted, and sometimes turned on its head.

THE POSTCOLONIAL STATE

While scholars of imperialism and literature have focused on different modes and arenas of domination, they have paid surprisingly little attention to the state. Perhaps this is because the state has conventionally been understood as an empirically given structure properly studied by political scientists rather than cultural critics. It is only recently that people have begun to understand the state as comprised of a set of discourses and practices that lend it to cultural analysis. In the following chapters, I examine how writers represent the postcolonial state. Here I want to address briefly some theoretical aspects of the postcolonial state: its material and historical continuity with the colonial state, its discursive contours, and its relationship to Enlightenment rationality and its optic.

Anthropologists, historians, and political scientists have drawn on diverse theoretical accounts to analyze the state. There is, of course, the liberal view—exemplified in the Indian Constitution—of the state as the protector of a secular ideal, guarantor of civic rights, and enforcer of the general will. Taking a more critical view, Max Weber famously defined the state as having a monopoly on legitimate violence. Charles Tilly takes a broader view of states as "coercion wielding organizations that are distinct from households and kinship groups and exercise clear priority in some respects over all other organizations within substantial territories."[17] Pierre Bourdieu extends Weber's definition to include "physical and symbolic violence over a definite territory and over the totality of the corresponding population."[18] Marxist scholars such as Nicos Poulantzas and Louis Althusser have viewed the state as an epiphenomenal domain of ideological and social relations. Moving away from an understanding of the state as a fixed, identifiable structure, other scholars offer a Gramscian account of the state as an unstable medium and product of class hegemony. In tension with this is a Foucauldian understanding of the state as the outcome of a general governmentalization of societies whereby in "specific ways human practices became objects of knowledge, regulation and discipline."[19]

While these influential critics focus on Western states, others attribute to the postcolonial state specific forms and agendas. Hamza Alavi, one of the first scholars to direct attention to the historical specificities of the postcolonial state in South Asia, presents a Marxist analysis that views the postcolonial state as inheriting from the colonial regime an overdeveloped repressive state apparatus.[20] This apparatus, including the police and military bureaucracy, takes on a relatively autonomous structure but at the same time mediates the interests of different elites. Mahmood Mamdani argues that the postcolonial state inherits a duality between a racialized citizenry and tribalized subjects from the colonial state. "This dualism juxtaposed modern and customary law, civil and traditional society, rights and custom, town and country, and crucially, citizens and subjects. The bifurcated nature of power was reflected in the contrast between a civil power claiming to guarantee rights for a racialized citizenry, and a customary power ('Native Authorities') claiming to enforce an ethnicized 'custom' on 'native' subjects."[21] The failure of democratization in postcolonial states is in effect a failure to deracialize civil authority and to detribalize native authority. Chatterjee concurs with Mamdani in arguing that postcolonial India lacks a well-developed civil society, and argues that one needs to look within the state rather than beyond it to identify progressive spaces and discourses.[22] Chatterjee argues further that the Indian state takes on the mantle of "development" from the colonial state, but asserts its mandate to pursue true development as opposed to the stunted progress caused by colonial rule.

The political theorists to whom I have referred tend to view the state as a distinct, empirically given structure that can be distinguished from civil society. Recently, following the "cultural turn" in the social sciences, scholars have attempted to analyze the state in terms of the discourses and cultural processes that mark it out as a domain in specific contexts. As the editors of a recent volume of essays put it, "Instead of talking about the state as an entity that always/already consists of certain features, functions, and forms of governance, let us approach each actual state as a historically specific configuration of a range of languages of stateness, some practical, others symbolic and performative, that have been disseminated, translated, interpreted, and combined in widely differing ways and sequences across the globe."[23] These critics set out to map the complex processes that produce the state as an idea as much as a form—and produce the notion of its autonomy from society and the economy. Timothy Mitchell argues, following Foucault's analysis of modern governmentality, that "government is a broader process than the relatively unified and functionalist entity suggested by the notion of the state."[24] He consequently asks why it is that the state appears as a unified, distinct entity if this is the case. That is, he calls for an investigation of the processes that make the state appear as a structure. I suggest that it is not only the practices of the state, but also the way that narratives represent the state that give it its seeming quiddity.

Postcolonial novels not only treat the repressive behavior of the state as a theme and a construct, they explore the way this repressive behavior is linked to the optic of the state—that is, to the way the state sees the world. James Scott, who charts the modes of apprehending the world that characterize the modern state, argues that above all it aims for legibility.[25] As Scott puts it in *Seeing Like a State*, "The functionary of any large organization 'sees' the human activity that is of interest to him largely through the simplified approximations of documents and statistics: tax proceeds, lists of tax payers, land records, average incomes, unemployment numbers, mortality rates, trade and productivity figures, the total number of cases of cholera in a certain district."[26] Scott shows this will toward legibility to operate in the wholesale transformation of land tenure and of forestry, as well as a host of other administrative practices. The postcolonial state, shaped as it is by specific histories of colonial administration, "sees" its subjects and territory in ways that render both into suitable objects of rational control and putative development. Postcolonial novels of intrigue explore the ways in which the state cognitively maps its domains of control.

THE NEW EMPIRE

The political landscape that postcolonial novels traverse is defined not only in terms of the state, but also in terms of the global geopolitical transformations of the late twentieth century. Critics have coined labels such as "Empire," "New Empire," "Super-empire," and "New World Empire" to signal the global reach as well as novel social, political and economic modalities of this "New World Order." Scholars and political pundits may disagree about its implications, but the broad contours of the New Empire are fairly clear. While the New Empire is characterized by unprecedented flows of capital, goods, people, and information, the United States is its dominant power because of its economic and military supremacy. At the same time, power is exercised at a global level not so much by the U.S. government but through international institutions, both political ones such as the United Nations and NATO, and economic bodies such as the World Bank and the IMF. The New Empire is committed to a liberal rhetoric of free markets and democracy, and indeed yokes the one to the other. Even so, it has presided over sharp and growing economic disparities between the North and the South, and frequently supports right-wing governments that maintain the status quo. Hand in hand with its touted commitment to democratic institution building goes an aggressive expansion of U.S. militarization. In this brave new world, where the Cold War has been replaced by a generalized "war on drugs" and now a "global war on terror," a shadowy web of extralegal prisons and torture centers operates alongside global police and intelligence networks.

Although the New Empire exercises its hegemony through economic and political means, its dominant powers still fight territorially based wars, as we see in Afghanistan and Iraq. Its global scope and power notwithstanding, it is the object of new modes and forums of resistance, seen perhaps most obviously in the activism around the World Social Forums of the last years. The slogan of the forums, "another world is possible," encapsulates the hopes of critics of the kind of neoliberal globalization promoted by the New Empire; in the name of "altermondialisme" they attempt to realize an alternative global vision of social, economic, and environmental justice.

The geopolitical changes of the last two decades and the emergence of the New Empire have been the subject of considerable theoretical scrutiny. One can broadly group the arguments about the New Empire along neoliberal, Marxist, and postmodern lines.[27] Neoliberal champions of the globalization of financial regimes and political governance see the New Empire as holding out the prospect of the expansion of markets, greater economic development, increased democracy, and the protection of civil rights. Some scholars and policy gurus go so far as to call for a revival of imperial realpolitik to advance the spread of modernity and civilization. Marxist critics view these geopolitical developments as the consequence of the forces of capitalist accumulation and expansion. They hold that "capitalism's limitless search for surplus value—albeit driven less by 'underconsumption' and more by crises of over-accumulation—constantly transgresses boundaries, and that the state, as a conduit for capitalists' interests, tends to employ its juridical and military resources to this end."[28] The present geopolitical conjuncture, then, constitutes yet another phase of capitalist development.

Postmodern thinkers see this conjuncture as qualitatively new, and argue that a new set of conceptual tools is needed to make sense of it. Michael Hardt and Antonio Negri's *Empire* is the most significant and fully developed statement of this view: "Imperialism was really an extension of the sovereignty of the European nation-states beyond their own boundaries. The passage to Empire emerges from the twilight of modern sovereignty. In contrast to imperialism, Empire establishes no territorial center of power and does not rely on fixed boundaries or barriers. It is a *decentered* and *deterritorializing* apparatus of rule that progressively incorporates the entire global realm within its open, expanding frontiers. Empire manages hybrid identities, flexible hier- archies, and plural exchanges through modulating networks of com- mand."[29] *Empire* is noteworthy for its bold vision of a world in which power operates in novel ways, producing new forms of sovereignty, biopolitical subjects, immaterial forms of labor, and new forms of re- sistance. At the same time, the book has been criticized on a number of grounds: its theoretical abstraction and lack of historical detail, its neglect of economics and an analysis of global capitalism, and its fail- ure to address the workings of militarism and of repressive apparatuses more generally. While the global Empire may have new elements and require new modes of analysis, I would like to underscore the repres- sive aspects of imperialism—war, militarism, territorial occupation, the plundering of resources—that accompany new modes of governance.

The anxieties of modern-day Empire are twofold. On the one hand, in Europe and North America one finds a heightened suspicion of Third World immigrants, and an expansion and consolidation of a North American security state as well as the emergence of "Fortress Europe." On the other hand, a so-called "war on terror" has legitimized the in- vasion and occupation by Western powers, especially the United States and Britain, of regions that lie outside their immediate purview. These twin developments suggest that modern Empire, while it may expand and change in the ways described by Hardt and Negri, shows marked forms of reterritorialization even while capital and sovereignty are to some extent deterritorialized. The United States is certainly the current imperial superpower and as such is anxious to shore up its borders and extend its security state. Its anxieties are above all focused upon putative terrorists, whom it proposes to defend itself against with the help of questionable legal instruments such as the Patriot Act and the Military Commissions Act. According to the ACLU, the Patriot Act 1) expands "terrorism" to include "domestic terrorism," facilitating monitoring and repression of political organizations; 2) expands the power of law enforcement agents to conduct secret searches; 3) allows the FBI to investigate American citizens without probable cause for "intelligence purposes; and 4) permits noncitizens to be detained in six-month increments on "mere suspicion," with no process of judicial review. Thousands of Arab and South Asian men, mostly Muslims, have been interrogated and detained in secret following the passage of the Patriot Act. In the United States, historically more receptive to immigrants, security concerns have ushered in, for example, novel forms of bio-identification. The most extreme expression of this hermeneutic of fear and its dehumanizing of the Other is the passage in October 2006 of the Military Commissions Act, which in effect abolishes the writ of habeas corpus for supposed suspects of terrorism.

We see, at the same time, the emergence of Fortress Europe: the increased expulsion and policing of immigrants, the curtailment of their cultural freedoms (with for instance the banning of the hijab in schools in France and in all public space in Holland), and the limiting of citizenship as happened in Ireland, where in June 2004 the country voted to restrict citizenship to those with at least one Irish-born parent. In Britain, the London bombings in July 2005 have led to an increase in violence against immigrants. Here, one also sees attempts on the state's part to increase its repressive powers by passing antiterrorist legislation greatly restricting freedom of speech and prolonging detention without trial.

What these measures suggest is that the colonial anxieties about subaltern migrants that I have sketched in relation to turn-of-the-century fiction find an echo in anxieties about the unruliness of migrants to Euro-America today. Arjun Appadurai, in his discussion of global migration in *Modernity at Large*, acknowledges the difficulties faced by migrants, but celebrates the emergence of a postnational era when subjectivities, or "imaginings" as he puts it, are being radically reformed.[30] A reflection upon the kinds of cultural anxieties evident in fiction of intrigue prompts more caution. We see in imperial fiction of intrigue the modern concern that "all that is solid melts into air" projected onto a global landscape. The "global ethnoscapes" that Appadurai contends are a feature of "modernity at large" are superintended by repressive apparatuses that surely mark imaginative possibilities. These transnational flows, rather than producing a "postmodern" frisson of pleasure in the imperial middle classes, generate entirely modern cultural anxieties even in the early twenty-first century, and the will to police such transnational migrations, and indeed the Third World at large, only appears to grow stronger. In the aftermath of Al Qaida's attacks, the vilification of Islam, never far from the surface, has become virulent.

As the European powers pulled out of the colonies, often following the policy of "divide and leave," they left bitter conflicts in their wake—in, for example, Ireland, Palestine, and India. Britain's presence in Ireland engendered the single longest-lasting insurgent movement in modern Europe. Furthermore, as newly liberated nation-states consolidated their political power, contestatory nationalisms remained, which then became the objects of counterinsurgent rhetoric. In South Asia, one thinks of Sikhs, Assamese, Tamils, Kashmiris, and so on. This is not to suggest that such insurgent movements are merely figments of rhetoric, but the rhetoric used to characterize them is certainly detrimental to the resolution of such conflicts.

The ethos of surveillance has taken on a global scope. After the end of the Cold War, one notices in public discourse a shift from the imagining of a world of polarized "spheres of influence" to the emergent perception of "terrorist threats" anywhere and everywhere. This newly dominant discourse has become the basis of extraordinary measures that legitimate surveillance and policing of borders within postcolonial states as well as by Western ones.

Equally a mark of the geopolitics of the present world system is a reversion to older forms of imperialism on the part of the superpower and its allies. Iraq and Afghanistan are at present under (largely) American occupation in the name of "the war on terror." The U.S.- and British-led second invasion of Iraq that began in March 2003 has had disastrous results: a study published in the British medical journal *Lancet* in October 2004 estimated that the risk of dying from violence was fifty-eight times higher than before the 2003 invasion, and that at least 100,000 Iraqi civilians had been killed, mostly by coalition forces.[31] In October 2006, the *Lancet* published a study by the same group of epidemiologists who estimate that as of July 2006, there had been 655,000 excess death of Iraqis as a consequence of the invasion.[32] Other aspects of the so-called "War on Terror" include illegal practices such as "rendition" or the "outsourcing of torture," as one writer describes it, indefinite detention in legal limbo in Guantanamo Bay, and the creation of a shadowy network of secret, globally dispersed prisons. Newly dubbed "the long war," this scenario bears a striking resemblance to the old imperialism of the nineteenth century, with ghastly postmodern shading.

In Britain, Robert Cooper spells out the rationale for the new wars, directly echoing the cadences of nineteenth-century imperial rhetoric. Cooper, who was British Prime Minister Tony Blair's foreign policy adviser and is now a senior adviser on security issues at the European Union, published a much-cited essay in 2002 in the *Observer* titled "The New Liberal Imperialism," extended and collected in 2004 in *The Breaking of Nations*. In it he argues that although imperialism is no longer the favored policy among so-called "post imperial, postmodern states who no longer think of security primarily in terms of conquest," it is called for in the face of threats to the world from the "pre-modern" world. He submits:

> The challenge to the postmodern world is to get used to the idea of double standards. Among ourselves, we operate on the basis of laws and open cooperative society. But when dealing with more old-fashioned states outside the postmodern continent of Europe, we need to revert to the rougher methods of an earlier era—force, pre-emptive attack, deception, whatever is necessary to deal with those who still live in the nineteenth century world of every state for itself. Among ourselves, we keep the law but when we are operating in the jungle, we must also use the laws of the jungle.[33]

Cooper champions what he euphemistically calls "the imperialism of neighbours": "What is needed is a new kind of imperialism, one compatible with human rights and cosmopolitan values: an imperialism which aims to bring order and organisation but which rests today on the voluntary principle." Such a "co-operative" imperialism would counter the "chaos" generated by "failed states": the civilizing mission redux. This benign mode of imperialism, he argues, is to be achieved by the imperialism of the global economy, on the one hand, and on the other, by interventions from neighboring states, preferably supported by the international community, when areas become unstable.

For my argument, what is telling here is not only the call to nineteenth-century forms of imperialism but the claim that such imperial intervention is needed because of threats to security. The "mission civilatrice" is not altogether absent from such imperial thinking, but it takes second place to threats to security from regions where "chaos is the norm and war is a way of life" and "in so far as there is a government it operates in a way similar to an organized crime syndicate." No analysis of the historical effects of imperialism and Cold-War politics here: "pre-modern chaos" is in this view a sort of ontological condition.

LITERATURE AND POSTCOLONIAL MODERNITY

I want to turn briefly to the implications of the political and philosophical issues that I have outlined for an examination of postcolonial literature. A number of postcolonial novels use plots of detection and pursuit to comment on the political landscape in South Asia and on the new global geopolitical dispensation. For example, in Michael Ondaatje's novel *Anil's Ghost*, a forensic scientist attempts to identify and explain the death in Sri Lanka of a single victim of political violence, whose body has been found at a site to which only the government had access. The detective in Amitav Ghosh's *The Circle of Reason* is an unenthusiastic functionary of a repressive state apparatus, and his supposedly "subversive" quarry is an innocent fugitive. Ghosh thus calls into question the ethos of surveillance that undergirds fiction of intrigue. In Rohinton Mistry's *Such a Long Journey*, the protagonist unwittingly becomes embroiled in an intrigue that involves the Research and Analysis Wing and underscores the gross corruption of Indira Gandhi's government. One of the principal characters of Mistry's *A Fine Balance* is a victim of the sterilization campaign that was such a notorious episode in the emergency rule of Indira Gandhi. Salman Rushdie offers imaginatively grotesque indictments of the abuse of state power in all his novels. In *Midnight's Children*, he lampoons Indira Gandhi's family planning campaign in his account of the Black Widow's meals of fried testicles. In *Shame*, Sufiya Zenobia becomes a monstrous embodiment of her nation's disgrace; and in *The Satanic Verses*, Saladin Chamcha is transformed into a defecating satyr in a police van in London in what is a literal instantiation of the racist discourse of the British state. These writers, like Doyle and Buchan, foreground the state's anxieties about order and control. Rather than confirm the legitimacy of the state, however, they interrogate the state's repressive actions. In the second part of this book, I analyze the ways in which Ghosh, Ondaatje, Arundhati Roy, and Rushdie portray through plots of intrigue the violence and corruption of social and political institutions in South Asia.

These writers also depict the experiences of globalization, migration, and the insertion of South Asians into an emergent geopolitical order. The second part of Ghosh's novel is set in a Middle East oil state, Al-Ghazira, where migrants from India and other parts of the Middle East try to do odd jobs and pool their resources to eke out a living. The novel represents the predicament of subaltern migrants to the Gulf states, where they are vulnerable to abuse, exploitation, and expulsion at the least sign of political organization. Ondaatje's novel *Anil's Ghost* is framed by the exigencies of transnational governance in the context of ethnic and class conflict. Anil, the protagonist of *Anil's Ghost*, is part of an international team of forensic scientists that investigates political killings under the aegis of the United Nations. The novel explores her complex relationship with Sri Lanka as a returning expatriate as well as a privileged employee of an international monitoring organization that has a tense relationship with none-too-scrupulous government forces embroiled in an internationally financed and orchestrated civil war. Roy's novel, while it focuses primarily on the repressive ideologies of caste and gender that operate in a small village in Kerala, presents a searing indictment of the effects of globalization on artistic culture, the landscape, and media. Rushdie's *The Moor's Last Sigh* explores the rise in Bombay of a global corporate class represented by Adam Braganza, and it ends with the Moor dying in exile in an imaginary dystopia in Spain among similarly deracinated migrants. Far from charting a deterritorialized Empire where labor is largely immaterial, these novels show the operation of borders and boundaries in a world where labor, gender, religion, and ethnic identity are negotiated in very material ways.

All of these writers rework the conventions of fiction of intrigue to reflect critically upon mechanisms of police and repression, on the state, on globalization, and on violence of a more or less political nature. They draw on the popular genres of detective fiction and crime thrillers for their characters and plots. Instead of validating the workings of the police and the enlightenment rationality that underpins and authorizes these workings, they turn a critical eye on the anxieties and coercive actions of the postcolonial state and of the New Empire. These postcolonial writers turn the generic conventions and topography of fiction of intrigue topsy-turvy so as to make both the oppressive and emancipatory impulses of postcolonial modernity visible.

At the same time, the novels I examine are all literary novels that foreground questions of interpretation even as they "provincialize" historical narratives. They point to the ways in which colonial state rationalities and colonial histories have marked South Asian modernity; yet they show such a colonial inscription to be contingent, partial, or even irrelevant. By using postmodern narrative techniques—pastiche, play, digression, fragmentation, irony, reflexivity, hybridization, nonlinear temporality, and the like—the authors whom I discuss write against the grain of historicism. They reflect upon the necessity of devising new modes of interpretation to make meaning of the postcolonial present. They use and transform the tropes and tools of imperial fiction of intrigue to address the realities of the postcolonial state and of the New Empire. Given that Empire is being revivified and transformed as I write, and that concerns about law and order, crime, police, and detection dominate European and American discussions of the Third World, I necessarily address not only literary developments, but also the political exigencies of the present.

SIX

Police and Postcolonial Rationality in Amitav Ghosh's *The Circle of Reason*

To be a postcolonial subject is to be an unbidden guest at the table of modernity. Its fruits are spread delectably before one: technological prowess, economic development, political freedom. Yet, as one reaches for these, one feels a hint of queasiness, for they evoke the postcolonial double bind: a desire to embrace the modern, but the knowledge that the dialectic of modernity has entailed the subjection of the colonized. What elements of the postcolonial contract entail the continuance of this subjection by other means? Is the postcolonial version of modernity inevitably marked as belated and inauthentic? Doubts about the salubriousness of the meal are compounded by the uncomfortable sense of being unwelcome—superficially, there is good cheer, a slap on the back, but this bonhomie is tinged with suspicion and arrogance. One will eat at this table if one is lucky enough to squeeze in among the habitual diners, but not without misgivings.

In this chapter, I explore the ambiguities of postcolonial modernity in a close reading of Amitav Ghosh's novel *The Circle of Reason*.[1] Appraising the character of modernity in India, Ghosh emphasizes the relation between Enlightenment rationality and police. When he traces the police activity of the postindependence Indian state in the face of luridly imagined political threats, Ghosh underscores the repressive aspects of colonial rationality that linger in the structures of postcolonial government. He suggests that the postcolonial state is heir to the anxieties about order and control that are characteristic of colonial regimes, and the full force of postcolonial rationality is seen in the state's response to insurgency and subaltern migrancy. At the same time, Ghosh's novel stages a succession of utopian projects that bear the imprint of Enlightenment reason. It points to the liberatory dimensions of reason and valorizes the characters' pursuit of these Enlightenment projects.

In juxtaposing so explicitly these themes of the progress and per-version of reason and the aggrandizement of police and national secu-rity in its depiction of postcolonial India, *The Circle of Reason* raises two sets of questions. The first concerns the relationship between En-lightenment discourses of reason and the apparatuses of police in the postcolonial context. Is there a necessary complicity between these? In other words, does the advance of reason authorize and rest upon a greater rationalization of police? Are the discourses and apparatuses of police inherited from the colonial state retained by the postcolonial nation? The second set of questions has to do with the ambiguous status of Enlightenment reason in postcolonial India. Ghosh suggests that reason in its postcolonial guise is both coercive and emancipato-ry. Are there multiple forms of reason, and can these be disentangled from the logic of police? Can an alternative, nonrepressive rule of rea-son be imagined in a postcolonial world?[2]

Ghosh explores these questions in *The Circle of Reason* by working with and against the genre of police fiction.[3] A genre that expresses anx-ieties about order and control, police fiction at the same time rehearses the power of the police through narratives of detection and pursuit. As I have argued in relation to Conan Doyle, the classic detective story en-dorses the bourgeois state and its social arrangements, and presents any challenge to these as threats to be allayed. Indeed, as I have also noted, D. A. Miller identifies a "policing function" in nineteenth century nov-els of all sorts, arguing that "the novel—as a set of representational techniques—systematically participate[s] in a general economy of polic-ing power" that brings the modern, liberal subject into being. And as I have suggested in the introduction to this book, there has been a recent spate of postcolonial novels that use the format of the mystery or detec-tive story, but tweak it or turn it inside out in what becomes a narrative of social detection, to borrow a phrase from Fredric Jameson, a "ve-hicle for judgments on society and revelations of its hidden nature, just as it refocuses the various individual or empirical events and actors into a representative pattern symptomatic of the social order as a whole."[4] These novels identify social and state practices as invidious, even vi-cious. In Arundhati Roy's *The God of Small Things*, the reader learns the story of Sophie Mol's death, and the subsequent torture and murder of Velutha, Amu's lover, by the police.[5] The novel reveals the brutal po-licing of caste boundaries and the unscrupulous operation of party po-litical machinery. Michael Ondaatje's novel *Anil's Ghost*, which I dis-cuss in the final chapter, traces the investigation by a forensic detective of human remains in a Sri Lanka riven by war between the government, insurgents in the south, and Tamil separatists in the north.[6] In Rohinton Mistry's *Such a Long Journey*, the protagonist becomes entangled during the 1971 Bangladesh war through a friend, a guileless and conscientious policeman who works for a corrupt state, with a scheme for money laundering and arms sales.[7] These novels cast suspicion on the repressive apparatuses of the state. *The Circle of Reason*, as it charts the warding off of an ostensible threat to the body politic in the name of "national security," similarly presents an unfavorable picture of the police and indicts the criminal behavior of the state's agents.

Critics have tended to overlook Ghosh's first novel in favor of *The Shadow Lines* and *In an Antique Land* because, I would suggest, the later novels more explicitly contend with the themes and problems that have dominated postcolonial studies recently: diaspora, migration, hybridity, and the like. Both of the later novels have received international attention, have been the subject of scholarly articles, and are making their way onto syllabi in North American and British universities.[8] *The Circle of Reason*, which was enormously popular in India, was less enthusiastically received in the West, where it soon went out of print for a time. *The Circle of Reason* deserves more critical consideration by scholars of postcolonial fiction than it has received because it points to the state rationalities that shape postcolonial experience.[9] Its conceptual focus on reason, as signaled by the title, makes it a particularly suitable text through which to explore the ambiguous legacy of Enlightenment rationality in postcolonial India. When its characters become migrants—and here the novel fully acknowledges the very different circumstances of bourgeois and subaltern migration—it is to escape the police, driven by the rationalities of the state. At the level of plot, the forces of police criminalize the protagonists and defeat their enlightened utopian projects. However, the narrative techniques that the novel employs go against the grain of the logic of repression that is embedded in classic police fiction. A deliberation upon intelligence gathering and policing in postcolonial India, the novel engages, disrupts, and parodies the generic conventions of police fiction in order to challenge its coercive logic. By turning the generic conventions of police fiction upside down, Ghosh critiques the repressive tendencies of Enlightenment reason

These tendencies are manifest in the mechanisms of *police,* a word that now primarily signifies the forcible maintenance of civil peace, but was used during the period of Enlightenment to refer broadly to laws and regulations that ordered everyday life. In order to explore the dual implications of *police,* it is helpful to turn to Pasquale Pasquino's discussion of the "science of police" in Europe in the eighteenth century, the century of Enlightenment. Pasquino identifies two disparate meanings of *police.* The modern notion of "police"—understood as "the maintenance of order and prevention of dangers"—emerged, Pasquino convincingly argues, during the late eighteenth and early nineteenth centuries. From the Middle Ages until the late eighteenth century, *police* referred more broadly to the administration of a population to promote happiness and the public good. The task of "police" was to be achieved by the application of specialized knowledge and practices. This administration in the interest of public happiness is the ostensible mission of the modern nation.[10]

Pasquino's distinction between the two concepts of police does not hold in a colonial context. Even in Europe, this regulation was accompanied by the surveillance and increased repression of "Others": the working classes, women, the insane, and so on. In Europe's colonies, where power and profit, not the population's happiness, were the chief objectives of colonial administration, the rational regulation of the population from the outset implied the prevention and suppression of challenges to the power of the regime rather than the enhancement of public well-being.[11] Several of the Subaltern Studies historians have traced the unhappy effects of colonial administration on the population of India.[12] Even when the motives were benign, the colonial regime's limited knowledge of local customs meant that "rational" administration could have adverse effects. "Rational" administration was premised upon general principles rather than local exigencies. Because, as Ranajit Guha puts it, "dominance was exercised without hegemony," the positive and negative senses of police cannot be distinguished in any clear way.[13] The administration of the population meant the maintenance of order and the prevention of dangers—dangers largely arising from a recalcitrant population. Rational administration necessarily implied the greater rationalization of police and other instruments of order, insofar as the exercise of reason meant the scientific organization of instruments of government. This kind of rational administration—what Foucault in one essay calls governmentality—carries over to postindependence India.[14] The postcolonial state, being in principle democratic and sovereign, holds out the promise of rational administration that will ensure the freedom and well-being of its citizens. Its mode of operation, however, is coercive, as Ghosh's novel underscores.

The Circle of Reason spans the middle decades of the twentieth century, the period of decolonization, and concludes in the 1980s. Much of the novel is set against the backdrop of the Bangladeshi war of independence in 1971.[15] Its meandering narrative tracks the misadventures of Alu, an orphan, who becomes embroiled in a feud between his foster father and the village strongman, also a police informant. Consequently, the police falsely identify him as a dangerous insurgent and set a special agent on his trail. When Alu flees to a Gulf kingdom, Assistant Superintendent of Police Jyoti Das, the police detective assigned to pursue him, eventually joins him and his companions in flight. Seamlessly interweaving descriptions of characters and events, the three parts of *The Circle of Reason* chronicle Alu's quixotic misadventures in India, Al-Ghazira, and finally Algeria. The reader's sympathies lie largely with Alu, who is an entirely innocent fugitive from the police, but they also extend to Das, who has been inducted into the police force only reluctantly—he is far more interested in observing and drawing rare birds than in tracking human quarry. By the end of the novel, Das abandons his pursuit, and indeed his job altogether.

In addressing the place of police in the postcolonial state, the novel raises questions about modernity in India. In liberal discourses, modern nations are broadly imagined in two ways: as political communities that are universally governed by a rule of law, assuring the duties and privileges of citizenship to all, and as "ethnic" communities that have a sense of shared history and culture.[16] In both kinds of images, the repressive aspects of the nation tend to be obscured. The nation-state form is energetically vested in newly decolonized countries with the promise of liberation from oppressive rule. It holds out the assurance of true equality and true fraternity. Yet the newly liberated nation inherits the repressive apparatuses of the colonial state, apparatuses that are freshly deployed against a "free" citizenry. As Partha Chatterjee puts it with reference to independent India, "the new state chose to retain in a virtually unaltered form the basic structure of the civil service, the police administration, the judicial system, including the codes of civil and criminal law, and the armed forces as they existed in the colonial period. As far as the normal executive functions of the state were concerned, the new state operated within a framework of universal rationality, whose principles were seen as having been contained (even if they were misapplied) in the preceding state structure."[17] One could make the argument that given their colonial derivation, these institutional embodiments of Enlightenment rationality were all the more coercive. After all, the implications of Enlightenment principles such as "reason" cannot be assumed to be identical for the West and for European colonies. In Europe and America, its enabling condition and ultimate goal was purportedly freedom.[18] In colonized countries such as India, where even in the view of "enlightened" intellectuals such as Raja Rammohun Roy the use of reason did not necessarily signify political freedom, the rational exercise of power could be doubly oppressive. Historians have documented the many areas of society that were subjected to the rationalizing force of colonial power: land revenue, social groupings such as caste, medicine, law, police—the list goes on.[19] Rendering these into domains of rational organization served to intensify colonial control and increase profit.

Indeed, Gayatri Spivak identifies a logic of colonial domination operating at the very heart of the discourse of Enlightenment thought. In *A Critique of Postcolonial Reason*, Spivak argues that "the end of the 'German' eighteenth century (if one can speak of 'Germany' as a unified proper name in that era) provides material for a narrative of crisis management: the 'scientific' fabrication of new representations of self and world that would provide alibis for the domination, exploitation, and epistemic violation entailed by the establishment of colony and empire."[20] Spivak traces the moments in the writings of Kant, Hegel, and Marx when the discursive instantiation of Enlightenment notions such as "Reason" and "History" are predicated upon the foreclosure of the figure of the native informant. She suggests that the colonial Other, which is not assimilable to the meaning-making processes of the West, is both excluded as well as recuperated as that which is to be reconstituted in the image of the West.

Nonetheless, the promise of Enlightenment, with its utopian cadences, is seductive. This promise is freedom—from material hardship, from political tyranny, and from superstition and ignorance—through knowledge of man and of nature.[21] As Dipesh Chakrabarty points out, while critiques of Enlightenment may be valid, Enlightenment rationality so powerfully informs modern India's desires that it cannot be dismissed as an external colonizing force.[22] The power of the discourse of Enlightenment rationality has indelibly marked Indians' own imaginings of their nation. In *The Circle of Reason*, the bureaucratic surveillance and regulation of the characters is not the only legacy of Enlightenment rationality. Interwoven with the narrative of Alu's run from the police is the story of his recruitment in various utopian schemes. While the narrative whorls and doubles back too much to permit straightforward schematization, the three parts loosely center upon three different idealistic projects. Each of these is an attempt at purification of one sort or another—be it a campaign against germs, a war upon the sullying effects of money, or a ritual purification of a dead body. Each of these projects becomes an occasion for dramatizing an Enlightenment discourse.

"REASON RESCUES MAN FROM BARBARITY"

The first part of *The Circle of Reason* concerns the efforts of Balaram, Alu's foster father, to introduce a rational program of hygiene in his village. This attempt to bring reason and order to his world is not Balaram's first. In his student days at Presidency College in Calcutta, he had, as president of the Society for the Dissemination of Science and Rationalism among the People of Hindoostan (whose motto was "Reason Rescues Man From Barbarity"), induced his classmates to follow Pasteur's principles of hygiene and wage a campaign against dirty underwear. Balaram was able to persuade his reluctant fellows, but the campaign was brought to an abrupt close when some bullies at the college proposed at a meeting to inspect *his* underwear, and he jumped off a balustrade and broke his legs. This is the first of several occasions in the novel when brutish might overcomes the forces of reason.

In characteristically ludic form, the novel both underscores the colonial origins of such a project as well as notes its hegemonic character—hegemonic in Gramsci's sense of involving both domination and consent.[23] Many Indians of the late eighteenth and early nineteenth centuries embraced the ideals put forward by Enlightenment thinkers. In using the word *reason* in the title of his novel, Ghosh invokes one of the key values of nineteenth-century Bengali culture.[24] Tapan Raychaudhuri writes, "Rational assessment of current needs and received traditions, both indigenous and alien, became the hallmark of Bengali thought in the nineteenth century. Arguably, this development marked a total discontinuity in the history of the region. A product of the colonial encounter, it was a development with explosive potentialities which acquired a measure of autonomy."[25] This importance given to the conscious invocation of reason was relatively novel, and can be traced to European Enlightenment thought, the influence of which was mediated by colonialism. During the late eighteenth and early nineteenth centuries, writers and social reformers in India criticized a blind adherence to custom and superstition. They urged their compatriots to order their lives along rational lines.

At the forefront of this movement was Rammohun Roy, founder of the Brahmo Samaj movement, and a central figure of the so-called "Bengal Renaissance." Rammohun sought to unite the best of Hindu, Muslim, and European culture using the principles of "reason" and "social comfort." He campaigned for the abolition of sati, the acceptance of widow remarriage, and for scientific and English education. An employee of the East India Company, he by no means challenged the legitimacy of colonial rule. Yet he was a critic of British administration on various fronts. Sumit Sarkar assesses his career:

> Rammohun managed to combine an impressive interest in and sympathy for liberal and nationalist movements in England, France, Naples, Spain, Ireland and even Latin America with a fundamental acceptance of foreign political and economic domination over his own country. Within this basic framework, Rammohun did blaze the trail, of course, for several generations of moderate constitutionalist agitation, focusing on demands like Indianization of services, trial by jury, separation of powers, freedom of the press, and consultations with Indian landlords, merchants, and officials on legislative matters.[26]

Rammohun's embrace of Enlightenment values went hand in hand with an acceptance of British hegemony, albeit with some criticisms of administrative policy. The intellectual culture that was promoted by the British furthered this hegemony. In spite of an emphasis on reason and useful knowledge, there was a lack in the university curriculum of scientific experimentation—the emphasis was on the humanities and social philosophy, subjects that molded attitudes about society. Subjects such as English inculcated in the Indian intelligentsia values, opinions, and tastes that accorded with those of the rulers, placing limits on the critical application of reason. Sarkar argues—and the point is debatable—that caste oppression was much less significant than colonial exploitation, yet it was the former rather than the latter that came in for attack from reformers such as Rammohun Roy.[27]

The discourse of reason had a mixed elaboration in colonial India. As in European Enlightenment culture, reason was invoked as a corrective to the grip of religious authority and tradition. A rational revaluation of social practices paved the way for reforms—in the status of women and in education particularly. In the case of Rammohun

Roy, who "combined rationalism, internationalism and sympathy for the peasantry with a pro-British stance," it did not lead to a critique of colonial rule.[28] And although Rammohun stressed "Mathematics, Natural Philosophy, Chemistry, Anatomy and other useful sciences," the colonial regime emphasized English and humanistic learning in the curricular changes they introduced, rather than science and technology. Also, as Raychaudhuri points out, the embrace of rational inquiry on every front also led to the development of "pseudo-sciences."

In Ghosh's novel, Balaram's obsession with both phrenology and hygiene points to this hybrid legacy. Recruited to teach at a village school close to what was then the border with East Bengal, Balaram had channeled his quest to bring order and intelligibility into phrenology, which he alighted upon as the key to the scientific interpretation of character. When Alu comes to live with him, he immediately subjects the boy to a phrenological examination and charts the peculiar bumps on Alu's head. Balaram's enthusiasm for phrenology suggests not only the hegemonic appeal of Enlightenment rationality but also its colonial belatedness.[29] We are told that Balaram had discovered the copy of *Practical Phrenology* that was to spark his interest on January 11, 1950, exactly the day Nobel Prize winner Irène Joliot-Curie arrived in Calcutta. Her presence signals the present state of scientific knowledge. Balaram is unable to recognize that phrenology has been long debunked, as has the criminal anthropology of Cesare Lombroso that he also champions.

The path of reason is not only skewed by a belated temporality, it is also hindered by the operation of base interest. Balaram's pseudoscientific line of investigation brings him into conflict with the school's headmaster, Bhudeb Roy, an unscrupulous profiteer. At a school festival put on by Bhudeb Roy, to which public officials and a priest have been invited, Balaram notices a growing cranial lump on a displayed figurine of Saraswati, the Goddess of Learning (caused by the heat of the lights inside the image's head), and loudly declares it to signify not learning but vanity. In this episode, different rationalities—those of science, the sacred, and the profane—come into ludicrous conflict. Balaram's pseudoscientific interpretation of the deformed religious icon exposes Bhudeb Roy's entirely worldly ambitions. It also earns him Bhudeb Roy's enmity, which becomes increasingly violent: Bhudeb Roy poisons Balaram's fish pond and his toughs threaten Balaram's maid, Maya. Coercive forces again begin to rally against Balaram's crusade to advance reason.

Undeterred by Bhudeb Roy's threats, if not spurred on by them, Balaram initiates an even more ambitious struggle for the rationalist cause. The story of Balaram's present tactics as he again conducts a battle against germs—he "douse[s] the village in waves of antiseptic" and at one point squirts Bhudeb Roy as well—is interwoven with that of his past campaign as president of the Rationalists.[30] This second war against germs, fought with carbolic acid, is credited later with saving many lives in Lalpukur. It occurs against the backdrop of the 1971 war for Bangladeshi independence as refugees from East Bengal stream across the border.[31] Against this cross-border invasion of refugees and against Bhudeb Roy's profiteering, Balaram tries to champion sanitary and moral order.

Balaram's confidence in the power of scientific rationality is not merely idiosyncratic, but rather has the colonial genealogy I have sketched earlier. It is a confidence shared by nationalist thinkers in the colonial world. Jawaharlal Nehru, first prime minister of India, is one forceful exponent in India of this faith in science. In *The Discovery of India*, he writes, "I am convinced that the methods and approach of science have revolutionized human life more than anything else in the long course of history, and have opened doors and avenues of further and even more radical change, leading up to the very portals of what has long been considered the unknown."[32] He sees in science the potential to transform India, where "a rational spirit ... is replaced by irrationalism and a blind idolatry of the past." Nehru's vision led directly to the setting up of the Department of Science and Technology in independent India, under which scientific and technological research and education were made national priorities and attained high levels for a country of India's economic resources. Balaram's promotion of science and its offshoots echoes the vision of postcolonial development set forth by Nehru. Ghosh clearly patterns Balaram's character upon historical figures such as Jawaharlal Nehru and Rammohun Roy who attempted to forward a progressive, rational program of social transformation.

When Bhudeb Roy closes down the school where Balaram teaches, Balaram decides to set up the Pasteur School of Reason, in which students can learn practical skills as well as more conventional subjects. It is from here that his campaign to sanitize the village is conducted. The money for Balaram's campaign comes from the sale of the material that Alu has learned to weave. Balaram intends to have Alu teach in the school as well. This endeavor is the peak of Balaram's ambition as a rationalist:

The School would have two main departments. After much careful
thought Balaram had decided to name one the Department of Pure Reason and the other The Department of Practical Reason: abstract reason
and concrete reason, a meeting of the two great forms of human thought.
Every student would have to attend classes in both departments. In the
Department of Pure Reason they would be taught elementary reading,
writing and arithmetic, and they would be given lectures in the history
of science and technology.... In the Department of Practical Reason, the
students would be taught weaving or tailoring. (p. 107)

In this literal interpretation of Kant's philosophical schema, Ghosh is
clearly parodying the grandiloquent claims of Enlightenment rationality. However, if Balaram's crusade in the name of Reason is at times
absurd, he also has an idealistic program of education and development. He proposes to harness Alu's talents as a weaver and his wife's
ability as a seamstress to formulate a course of education that is at
once reasonable and useful. That is, he proposes to reinterpret Enlightenment rationality to serve the needs of an impoverished postcolonial
society. From the profits of their work, he inaugurates the Department
of the March of Reason, which undertakes to disinfect the entire village—Balaram's ambitions circle back to his earlier zeal for eradicating
germs. This new department embodies "Reason Militant":

A school, like Reason itself, must have a purpose. Without a purpose Reason decays into a mere trick, forever reflecting itself like mirrors at a fair.
It is that sense of purpose which the third department will restore to our
school. It will help us to remember that we cannot limit the benefits of our
education and our learning to ourselves—that it is our duty to use it for
the benefit of everybody around us. That is why I have decided to name
the new department the Department of the March of Reason. It will remind us that our school has another aspect: Reason Militant. (p. 117)

Balaram repudiates an abstract development of reason and argues instead for the harnessing of reason to praxis—to practical activity directed toward social transformation. Otherwise, reason can undergo an in-
finite regression, "forever reflecting itself like mirrors at a fair." Balaram
proposes to fashion the educational program of the Pasteur School of
Reason in such a way that reason advances material well-being.

Ultimately, the text is equivocal about the potential of reason. It
playfully mocks the more bizarre manifestations of doctrines of reason

in its treatment of Balaram's obsessions with phrenology and with hygiene and his use of carbolic acid to free the entire village of germs. At the same time, it urges with a grain of seriousness the quest for a novel rational praxis in its portrayal of Balaram's School of Reason. Balaram has earlier discovered Alu's natural propensity for weaving, and, when Alu has refused to go to school, has apprenticed him to a local weaver who has a stolen knowledge of the mysteries of jamdani technique. Alu's extraordinary ability epitomizes the potentialities of reason.

> Man at the loom is the finest example of Mechanical man; a creature who makes his world as no other can, with his mind. The machine is man's curse and his salvation, and no machine has created man as much as the loom. It has created not separate worlds but one, for it has never permitted the division of the world. The loom recognizes no continents and no countries. It has tied the world together with its bloody ironies from the beginning of human time.... It has never permitted the division of reason. (p. 55)

Weaving is presented here as a complex figure for human experience.[33] The passage emphasizes the ambiguities of human agency, as seen in his working of the loom. Man at the loom functions as a metonym for man in his total capacity to transform his world—for better and for worse. This transformative capacity is so profound as to affect human subjectivity itself: "no machine has created man as much as the loom." History itself, or "human time," is the bloody and contradictory cloth of the loom. The figure disavows a number of divisions: those of mind and body, of continents and countries, of history, of reason itself. The narrator, in propounding a vision of praxis through this figure of weaving, is fully cognizant of the history of imperial exploitation that inheres in its forms—as is clear from the brief excursus in the novel on slavery, colonialism, and weaving. "It is a gory history in parts; a story of greed and destruction. Every scrap of cloth is stained by a bloody past." However, the novel imagines the possibility of reconstituting these forms for liberatory ends—hence the repeated valorization of weaving. "But it is the only history we have and history is hope as well as despair. And so weaving, too, is hope; a living belief that having once made the world one and blessed it with its diversity it must do so again. Weaving is hope because it has no country, no continent.... Weaving is Reason, which makes the world mad and makes it human" (p. 58). In positing human experience, equated here with both weaving and reason, as universal, heterogeneous, and interwoven, the narrator repudiates the Eurocentrism of Enlightenment discourses of reason. In this view, weaving/reason can be rescued from the determinations of colonial domination and can take new, emancipatory forms.

The figure of the circle also works against the linear logic of modernity and of Enlightenment rationality. Circling is invoked in three ways: in the title, in the form of the narrative, and in terms of travel. It is contrasted with the straight lines that have the quality of a fetish for Bhudeb Roy.

> The time has come, he said, his tears drying on his cheeks, for straight lines. The trouble with this village is that there aren't enough straight lines. Look at Europe, look at America, look at Tokyo: straight lines, that's the secret. Everything is in straight lines. The roads are straight, the houses are straight, the cars are straight (except for the wheels). They even walk straight. That's what we need: straight lines. There's a time and an age for everything, and this is the age of the straight line. (p. 99)

Here linearity is linked with the modern and the prosperous: Europe, America, Tokyo. Development is conceived in the image of "the straight line." The village, by contrast, is a place with "unrepaired cycles" resting against a banyan tree, "the rickety shed of the pharmacy," "ponds mildewed with water-hyacinth and darkened by leaning coconut palms"—a place of disorderly rural beauty. This sense of disorderliness is enhanced by the circling, perambulatory quality of the narrative, which moves between past and present, the city and the country, and from character to character in a highly associative way. As the story develops, Alu himself moves, again without any clear purpose or sense of direction. The novel's formal and thematic disruptions of linearity are another way of refuting the neat closure of the detective narrative and the corresponding logics of domination.

The novel circles around the concept of reason, exploring its various meanings via philosophical categories and metaphorical figures: Pure Reason, Practical Reason, Reason Militant, the Circle of Reason, and reason as weaving. We have, in the novel, a rejection of reason as an unworldly abstraction. Rather, reason is prescribed a secular role, a role that involves the creative use of the intellect in the practices of everyday life. When he uses the Kantian phrases "Pure Reason" and "Practical Reason," though, Ghosh does not merely refer to intellectual application—he invokes the discourse of Enlightenment reason with all its connotations. In lampooning a world of "straight lines," Ghosh hints at the oppressive qualities of a concretized reason that in its linear, forward movement is inimical to difference. It is to counter this that he also elaborates the concept of reason through the figure of the circle and the process of weaving. However, Ghosh suggests, this more complex, fractal kind of reason is vulnerable to the action of the police.

ENLIGHTENMENT REASON AND POLICE

The picture that Ghosh presents of the doings of the police could not be further removed from the Hegelian ideal of the state as an embodiment of reason, directed at ensuring happiness and freedom. The postcolonial state is portrayed in Ghosh's novel as an administrative machine unconcerned with the well-being of the populace. The government's interventions are by and large represented unfavorably. Balaram's attempts to introduce a suitably reformulated program of reason, one that has practically beneficial applications, fail both when he is at Presidency College and years later in the village of Lalpukur. In both instances, the strong-armed forces of unreason overpower him. Reason, it turns out, cannot be protected from the base operation of interest. Balaram's opponent in Lalpukur, Bhudeb Roy, has successfully represented the doings of Balaram and his household to the police as an insurgent plot, a perception that accords with the police's need for subjects to monitor. Balaram barricades himself against Bhudeb Roy and the police behind barrels of carbolic acid, the medium through which he has crusaded to introduce hygiene. Balaram's weapon is ineffectual, but without his knowledge another member of the household, Rakhal, has homemade bombs in which he traffics, which do the job. When tensions come to a head, the police aim a warning flare at the house, unwittingly sending it up in flames. Only Alu, who is away, survives. The episode brings home the point that an interest in profit, backed by force, easily overpowers individual efforts to bring about enlightenment and social improvement. Moreover, through this episode the novel depicts the state and its forces of police as an impediment to the proper exercise of reason.

The incineration of the School of Reason is not the first instance in the novel in which an ameliorative venture is defeated by the intervention of the police. A pessimistic view of the state—both as an embodiment of rationality and as an institution—is strikingly evident in a chapter on "Signs of the Times." The villagers of Lalpukur experience a windfall of war—a plane literally drops down out of the sky. This incident makes more of an impression upon the people of the village than the events of the war, the creation of a new nation, or the dispersal of refugees. They speculate about the significance of the crash:

> After the crash things took a new turn. The numerologists assumed the leadership of the End of the World Signaled camp and heaped scorn on the palmists and their theory of Signs of New Times. Whose palm do you read an aircrash on? they sneered. God's? The astrologers, warily neutral for once, took the conservative view that it meant nothing at all: crashes and tempests and earthquakes were normal in Kaliyug. What else could you expect in the Age of Evil?
>
> But they're wrong, said Balaram, telling Gopal the story on his veranda in Calcutta. If it has no meaning, why would it happen? Of course it has a meaning, but the meaning must be read rationally—not with the hocus pocus of these Stone Age magicians. (p. 87)

The fallen plane invites philosophical speculation from different groups—preachers of doom, optimists, and stoics. In fact, these traditional philosophers fail to provide the more prosaic and rational interpretation that is required: the plane becomes a source of profit for Bhudeb Roy, who is quick to take possession of it. Bhudeb Roy proceeds to sell parts of the plane to the villagers: the metal sheets of the fuselage to convert into a roof; the wings to make bridges; and glass, rubber, and nuts and bolts. The multiple meanings of modernity are implied in this episode—a war machine, emblem of modern technological development, is transformed into modern materials for the village. Bhudeb Roy also collects insurance for the school that is destroyed by the plane. A few days later, two jeeps of uniformed men appear, intent on retrieving the scrap, all of it "government property."

> Nobody ever really learned what happened there, but over the next two days the blue-uniforms went unerringly to the shops with sheet-metal roofs, the canals bridged by reinforced steel, the rickshaws decorated with shiny bolts, and recovered every last bit of scrap the plane had deposited in the village. All that anyone knew was that when the jeeps drove out ranks of blue-uniformed arms appeared in the windows waving cordially to Bhudeb Roy, and he waved back, smiling happily. (pp. 96–97)

The villagers of Lalpukur pay for even the scraps of the modern that fall upon them out of the sky, and which they incorporate bricoleur-fashion into their everyday lives. Even so, these scraps are quickly wrested away by the "blue uniforms" of the state.

At the point in the novel when things begin to heat up in Lalpukur, the reader is introduced to police detective Jyoti Das. Das is an improbable professional detective, with no particular appetite for his job. He has been relieved to be admitted to the Union Secretariat, the intelligence branch, where he can analyze files and write reports rather than "rushing about catching dacoits" (p. 126). He is especially pleased to discover that he is able to pursue his true interest: drawing and painting birds. Das's lack of esprit de corps does not deter the local police from besieging Balaram's compound and unwittingly setting it ablaze. At the same time, his reluctance does distance the reader from the enterprise of policing.

The police do not stop with the destruction of the School of Reason in what they describe as "an encounter with an extremist group." Having been mobilized, they embark on a pursuit of Alu, whom they falsely identify as an insurgent with ties across the border. The state's power and self-serving paranoia are evident in the way its agents attempt to track down Alu; they draw on informants, produce intelligence reports, and ultimately authorize an international search. The postcolonial state shares the anxieties about insurgency and potential disorder that we saw on the part of the colonial state in the earlier chapters of this book. As I have suggested, the logic of domination inherent in Western Enlightenment versions of nationhood has been emphasized by critics such as Partha Chatterjee. In *Nationalist Thought and the Colonial World*, Chatterjee claims that because nationalism is so entangled in the logic of Enlightenment rationality, it has a colonial logic inherent to it.[34] Ghosh underscores the repressive dimensions of the nation and its apparatuses in his fiction.

One episode underscores in a pointed way the problematic character of state rationality in the novel. After his home and family are destroyed, Alu flees Lalpukur and travels to the south of India, from where he eventually departs by sea for Al-Ghazira. On the boat that Alu takes is a very pregnant woman who, much to the consternation of her companions, refuses to deliver her baby unless she is given forms to sign. One of the passengers, Professor Samuel, discovers that the woman is convinced that her child's birthright to future prosperity is in jeopardy. "She says she won't deliver without signing the forms. That's what she says. She says she'll keep it in for as long as she has to.... She says that she knows that the child won't be given a house or a car or anything at all if she doesn't sign the forms. It'll be sent back to India, she says, and she would rather kill it than allow that to happen; kill it right now with a bottle while it's still in her womb" (p. 177). Ultimately, the professor dupes the delirious woman by donning a jacket and presenting to her a page torn from a copy of a book. "Alu took out the copy of *The Life of Pasteur* that Gopal had given him and very carefully tore off a page. Despite its age the paper was stiff and crisp. The Professor snatched it from him and, taking a pen out of his jacket, drew a straight line at the bottom of the page. Beside it he wrote in English: 'Signed'" (pp. 186–87). The woman credulously scrawls her name upon the page, then goes into labor. In fact, the book from which the page is taken is referred to repeatedly in the novel and given a special significance. It embodies the heroic potential of science. In this farcical episode, this testament to the possibilities of scientific reason literally doubles as a form for the inscription of a state rationality that affords the newly born infant a legitimate identity. The novel lampoons this subjection of reason to the rationality of the postcolonial state.

The Circle of Reason resists the narrative logic of police, one typified for example by the Sherlock Holmes stories, by making Alu and not Das the central character. In fact, the description of Alu's flight as an unwitting fugitive from the police elicits the sympathy of the reader. Alu is depicted as something of a misfit, with his strange cranial bumps, his solitary nature, and his passion for weaving. Yet the narrative respects his "difference," rather than making him an object of knowledge to be apprehended and explained. The reader comes away with little sense of Alu's thoughts and feelings. Alu's very opaqueness as a character, his unknowability, can be seen as yet another way in which Ghosh marks the limit of Enlightenment reason and its guarantee of epistemological transparency. Alu is elusive not only to the reader, but also to the police who attempt to pin him down. The novel counterposes to the workings of the police apparatus a shadowy network of Chalias or weavers from Kerala, who embrace Alu and help him evade the police, at the cost of being taken in by the police themselves. The tendency of police fiction is to bring to light the motives and movements of he who is pursued. Ghosh, in making us privy to Das's police files, presents Alu to us as an object of pursuit, but allows him to remain in the shadows.

MIGRANCY AND UTOPIA

While *The Circle of Reason* goes some way toward unraveling the rationality of police, this deconstruction mostly occurs outside India, in a space depicted as extraneous to the bounded and closely regulated territory of the nation. The second part of the novel concerns the flight of Alu to the Gulf state of Al-Ghazira, where he becomes part of a community of migrants. Jyoti Das, as a Deputy Central Research Officer whose area of expertise is police intelligence, pursues Alu. En route by boat, Alu meets the cast of characters whose doings and histories comprise this segment of the novel: Zindi; Karthamma and her newborn baby, Boss; Kulfi; Chunni; the Professor; and Rakesh. In Al-Ghazira, all these migrants join Zindi's household, paying a moderate rent and finding work with her assistance. Alu once again narrowly escapes from a catastrophe: he is presumed dead when a building in which he is working collapses, but his voice is heard in the rubble and he is pulled out two days later, alive and unhurt. The experience is cataclysmic—his reflections inspire the other inhabitants of the Souq to repudiate the use of money and to resist the exploitation of day laborers. Zindi, meanwhile, has been trying to buy a tailoring shop run by Forid Mia and owned by Jeevanbhai Patel, who also lives in Zindi's house. Jeevanbhai traffics in intelligence with the police and also with the old Malik of Al-Ghazira, who is kept virtually confined in his fort by the oil-hungry British who control the kingdom. Jyoti Das, who is still in pursuit of Alu even though he doubts that Alu is an insurgent, interviews Jeevanbhai. Just as Zindi is about to conclude the purchase of the tailoring shop, Forid Mia betrays his employer Jeevanbhai's meeting with the Malik; Jeevanbhai is apprehended by the police and hangs himself. The rest of Zindi's household proceeds on a planned shopping expedition, but they are ambushed by uniformed men. Zindi, who has anticipated something of the sort, shepherds the survivors, including Alu, onto a boat and they flee.

Ghosh by no means idealizes the circumstances of economic and political marginality in which the characters in Zindi's household live. These characters are all displaced in one way or another. Salman Rushdie in *Shame* characterizes the condition of migrants well: "All migrants leave their pasts behind, although some try to pack it into bundles and boxes—but on the journey something seeps out of the treasured mementos and old photographs, until even their owners fail to recognize them, because it is the fate of migrants to be stripped of history."[35] Alu and his companions have, like the migrants Rushdie describes, traveled light. They say little about the places and people they have left behind, and make do with the odd jobs and moments of fellowship that happen their way. Liberated from the repressive structures and narratives of the nation, they are also stripped of its protections and comfort.

This representation runs against the grain of current discourse about migrants, which is largely celebratory. For example, in his book *Global Diasporas*, Robin Cohen represents global migration in largely favorable terms, stressing its liberatory and ameliorative aspects.[36] According to Cohen, diasporic migrants experience an advantage in the present era of globalization. Cohen identifies five aspects of globalization that bear upon diasporas: 1) a world economy shaped by new technologies, a new division of labor, transnational corporations, and free trade policies; 2) forms of international migration that are temporary; 3) the development of global cities; 4) the creation of cosmopolitan and local cultures; and 5) a deterritorialization of social identity. Although Cohen is suspicious of what he calls "global babble," he concludes that diasporas are advantaged by globalization because they are both materially and psychologically in step with its imperatives. For example, diasporic kin and family ties facilitate global trade, and deterritorialized social identities allow for multiple affiliations and associations, according to Cohen. While his assessment rings true for a migrant bourgeoisie, it is less convincing in the case of subaltern migrant workers such as those depicted in *The Circle of Reason*, who do not have the sort of room to maneuver that Cohen ascribes to diasporas. These migrants are illegal, economically marginal, and do not have recourse to the kinship and family structures that bourgeois migrants have.

At the same time, their interstitial existence does give them the chance to fashion their lives in creative and unorthodox ways, particularly with regard to family relations and to labor. These subaltern migrants, who neither are part of an imagined national community nor are served by a traditional immigrant family structure, express their solidarity in communal units that approximate the family form. However, Zindi's makeshift family of lodgers is far from typical. It is a matriarchally governed agglomeration based on mutual need and chance, rather than a patriarchal structure linked by lineage and property relations. The character of Zindi's household contravenes the ideology of domesticity that prevailed in modern Europe and was recast for nationalist ends in India in a separation of "the home" and "the world."[37] In the latter view, the chaste middle-class Indian woman was the guardian of national authenticity. This representation of woman as at once bearing the standard of cultural authenticity and being at home in the modern world is equally pronounced in diasporic immigrant communities in the twenty-first century.[38] The figure of Zindi, a large-bodied, rough-tongued, tough Egyptian migrant, could not be further removed from this ideal of the demure, respectable, chaste homemaker. Zindi, whose name in Urdu means "alive," is the heart of the household—not as the modest, unsullied bearer of tradition but as the big-hearted den mother who bullies, cajoles, wheels, and deals to keep her family intact and afloat.

Nor is her fabricated family united purely by affect rather than monetary interest, for Zindi helps her lodgers find jobs and charges them rent. Her domestic arrangements underscore the fact that the split between private and public does not obtain for subaltern migrants, who do not enjoy full political and economic subjecthood in the public sphere. In *The Circle of Reason*, the public business of contractual relationships and economic transactions is brought into the loosely familial private domain of Zindi's household, where there are continual references to labor and money. For example, when neighbors gather, Zindi is quick to make a profit from the sale of tea. Zindi cannot sustain her family from within, however, and, faced with their gnawing economic insecurity, she tries to buy a tailoring shop to run as a family business.

It is at this point that the family ceases to function as a utopian alternative to the state. As part of the exchange for the shop, Jeevanbhai asks Zindi to provide information about Alu. She responds, "Police, I suppose? No I can't. You know that's one thing I couldn't do to them. Whatever happens in the future, in the past they all ate my bread and salt. They've become part of my flesh" (p. 304). Zindi refuses to betray the familial ties that the communal sharing of bread has created. The center of this family, which appears to be transgressive both because it is associationally rather than biologically constituted and because it deconstructs the opposition between private and public, does not ultimately hold. Jeevanbhai persuades Zindi to point out her family to Jyoti Das, ostensibly a "friend" from India, though it is not clear whether Zindi believes that he is not a policeman or she is willingly deluded. In any case, the police penetrate the circle of subaltern migrants who in a provisional way constitute a counter-community outside the aegis of the state. In fact, Zindi's family is the medium through which a subaltern migrant such as Alu becomes visible to authority.

Even as Zindi negotiates for the tailoring shop, the subaltern migrants who make up her household attempt to establish a utopian community that is far more transgressive than Zindi's ultimately compromised if reconstructed family. Trapped in the ruins of a shopping complex built of adulterated cement that has crumbled—an event that symbolizes the collapse of capital because of its rotten foundations—Alu has an epiphany. As he later explains to his companions, Pasteur's struggle against germs was spurred by a quest for purity, but this quest was frustrated because Pasteur had failed to discover the breeding ground of germs—which, according to Alu, is money. Alu then proposes, "We will drive money from the Ras, and without it we shall be happier, richer, more prosperous than ever before"(p. 281). Inspired, as Balaram was, by Pasteur, Alu is as zealous as his foster father had been in his mission to rid his community of germs. Professor Samuel devises a scheme to provide "from each according to his ability to each according to his need," whereby the inhabitants of the Ras are to pool their earnings and jointly buy goods and services from the Souq through a designated agent, and put an end to profit-making commerce in the Ras.

This scheme is reminiscent of Robert Owen's practical attempts at social reform in early nineteenth-century England. Owen, a prosperous mill owner in the Scottish village of New Lanark, reorganized his factory to improve working conditions and also established model schools and preschools for his employees. At first offering a conservative resolution to the opposition of labor and capital, Owen became more critical of classical economics and argued for the rights of workers to the full yield of their labor.[39] One of his proposals was to do away with money bound to a gold standard and to issue units of exchange representing labor time. The vision of Alu and his companions is equally ambitious, and like Owen, they predicate an entire social and moral transformation upon their scheme of economic reform.

Once again, however, the police put a forcible end to a revolutionary project: when Alu and his companions leave the Ras and enter the town to spend their pooled earnings, uniformed men with guns ambush them. The composite, diasporic community that migrants have forged beyond the repressive structures of their postcolonial nations proves to be vulnerable to the forces of capital and of police, forces that are global in scope. The presence of these forces is felt at this point as narrative attention shifts to police, from whose perspective the reader learns of Alu's inspiration and the planned shopping trip. The men who ambush Alu and his companions are employed by the new regime that is now exploiting Al-Ghazira. With its newly discovered reserves of oil, Al-Ghazira is exemplifies the workings of neocolonialism: we learn in one of the many tangential stories that oilmen from abroad have imprisoned the Malik and have installed his American-educated brother as oil minister and minister of public works. When Alu and his friends challenge in even a mild way the economic terms of this arrangement by banding together as workers and consumers, the regime responds with a show of force. The fact that a crisis is precipitated by their shopping trip is itself telling—the residents of the Ras want to enter the market on their own terms, and that of course is not acceptable to the neocolonial rulers of Al-Ghazira. In their encounter with the police, many of Alu's friends are killed, and the survivors are rounded up and deported. Alu himself escapes with Zindi, Kulfi, and Boss, but is forced once again into migratory flight.

LAST RITES

The last part of the novel focuses on the place of religion in postcolonial societies, societies that have emerged out of a negotiation with European modernity. It also considers the character of socialism, but this time as it is championed by members of the Indian bourgeoisie, and once again it explores the experience of diasporic migration. The setting is a small town in Algeria, El Oued, where Zindi, Boss, Alu, and Kulfi have come, still pursued by Jyoti Das. An Indian doctor in the town, Mrs. Verma, recruits the refugees to act in a religious play by Tagore, *Chitrangada*, at the local hospital. She wants to present the play rather than endure a repeat of a public speech by her colleague Dr. Mishra, whose socialist rhetoric is hollow and self-promoting.

Unknown to Zindi and her friends, Jyoti Das has also been recruited to act in the play, and he becomes infatuated with Kulfi at first sight. Yet again a calamity occurs: Kulfi dies of a heart attack in the middle of a rehearsal. Mrs. Verma arranges a performance of last rites and a cremation, in the face of Dr. Mishra's gibes about her unmodern, irrational, and makeshift adherence to religious tradition. In the final passages of the novel, the renegade policeman travels with Alu, Zindi, and the baby, Boss, to Tangier. There they go their separate ways, ways that are determined by the economic and political circumstances that underpin diasporic migration. Jyoti Das intends to migrate to Dusseldorf while Zindi and Alu wearily but hopefully turn their steps back toward the Indian subcontinent.

In making the performance of *Chitrangada* the centerpiece of this part of the novel, Ghosh points to how national identity is staged in bourgeois diasporic communities through public displays of cultural patrimony. A group of Indians plan the play for an audience of Algerian colleagues. Mrs. Verma's desire to put forward an exalted representation of Indian culture is undercut by the circumstances in which the performance is cobbled together. The play is based on a legend in the Mahabharata, in which the noble but plain Chitra is able to seduce Arjuna with the beauty she is granted for a year, but ultimately wins his heart and retains his love even when her beauty fades. The renegade policeman Das, who is to play Arjuna, is smitten with lust for Kulfi, who is to be Chitra. Das's visceral desire departs markedly from the ideal of a love that, inspired by beauty, develops in *Chitrangada* into a regard that survives the loss of physical beauty. Kulfi is herself a travesty of the character of Chitra. In the play, Chitra, although she initially enchants Arjuna with an assumed beauty, is renowned for her high ethical character and wins him with her inner grace. Kulfi, who has in the past been forced to work as a prostitute by her husband, attempts to beguile Das with her decidedly erotic charm. Ghosh's playful undercutting of a "high" cultural discourse by introducing absurd and idiosyncratic elements is in keeping with his treatment of utopian projects in the earlier parts of the novel, though here it is a quasi-religious cultural project that is mildly lampooned.

Dr. Mishra objects that the cultural representation put forward by *Chitrangada* is quaint and outdated in its quasi-religious character. His opposition to the performance of *Chitrangada*, couched as the opposition of a forward-thinking, secular champion of reason, anticipates the argument between him and Dr. Verma that follows Kulfi's abrupt death. When Dr. Verma proposes to erect a pyre and perform last Brahminical rites, Dr. Mishra scoffs at first, her religiosity, and second, the makeshift manner in which she proceeds. He argues that the rites are incongrouous with a modern, secular outlook, and that they become absurd when tap water is substituted for Ganges water and broken furniture suffices for a funeral pyre. Dr. Verma's response is a comment on the place of religion in modern India. She insists that it is the spirit rather than the letter of religious doctrine that matters, and that she and her companion owe it to the dead Kulfi to adhere to religious tradition. Dr. Verma views religion not as a set of dogmatically adhered-to rules and prescriptions that constrain everyday actions, but rather as a historically contingent form of cultural practice that expresses deeply felt sentiments. Dr. Mishra's narrowly doctrinal understanding of religion and his excessive valorization of rationalism allows no room for such sentiments. Here Ghosh echoes the view of critics such as Ranajit Guha of the irreducibility and importance of religious consciousness in postcolonial India.[40]

Dr. Mishra opposes Dr. Verma's plan to stage *Chitrangada* not only on rationalist grounds but also because he wishes to repeat the rousing socialist speech he delivered on a similar occasion the year before. Dr. Mishra has held forth on the subject of social justice and equality. When he proposes to do the same once again, Dr. Verma challenges his political commitment. She recalls Mishra's father's comfortably self-serving left positions and suggests that Mishra's rhetoric is hollow. Her own father has lived by and suffered for his socialism. Ghosh here queries the political stances of an economically comfortable leftist bourgeoisie. Mishra's socialist bombast contrasts with the practical, lived socialism that Alu and his companions have adopted.

This divergence between bourgeois and subaltern articulations of the same project or phenomenon is seen finally in the representation of migration. The theme of migration is explicitly raised in the novel with reference to Jyoti Das, who, as an amateur ornithologist, is preoccupied with the migration of birds. While this whimsical pursuit marks Das as less pragmatic and materialistic than his peers, it also identifies him as a middle-class person who enjoys leisure, education, and a love of knowledge for its own sake. Moreover, it is a figure for his own pleasurable mobility. This mobility contrasts sharply with the forced, desperate movement of subaltern migrants such as Alu and Zindi. Earlier in the novel, Das is congratulated by a fellow police officer on his coming "foreign trip." His quarry Alu has, by contrast, been forced to migrate to Al Ghazira to elude the police. Although Jyoti Das becomes increasingly alienated from his colleagues and ultimately abandons his pursuit, and for a time travels with Alu and Zindi, his experience of migration is clearly represented as different from theirs. When the lapsed policeman runs out of funds in Al Ghazira, he is able to obtain money by wire from an uncle in Dusseldorf. In the last pages of the novel, Jyoti Das buys a ticket with the intention of migrating to Germany. As he waves goodbye to Zindi and Alu he exults in his freedom and the prospect before him.

> By the time the sleek Spanish ferry drew away, churning up the harbor, Jyoti Das was already on deck, waving. He was sure he could see them among the trees of the Avenue d'Espagne, so he kept waving as

the lovely white town cradled in its nest of hills shrank away. Then he looked down and saw a humped back caracoling through the water. Then he saw another and another and suddenly there was a whole school of dolphins racing along the ferry, leaping, dancing, standing on their tails. He looked up at the tranquil sky and gloried in the soaring birds, the sunlight, the sharpness of the clean sea breeze and the sight of the huge rock glowing in the distance.

It was very beautiful and he was at peace.

When the ferry entered a bay and turned away from the rock of Gibraltar towards the shiny oil-tanks of Algeciras, Jyoti Das turned back to wave for one last time. But all he saw there was a mocking gray smudge hanging on the horizon, pointing to continents of defeat—defeat at home, defeat in the world—and he shut his eyes, for he had looked on it for too many years and he could not bear to look on it any longer.

And so he turned to face the land before him, now grown so real, and dizzy with exultation he prepared to step into a new world. (p. 423)

The pleasure of migration is conveyed in Das's perception of the land-scape—the racing dolphins and soaring birds signify his own sense of speed and weightlessness. Das experiences an enhancement of his sensory capacities. The sunlight, the sea breeze, and the Rock of Gibraltar take on an intensely real quality. The passage describes the possibilities open to the bourgeois migrant in euphoric terms. This sense of euphoria is contrasted to his feelings for his past "home"—signified as a "mocking gray smudge." He is able to turn his back on the "continents of defeat" that he has left behind.

The subaltern migrants are much more vulnerable and desperate. When they arrive in El Oued, for example, Boss has a fever that has been untreated for ten days. On the way, they have passed through Egypt and have returned to Zindi's village, but she has been taunted and driven away. In the last passages of the novel, Alu, Zindi, and Boss, who comprise an unlikely holy family of surviving subaltern migrants, experience a sense of resignation rather than exultation. They turn away from the Mediterranean vista toward which Das faces.

But Boss was looking the other way, towards the Atlantic, and soon they were looking there, too, scanning the waters. They saw nothing except sleepy, crawling oil-tankers. So, drowsily warmed by the clear sunlight, they settled down to wait for Virat Singh and the ship that was to carry them home. (p. 423)

The description conveys a sense of lethargy and immobility that is the very opposite of the ebullience of Das's vision. Although the novel ends with the statement, "Hope is the beginning," the reader is left with the strong sense that the bulk of the hope lies with bourgeois migrants.

The emergence in the late 1980s of transnational and global cultural studies alongside postcolonial studies bears witness to a move to understand cultural relations between "the West and the rest" not in terms of a metropole/periphery frame but in terms of more complex, shifting, variegated patterns brought about by the global flows of peoples, goods, and information. *Public Culture,* the most prominent of the journals devoted to this vision of cultural studies, for example, "seeks a critical understanding of the global cultural flows and the cultural forms of the public sphere which define the late twentieth century."[41] While critics working in the field of postcolonial studies have been unmitigatedly critical of the coercive legacies of colonial regimes, those in transnational and global studies are somewhat more celebratory of the fluctuating, hybrid cultural terrain that they analyze. In Appadurai's *Modernity At Large,* for instance, one detects a note of wonderment at the disjunctive global flows that constitute various ethnoscapes, ideoscapes, technoscapes, financescapes, and mediascapes.[42] In such discussions, the possibilities of modernity rather than the problems tend to be writ large. No longer do we find in such scholars the rhetoric of resistance to the cultural forces of domination; instead we find a discourse of improvised self-fashioning in the face of the exigencies of the present. While such a shift in scholarly focus is an understandable response to the material and imaginative transformations that Appadurai sketches, I would suggest that in South Asia the experiences of colonialism and neocolonialism so strongly mark "alternative modernities" as to render an excessive emphasis on the notions of "contingency" and "disjuncture" somewhat questionable.[43]

CONCLUSION

Fiction of intrigue typically closes with a recapitulation of the steps the detective has followed in solving the mystery and apprehending the wrongdoer. In the final passages of *The Circle of Reason,* the remaining characters disperse, in what is described as a beginning rather than an ending. The narrative's "movement" is to wriggle out of the skin of the detective plot. Ghosh gives the detective only a subsidiary part in the narrative. From the outset, Ghosh's detective has been a reluctant sleuth, and has felt little appetite for the chase. In the course of an interrogation, when he has been expected to brutalize a witness, he has felt the bile churn at the back of his throat. Well before the end of the novel, Das abandons his duties as a police detective. By constructing the detective's character and role in this way, Ghosh divests his parodic rewriting of fiction of intrigue of the gratifications of heroic detection. He consequently undercuts the ethos of enlightenment and police that drives fiction of intrigue.

The Circle of Reason combines a critique of the repressive aspects of postcolonial societies with a qualified hopefulness about the possibilities of postcolonial modernity. It articulates this critique at both a philosophical and social level, dwelling on the oppressive as well as emancipatory aspects of Enlightenment reason and at the same time sketching the role of force in the state and civil society. It imagines ways of superseding a repressive postcolonial modernity by presenting an account of alternative utopian projects. This sense of possibility is conveyed by the figure of weaving, a figure that emphasizes the imbricatedness of people's lives and their capacity creatively to transform these lives. The novel also explores the phenomenon of migration, seeing in the experience of the nomad an escape from the repressive elements of modern rationalities and social forms. However, it does not idealize migration per se, and carefully distinguishes between the liberatory experiences of bourgeois migrants and the much harsher circumstances of subaltern migrants.

The Circle of Reason does not ultimately provide neat answers to the questions it raises. On the one hand, Ghosh points to the complicity between the discourses of reason and the apparatuses of police in the postcolonial nation-state.[44] He dramatizes the workings of the legal-bureaucratic apparatus of the state and depicts the unsuccessful attempt by subaltern peoples to enter the domain of civil society. On the other hand, Ghosh imagines other forms of subaltern "associational life" that signify interstitial and transnational alternatives to civil society. It is in these interstices that Ghosh locates postcolonial agency. Ghosh also eviscerates the narrative form of detective fiction, and voids the legal-bureaucratic apparatus of gravity. In so doing, he severs the thread between "the novel and the police." In sum, a close reading of *The Circle of Reason* suggests that the logic of domination is strongly embedded in postcolonial rationality. This logic has, however, a seductive utopian dimension. By parodying and subverting a narrative of police, yet acknowledging the allure of the discourse of Enlightenment rationality, Ghosh conveys both the challenges and pitfalls faced by modern, postcolonial India.

SEVEN

"Deep in Blood"

Roy, Rushdie, and the Representation of State Violence in India

In the field of postcolonial studies, most recent analysis of the nation-state has focused on the way people imagine the nation. Following Benedict Anderson's work on the cultural processes that have produced the nation as an imagined political community, a number of critics have explored the question of what kind of national imaginary—a nation's sense of self—novels produce, and how national identities are fashioned in and through literature.[1] Others have characterized the nation-state as a political unit that is of declining importance, and have focused rather on "transnational flows," "global ethnoscapes," "diaspora," and the like. The consequence of this tendency to focus on the relationship between "nation and narration," or, beyond the nation, on transnational and diasporic literature and culture, has been a relative neglect of the representation of the postcolonial state.

In this chapter, I analyze the way the apparatuses of the state and state violence are imagined in two recent novels, Arundhati Roy's *The God of Small Things* and Salman Rushdie's *The Moor's Last Sigh*. Indeed, "state violence" is a rather broad term. It can be taken to include the violation of human rights, the illegitimate functioning of the police and the military, or the imposition of development plans that displace and economically marginalize millions of people. Here I use the phrase to refer to the use by state apparatuses of physical violence and intimidation above and beyond the "rule of law."

The God of Small Things and *The Moor's Last Sigh* both foreground the complicity of the Indian state in caste and communal violence. In *The God of Small Things*, the reader is gradually initiated into the mystery of the accidental death of Sophie Mol, a favored English child. Velutha, a lower-caste carpenter who transgresses the bounds of class, caste, and sex, is made a scapegoat for this tragedy, paying the price for it with his brutal death at the hands of the police. In *The Moor's Last Sigh*, Moraes Zogoiby, or "the Moor," becomes an agent of the criminal, fascist organization the Mumbai Axis. He uses his deformed fist, for which he is nicknamed "the Hammer," to beat the Axis's victims into submission. The novel, rather than representing this violence from a vantage point of critical distance, puts the protagonist in the position of an agent of the Hindu right—we are presented with an intimate account of violence. The Moor discovers, moreover, that his own father is the kingpin of a criminal nexus of the underworld and the business elite.

Roy and Rushdie use narratives of intrigue to expose the logic of state violence. Again, by fiction of intrigue, I mean fiction that foregrounds the solution of a mystery, be it a crime or a threat to national security. Novels of intrigue exemplify the narratives of social detection of which Fredric Jameson speaks. However, unlike in the Sherlock Holmes stories and other classic detective fiction, the criminal element in question is not located in an "Other" and expunged. Rather, the protagonist eventually perceives the corrupt core of social and political institutions, and in some instances becomes their creature. Such fiction of social detection becomes a "vehicle for judgments on society and revelations of its hidden nature."[2] The secret abuse of state power by the government and by elites is an important theme in contemporary fiction, and one that, as I said, has been strangely neglected by critics. It is an especially consistent preoccupation of contemporary South Asian writers in English, who have moved away from earlier more celebratory representations of the fledgling nation and its state, to a more critical appraisal.

THE STATE, CULTURE, AND NARRATIVE

The moment is especially ripe for critics of South Asian literature to direct attention to the imagining of the state, in view of the horrific state-mediated and organized violence in Gujarat in the spring of 2002. Between the end of March and May, following upon the torching of a train compartment in Godhra and the death of fifty-nine Hindu activists who were returning from an attempt to build the Ram Temple on the former site of the destroyed Babri Mosque, the Hindu right conducted what can most accurately be described as a pogrom. Two thousand people, mostly Muslims, were killed in the most invidiously brutal ways, and over one hundred thousand people, again mostly

Muslims, ended up in refugee camps. The police stood by and watched; they refused victims fleeing the massacres entry to police stations. The killers were able selectively to target Muslims using voter registration lists. What is chilling about this genocide was the systematic and efficiently brutal way in which it was carried out, with the collusion of the state. The genocide in Gujarat forces us to ask: what kind of state is produced in the conditions of postcolonial modernity?

One such process, I would suggest, is the representation of the state in literature. In *The Circle of Reason,* which we examined in chapter 6, and in *Anil's Ghost,* which I discuss in the next chapter, the state is imagined as a bureaucratic, violent entity that follows its own logic at the expense of fragile individuals. The diversity of understandings of the postcolonial state, as well as the different preoccupations of writers, forestalls easy generalization about the significance of literary representations of the state. This diversity notwithstanding, I propose to explore the representations of apparatuses of the state in *The God of Small Things* and *The Moor's Last Sigh* in an effort to work toward an analysis of state violence in postcolonial fiction of intrigue more broadly. I argue that while Roy and Rushdie have rather different visions of the nation, they concur in representing the state as a threat to particularity and plurality, in its introduction of a modern bureaucratic rationality coupled with the violent policing of social boundaries. With regard to the objects of its supervision, the state favors the general and the singular to the particular and the plural because the former better serve the logic of administration. Both Rushdie and Roy use postmodern literary styles to foreground the value of the particular and the plural; and they both portray the state's drive toward legibility as inimical to pluralism and to justice.

SMALL THINGS AND THE STATE

The God of Small Things may not at first glance appear to be a novel of intrigue, but in fact it unfolds as a narrative of mysterious death and violent retribution. It begins with the funeral of a child, Sophie Mol, whose death is not explained. We then quickly learn of a man dying in a police cell. As the fragmentary narrative unfolds, the mystery of these deaths is gradually revealed to the reader. In elucidating the events that have led to Velutha's killing, the narrative assigns implicit blame to each of the characters in the novel. In different ways and to different degrees, Mamachi and Baby Kochama, Velutha's father Vellya Paapen,

Chacko, Margaret, and Comrade Pillai have either moved to inculpate Velutha or have failed to intervene when he is scapegoated. Although there is no detective figure in it, the novel is akin to the kind of narrative of social detection that Jameson analyses, in that the reader is made privy to the wholesale personal, political, and social corruption that "causes" Velutha's death. By keeping us guessing about "who done what," Roy casts suspicion on all the social hierarchies that organize the community: those of caste, class, gender, and race. At the same time, Velutha's murder is not, in the last instance, an act of private, domestic revenge or a party-political elimination; rather, it is carried out by the village policeman as a representative of the historical forces of order. In the final analysis, she reveals the state to be the brutal enforcer of these hierarchies.

The terms in which Velutha's fatal beating is represented are worth looking at closely because they show his killing to be part of a larger rationality, the rationality of the state. The chapter begins with a description of "the posse of Touchable Policemen" crossing the Meenachal River, itself complexly coded in the novel as a concretization of the spirit of place, as well as a symbol for the social and caste boundaries that the characters cross. In coining the adjective "touchable" in contradistinction to "untouchable," Roy underscores the authority and social legitimacy invested in the police. In her description of the men, Roy uses the simple, staccato language that sometimes gives the novel the tone of a children's storybook: "There were six of them. Servants of the State... The Kottayam Police. A cartoonplatoon. New-age princes in funny pointed helmets." This slightly comical account of the police is followed by a whimsical description of the lush vegetation and animal life: "Crimson dragon flies mated in the air. Doublecheckered. Deft. The admiring policeman watched and wondered briefly about the dynamics of dragonfly sex, and what went into what. Then his mind clicked to attention and Police Thoughts returned."[3] The fantastic flora and fauna, described at length here, serve as icons of an alternative, more vital rationality, the religion of small things. The book celebrates this creed, but shows its vulnerability to the violent domination of the police. The rationality of governance, the legacy of the European Enlightenment, threatens the way of being of small things, things that are particular, fragile, marvelous. As the police approach their quarry in the history house, they become more and more depersonalized: "Then together, on their knees and elbows, they crept towards the house. Like film-policemen. Softly, softly through the grass. Batons in their hands.

Machine guns in their minds. Responsibility for the Touchable Future on their thin but able shoulders." Both the beautiful description of the landscape, and the slightly comic portrayal of the policemen, make the assault on Velutha all the more disturbing by contrast. The figure of the bumbling policeman, a commonplace of detective fiction, is a trope that is designed to humanize state power. Here Roy uses the trope to expose the actual effectiveness of the state. The police are described not as brutal and cruel, but as dutiful functionaries meting out a just measure of pain: "Unlike the custom of rampaging religious mobs or conquering armies running riot, that morning in the Heart of Darkness the posse of Touchable Policemen acted with economy, not frenzy. Efficiency, not anarchy. Responsibility, not hysteria." Roy ironically comments on how the measured violence of the police serves the advance of postcolonial modernity, and must be distinguished from the violence of past elites—conquering armies in riot—or of atavistic mobs: "After all, they were not battling an epidemic. They were merely inoculating a community against an outbreak." In using the language of disease and public health, Roy ironically invokes the language of governmental rationality, that is, the reasoning behind practices of government, to present the state's view that its interventions further the well-being of the community.

Roy similarly shows the state's controlled violence to operate in the name of public order in an account of Ammu's visit to the police station in Kottayam. As Velutha lies dying in a police cell, Ammu comes to the police station to intervene. There she asks the Station House Officer if she can see Velutha, and says that she wants to make a statement.

> He said the police knew all they needed to know and that the Kottayam Police didn't take statements from veshyas or their illegitimate children. Amma said she'd see about that.
>
> Inspector Thomas Mathew came around her desk and approached Ammu with his baton.
>
> "If I were you," he said, "I'd go home quietly." Then he tapped her breasts with his baton. Gently. Tap tap. As though he was choosing mangoes from a basket. Pointing out the ones that he wanted packed and delivered. Inspector Thomas Mathew seemed to know whom he could pick on and whom he couldn't. Policemen have that instinct.
>
> Behind him a red and blue board said:
>
> Politeness
> Obedience

Loyalty
Intelligence
Courtesy
Efficiency

The passage occurs at the very beginning of the novel, though the episode follows upon Velutha's capture and brutalization. In reversing the order of the event and its narration, Roy underscores the power of the police—they have already established their control even as the story of multiple transgressions begins. The measured syntax mimics Inspector Mathew's deliberate exercise of authority. The terms in which he denigrates Ammu are those of caste as well as gender. He denies her a legal voice on the grounds of a loss of caste ("the Kottayam Police didn't take statements from Veshyas or their illegitimate children"). He also sexually humiliates her with an object that is both an instrument of the state's repressive function and a phallic icon—a police baton. By likening the policeman's action to the purchase of mangoes, Roy invokes a simile that is a cliché in India—a desirable woman's breasts are like ripe mangoes—but gives it a macabre overtone by taking it to the logical extreme of commodification and evoking a picture of the mangoes/breasts being picked, packed, and delivered. The inspector's violent policing of illiberal social norms is ironically offset by the sign that spells out the codes of governmental civility. By making us see the sign as Ammu would have, Roy draws us into the space of the "police" with all its contradictions.

Roy uses a narrative of social detection to mount a critique not only of the state and its rationalities, but also of the political landscape of contemporary India more broadly. She casts a sharply critical eye on the social borders and boundaries that persist in constraining the lives of those who are deemed to be marginal: women, untouchables, the working poor. She offers an especially damning indictment of the social policing of caste and gender in her representation of Ammu's and Velutha's lives and their affair. Roy also presents in a negative light the other Big Things that bruise the lives of small people. She mounts a broadside against left party politics: although the Communist Party is avowedly the champion of the worker, when Velutha comes to Comrade Pillai, the local party head, for help, Pillai readily sacrifices him to serve his own political expediencies.[4]

The mandate of industrialization and development to which the postcolonial Indian state lays claim also comes in for a harsh portrayal. In a chapter ironically titled "God's Own Country," Roy describes the desecration of the river Meenachal, "no more than a swollen drain now" for shit and factory effluents. In the same chapter, she describes the recent incarnation of the History House, an edifice that is heavily symbolic throughout the novel of cultural politics, as an international tourist resort. Earlier the home of a colonial planter-gone-native with a young Indian lover, then a semi-ruined repository of memories of the Raj and the scene of Ammu and Velutha's passion and of Velutha's capture, the History House—now called "Heritage"—has become a resort for affluent tourists who watch truncated Kathakali performances to suit their short attention spans: "So ancient stories were collapsed and amputated. Six-hour classics were slashed to twenty-minute cameos" (p. 121). Roy lambastes the extreme commodification of India's "cultural heritage" by a global tourist industry. The political and economic path taken by the new post-liberalization India has, in Roy's view, compounded the constraints upon the lives of small people and further depleted the land.

Although Roy presents a bleak view of the social landscape in the novel, she does gesture toward certain possibilities of liberation. She especially emphasizes two domains of experience that are antithetical to the crushing power of the Big Things, and particularly to the straitjacket rationality of the state: the domain of nature and the realm of the erotic. She repeatedly portrays the natural environs of Ayamenem as lush and fecund, and in the case of the river Meenachal, dangerously potent. In her description of Ayamenem in the first pages of the novel, the flora and fauna have an irrepressible presence in the built landscape.

> But by early June the southwest monsoon breaks and there are three months of wind and water with short spells of sharp, glittering sunshine that thrilled children snatch to play with. The countryside turns an immodest green. Boundaries blur as tapioca fences take root and bloom. Brick walls turn mossgreen. Pepper vines snake up electric poles. Wild creepers burst through laterite banks and spill across the flooded roads. Boats ply in the bazaars. And small fish appear in the puddles that fill the PWD potholes on the highways. (p. 3)

Roy describes a physically transformed environment with blurred boundaries where built spaces and objects are invaded by extraneous living beings. Colors change, moods shift, and boats and fish appear in strange places. The PWD, or Power and Works Department, is characterized in relation to its ineffectuality, as a purveyor of pot-holes that are in turn taken over by living creatures. Such portrayals of the fecund and transgressive power of nature abound in the novel; another example can be seen in the description above of the mating dragonflies that distract the policeman from his quarry. As Scott notes, the state tries to impose regularity upon the lived world, even though "a human community is surely far too complicated and variable to easily yield its secrets to bureaucratic formula."[5] The over-grown, riotous natural world in *The God of Small Things* represents a challenge to the state's vision.

Velutha is an embodiment of this antithesis to the vision of the state. The leaf imprinted on his back is symbolic of his connection to the natural world. He is described as a force of nature:

> As he rose from the dark river and walked up the stony steps, she saw that the world they stood on was his. That he belonged to it. That it belonged to him. The water. The mud. The trees. The fish. The stars. He moved so easily through it. As she watched him she understood the quality of his beauty. How his labour had shaped him. How the wood he fashioned had fashioned him. Each plank he planed, each nail he drove, each thing he made had molded him. Had left its stamp on him. Had given him his strength, his supple grace. (pp. 315–16)

Velutha is described as one with the natural world, completely un-alienated from it. The measured syntax and repetitive phrasing con-vey a sense of Velutha's deep and steady connection to the material world. The passage also refers to his craft, and how his work with his hands and wood has shaped the man. Velutha embodies what James Scott terms "metis," from the Greek word that means "natural cun-ning," referring to the faculty of practical intuitiveness. An expert car-penter, Velutha fashions all sorts of things with his hands, and is able to keep the pickle factory running and repair the machinery when it breaks down, using his diverse skills and his ability to improvise. His desirability and his dangerousness both derive from his being quietly outside the rationality of the state.

The most important form in which a transgression of oppressive norms takes places is that of erotic relationships. Here, the liaison be-tween Ammu and Velutha is of course the most significant. As an act, their union is transgressive of sexual, class, and caste boundaries. We know that the power of these boundaries is so great that they have no more than the immediate, the small things, to share, but the structure of the novel asserts the fleeting hopefulness of their union. They end each rendezvous with the solitary word "tomorrow," as if to speak into being a future for a relationship that has none. The narrative trajectory of the novel (what Todorov calls the fabula) ends with a scene of their passion and with this word, "tomorrow," although the *sujet* or sequence of events has already closed off all tomorrows.[6] This assertion of the power of desire in the face of the social impossibility of its fulfillment is an act of willful optimism.

An understanding of the significance of erotic transgression as a negation of oppressive social norms also helps make sense of one of the more puzzling episodes in the novel: the sexual tryst between Rahel and Estha. Buffeted about by the winds of fortune, they come together in an embrace that is described so obliquely that the reader might miss it altogether. This moment is not so much a turn to sex as a turn against the defining terms of culture. Levi-Strauss characterizes the incest taboo as "natural" because it is universal. It ensures exogamy and is hence a guarantor of culture. Derrida deconstructs Levi-Strauss's opposition between nature and culture, arguing that the incest taboo confutes this opposition because it is both "natural" (because universal) and "cultural" (because a prohibition). At the same time, Derrida argues, the incest taboo lies on the cusp between nature and culture and is in fact the placeholder for "culture." Rahel and Estha, in violating the incest taboo, reject the terms of culture. Their union returns them to a moment of intimacy that they have shared as twins in the womb, a space unmarked by social norms, a space before difference. Roy "dreams the impossible dream" of the rejection of the social norms that take their most unbending form in the modalities of the state.

Roy is known as an engaged intellectual for her political writing and activism rather than her novel. Yet *The God of Small Things*, with all its intricacies of diagesis, and its sumptuousness of language, expresses in a literary register the criticisms of the Indian state for which she has become well known. The novel is a paean to the small things and an indictment of the political juggernaut that rolls over them. Her activism, too—be it against nuclear testing, big dams, militarism, or the state's collusion in communal violence—is aimed precisely at this rational operation of the state to crush those who are weak. In "The Greater Common Good," a sharp critique of the Indian government's decision to carry through with the Sardar Sarovar Dam project despite its displacement of thousands of people, Roy spells out her view of the Indian state:

> It's time to spill a few State Secrets. To puncture the myth about the inefficient, bumbling, corrupt, but ultimately genial, essentially democratic, Indian State. Carelessness cannot account for fifty million disappeared people. Nor can Karma. Let's not delude ourselves. There is method here, relentless and one hundred percent manmade.
>
> The Indian Sate is not a State that has failed. It is a State that has succeeded impressively in what it set out to do. It has been ruthlessly efficient in the way it has appropriated India's resources—its land, its water, its forests, its fish, its meat, its eggs, its air—and re-distributed it to a favoured few (in return, no doubt, for a few favours). It is superbly accomplished in the art of protecting its cadre of paid-up elite. Consummate in its methods of pulverizing those who inconvenience its intentions.[7]

Roy calls into question the canard that the Indian state is an inefficient, ramshackle, corrupt but essentially benign entity that stewards the people as best as it can. In her fiction as well as her political writing, she shows that the ostensibly innocent though ineffectual state is in fact guilty of systematic social and economic violence. She characterizes the state as a modern apparatus that efficiently maintains the economic and political domination of elites, polices social boundaries, and ruthlessly destroys those that stand in its way. Violence is not an aberration but one of its key instruments. The state is the powerful entity that crushes the Small; the stakes arrayed around Velutha are precisely the coercive instruments of a rigid and oppressive social and economic structure.

What one has here is the confluence of a modern bureaucratic rationality with a tribalized power structure. The postcolonial state in India, as in other former colonies, has inherited overdeveloped police and military bureaucracies from a colonial state. This bureaucracy is used efficiently to enforce extremely oppressive hierarchies of class, caste, gender, and religion, and dispossess those who are subordinated by them. At the same time, Roy expresses a certain degree of willed optimism, writing in "The Greater Common Good," "Who knows, perhaps that's what the twenty-first century has in store for us. The dismantling of the Big. Big bombs, big dams, big ideologies, big contradictions, big countries, big wars, big heroes, big mistakes. Perhaps it will be the century of the Small."

"I HAVE BROUGHT VIOLENCE TO MANY DOORSTEPS"

Salman Rushdie also explores the place of violence in postcolonial India. Violence is in fact a prominent theme in all his novels of South Asia. In *Shame*, Sufia Zenobia becomes the embodiment and nemesis of the political violence of Pakistani elites as well as the nation's social violence against women when she turns into a marauding monster. In *Midnight's Children*, violence marks the genesis of the Indian nation and punctuates its "development," most memorably caricatured in "the Black Widow's" castration of her victims in the name of Family Planning. *The Satanic Verses* begins with the violent explosion of a plane by terrorists during the transoceanic passage that launches Chamcha's and Farishta's transformations. In all these novels, violence has a variety of valences: it can be retributive, destructive, cathartic, generative, or transformative. It is also distributed over a range of social and political locations, including the state, the family, and the community. In *The Moor's Last Sigh*, while violence is again wide-ranging in its significance and its location, Rushdie focuses specifically on the violence of the Hindu right in Bombay. Rushdie takes a somewhat different view of the Indian nation and the threat of state violence than does Roy in *The God of Small Things*. He celebrates the Juggernaut, the chaotic multiplicity of India, a humungous heterogeneous entity of which violence is an organic part. For him, the danger lies in reducing this multiplicity through state violence.

In *The Moor's Last Sigh*, Rushdie sketches the uneven fortunes of Moraes Zogoiby, the embodiment of the nation's hybrid religious and cultural identity. Violence pervades the world of the novel, from the brutal rivalries of Moor's forebears, the Menezes and Lobo clans, to the social violence Aurora Zogoiby depicts in her paintings. Yet in the first part of the novel, violence is but one element of the hybrid, plural, complex, chaotic, vibrant character of the nation. Aurora bears witness to this multiplicity in her painting of Mother India. "Mother India" was a common icon for the emergent Indian nation in the early part of the century in both colonialist and nationalist discourse. The phrase is echoed in the nationalist slogan "Bharat Mata ki Jai" or "Long Live Mother India," and is the title of a landmark Bollywood 1957 film, to which Rushdie refers repeatedly in the novel. The narrator describes Aurora's painting of Mother India—a representation of the motherland as a cornucopia that is violent, yet vital:

> Every inch of the walls and even the ceiling of the room pullulated with figures, human and animal, real and imaginary, drawn in a sweeping black line that transformed itself constantly, that filled here and there into huge blocks of colour, the red of the earth, the purple and vermilion of the sky, the forty shades of green; a line so muscular and free, so teeming, so violent, that Camoens with a proud father's bursting heart found himself saying, "But it is the great swarm of being itself"... and it was all set in a landscape that made Camoens tremble to see it, for it was Mother India herself, Mother India with her garishness and her inexhaustible motion, Mother India who loved and betrayed and ate and destroyed and again loved her children, and with whom the children's passionate conjoining and eternal quarrel stretched long beyond the grave.[8]

Rushdie both naturalizes and aestheticizes violence in this passage. His use of natural imagery to portray India makes the state, and state violence, appear to be natural forces. "The great swarm of being" brings to mind the movement of bees, with their social tendencies as well as their capacity for violence. The figure of the devouring mother also imputes to the nation a violence that is contained within a regenerative cycle. Rushdie also aestheticizes violence with his references to "huge blocks of colour," a surfeit of shades, and a violence of line. He celebrates the exorbitant energy of India in this description of sensory excess and of pulsing movement. In this vision, Mother India's violence—her propensity to love, but also to consume, betray, and destroy her children—is but one element of "the great swarm of being" rather than a dominating force.

Rushdie affirms India's vibrant multifariousness in an essay commemorating the fiftieth anniversary of independence: "In the modern age, we have come to understand our own selves as composites, often contradictory, even internally incompatible. We have understood that India is many different people ... India has taken the modern view of the self and enlarged it to encompass almost two billion souls. The selfhood of India is so capacious, so elastic, that it manages to accommodate one billion kinds of difference."[9] Here Rushdie projects the postmodern understanding of subjectivity onto the nation as a whole, applauding the country's openness to difference. He emphasizes this plurality in *The Moor's Last Sigh* in three ways: in his language, in his characterization, and in his treatment of setting. In the first part of the novel, he uses all his characteristic rhetorical sparkle and fizz to convey the sumptuous polyvocality of the nation—indulging in a playful and creative violence to the English language. His use of puns, allusions, fantastic imagery, Indianisms, linguistic mixes, idiosyncratic diction, and acrobatic syntax reproduces in the form of his discourse the admixture and excess that he celebrates. He embodies that excess, hybridity, and even freakishness in the person of Moraes, or the Moor. The Moor is part Christian, part Jewish, and possibly part Muslim and Hindu (his paternity is tantalizingly uncertain); he has a deformed hand; and he grows at an accelerated pace to an enormous size. Finally, Rushdie applauds the ethos of chaotic multiplicity in relation to the city of Bombay—and not Mumbai, which for him signifies an entirely different cultural and political landscape.

The city of Bombay occupies a privileged place in Rushdie's oeuvre, representing India's hybrid origins and character more than any place. At the same time, Rushdie suggests that while its pluralism makes the city an exemplar of the multicultural aspirations of the nation as a whole, it is this very condition of culture admixture that makes what one might call unicultural politics appealing. In the first part of the novel Bombay is characterized as a consummately composite city.

> Bombay was central, had been so from the moment of its creation: the bastard child of a Portuguese-English wedding, and yet the most Indian of Indian cities. In Bombay all Indias met and merged. In Bombay, too, all-India met what-was-not-India, what came across the black water to flow into our veins. Everything North of Bombay was North India, everything South of it was the South. To the east lay India's East, and to the west, the world's West. Bombay was central; all rivers flowed into its human sea. It was an ocean of stories; we were all its narrators; and everybody talked at once. (p. 350).

This is the first of a series of passages in which Rushdie mourns the historical transformation of Bombay from the most hybrid and cosmopolitan of Indian cities into a stronghold of the Shiv Sena, part of the family of Hindu chauvinist parties that dominates politics in India. Given as part of Catherine of Braganza's dowry to King Charles II of England in 1661, Bombay grew through a process of land reclamation from a cluster of seven islands into the megalopolis of many million people that it is now. In this passage as elsewhere, Rushdie draws on a mixture of tropes to characterize Bombay, and by extrapolation, the nation. On the one hand, he describes Bombay here as a crossroads. The part of the novel from which this excerpt is taken, "Bombay Central," is titled after the main railway station in the city, an entrepôt for travel to and from every part of the country. At the same time, he uses the trope of illegitimate birth to portray the city as an illicit and hybrid offspring of Europe. The allusions to merging and to the flowing of rivers into its human sea imputes to Bombay a syncretic quality. Finally, in the last sentence of this passage, Rushdie echoes the title of his own novel, *Haroun and the Sea of Stories*. He portrays Bombay as a polyvocal, cacophonic mix of narratives, the model for and favorite subject of his own fiction.

The various tropes that Rushdie uses give slightly different inflections—those of multiplicity, plurality, and hybridity—to the city and the nation. Whereas plurality, conveyed by the figure of a crossroads, implies separate ethnicities under one nation, hybridity, suggested by the figures of bastardy and of merging rivers, implies syncretic fusion. Rushdie's rhetorical inconsistency on this score speaks to an ambiguity in his conception of India as a nation. It is not clear whether the many fuse into one, or whether the many coexist in a mix with a preservation of differences: melting pot or mosaic? This tension notwithstanding, Rushdie suggests that Bombay has historically and geographically been a city that has accommodated difference.

As the novel proceeds, the capacious and polyphonic character of the city—and, by extrapolation, of the nation—comes under assault with the political takeover of the Hindu right, "the alphabet soup of RSS, VHP, BJP," as Rushdie calls it, both within Bombay and at the level of the central state. Rushdie identifies the destruction of the Babri Masjid in Ayodhya as a key moment in this attack on the polyvalent character of the nation. The mosque, built by the Mughal emperor Babar in the sixteenth century on the supposed site of a temple marking the birthplace of the Hindu god Ram, was destroyed by recruits of Hindutva, or the movement for Hindu supremacy, on December 6, 1992, precipitating the greatest internal crisis that India had faced since independence. During the riots that followed in Bombay in December 1992 and January 1993, over a thousand people were killed, thousands more were wounded, and 150,000 people were displaced.[10] Thousands of traumatized and dispossessed people—largely Muslims and non-Marathi speakers—camped on the platform of "Bombay

Central" train station, waiting to leave. In March 1993, a series of bomb blasts shook the city. It emerged that members of Muslim gangster organizations orchestrated these explosions.

The riots and bombings, which Rushdie portrays in a cartoonish fashion in *The Moor's Last Sigh,* were in fact a severe blow to the common perception of Bombay as India's most diverse, cosmopolitan, "modern" city. They also posed a direct challenge to the image of the postcolonial state as a politically neutral, ethical structure because of the very problematic role the Bombay police played in the riots; they did little to stop violence against Muslims and in some instances even furthered it. Thomas Hansen, in an excellent ethnographic study of the riots, argues that the violence precipitated a crisis of political legitimacy, to which the state responded by setting up an independent commission headed by Judge Srikrishna to investigate the circumstances of the violence. Evidence mounted showing the Hindu nationalist party Shiv Sena's role in the violence. However, soon after the Shiv Sena came to power in Bombay in 1995, the Srikrishna commission was dissolved, though it was later reinstated under pressure from the central government. Shiv Sena leader Bal Thackeray was not prosecuted for any of the over twenty cases that were brought against him for inciting violence. Running through the testimony of policemen is "the perception that Muslim anger or 'aggression' justified police brutality and later Hindu 'retaliation.'"[11] By contrast to the lax treatment of perpetrators of violence against Muslims, hundreds of people, mostly Muslims, were charged in connection with the bomb blasts under the Terrorist and Disruptive Activities Act, aggressively prosecuted, and given long prison sentences.[12]

In the fortunes of the city and of his protagonist the Moor, Rushdie maps the changes in Bombay, and in the country, with this historical shift to the right.

> Bombay was central. In Bombay, as the old, founding myth of the nation faded, the new God-and-Mammon India was being born. The wealth of the country flowed through its exchanges, its ports. Those who hated India, those who sought to ruin it, would need to ruin Bombay: that was one explanation for what happened. Well, well, that may have been so. And it may have been that what was released in the north (in, to name it, because I must name it, Ayodhya)—that corrosive acid of the spirit, that adversarial intensity that poured into the nation's bloodstream when the Babri Masjid fell and plans for a mighty Ram

temple on the god's alleged birthplace were, as they used to say in the Bombay cinema houses, filling up fast—was on this occasion too concentrated, and even the great city's powers of dilution could not weaken it enough. So, so; those who thus argue have a point, too, it cannot be denied. At the Zogoiby Bequest, Zeenat Vakil offered her usual sardonic take on the troubles. "I blame fiction," she said. "The followers of one fiction knock down another popular piece of make-believe, and bingo! It's war. Next they will find Vyasa's cradle under Iqbal's house, and Valmiki's baby-rattle under Mirza Ghalib's hang-out. So, OK. I'd rather die fighting over great poets than over gods."

> . . . and if Bombay was central, it may have been that what transpired was rooted in Bombay quarrels. Mogambo versus Mainduck: the long-awaited dual, the heavyweight unification bout to establish, once and for all, which gang (criminal-entrepreneurial or political criminal) would run the town. (p. 351)

I quote this long passage because its movement disavows the shift to a single narrative that Rushdie decries. The narrator tries to explain the carnage in Bombay during the weeks after the destruction of the Babri Masjid. Instead of a definitive explanation, the narrator gives us a number of accounts of why the riots have taken place—as if to refute the tendency toward discursive simplification that the character Zeenat parodies. He identifies a shift from the "old" secular, Nehruvian socialist or Gandhian vision of India to a "new" India ruled by the avowedly pro-Hindu Bharatiya Janata Party (BJP) and, after 1991, open to foreign capital and the privatization of state industry. The attacks on Bombay are an attack on this new nation, possibly from its neighbor to the West. The narrator also tentatively faults that "corrosive acid of the spirit"—communalism. In this context, "great poets" signify a secular state as opposed to the "gods" of a religious state. Interestingly, he characterizes communalism as a poison poured "into the nation's bloodstream," articulating an essentialist notion of the nation as a tribal affiliation of blood. That is, he turns the rhetoric of impurity, often deployed by communalists, on its head to discredit communalism.

Finally, Zeenat Vakil, who also appears in *The Satanic Verses*, where she chaperones Saladin Chamcha around the city, depicts the riots as the culmination of a stand-up fight between stories—rather than a sea of stories with everyone talking together, one has a pugilistic contest for the supremacy of a single narrative. This "heavyweight unification" is carried out both in the domain of narrative and in the empires of the political and business tycoons. In his novels, Rushdie represents the Indian state as a criminal assemblage of political and business elites that have rationalized their abuse of power with the modern instruments of efficiency and organization.

Here as in the description above of Aurora's painting, Rushdie uses metaphorical, even cartoonish language to depict violence: "Mogambo versus Mainduck" and "heavyweight unification" give the contest between the different forces in the city a slapstick quality. The different discourses that Rushdie employs point to competing forces in the city, but also to competing narratives of the nation.

The change in the character of Bombay with the rise of the Hindu right is mirrored in the novel by the new career of the Moor, who joins the Mumbai Axis and becomes an agent of Mainduck, a thinly veiled portrait of Bal Thackeray, the Shiv Sena leader. While in the other novels that I mentioned earlier, the narrator takes a position of critical distance toward state violence, *The Moor's Last Sigh* presents us with the point of view of an enforcer for the Hindu right. Unlike the spy in Buchan's novels who goes undercover but retains (though with a certain amount of psychic strain) his allegiances, Rushdie's Moor embraces his new identity wholeheartedly. Rushdie tries to get into the head of one of the many young men who have embraced the Shiv Sena, and also demands that we as readers contend intimately with their view of the world. These views are epitomized in those of Mainduck:

> He was against unions, in favour of breaking strikes, against working women, in favour of sati, against poverty and in favour of wealth. He was against the "immigrants" to the city, by which he meant all non-Marathi speakers, including those who had been born there, and in favour of its 'natural residents, which included Marathi-medium types who had just stepped off the bus. He was against the corruption of the Congress I and for "direct action" by which he meant paramilitary activity in support of his political aims, and the institution of a bribery system of his own. (pp. 298–99)

We have in this passage, and I would argue in the third part of the novel as a whole, a shift to a much more realist narrative in this un-varnished account of the Shiv Sena's platform. Given that the Shiv Sena came to power in 1996, in Bombay, and the BJP to national power, this now represents the vision of the state. The simplification of prose mirrors that of the worldview, which is structured in terms of binary oppositions, in which the term associated with rightist stances is invariably privileged: no "play" or "bricolage" here. At this juncture of the novel, the Moor embraces violence and lauds the pleasures of simplification:

> I admit it: I am a man who has delivered many beatings. I have brought violence to many doorsteps, the way the postman brings the mail. I have done the dirty as and when required—done it, and taken pleasure in the doing....
>
> ...Can you understand with what delight I wrapped myself in the simplicity of my new life? For I did; I reveled in it. At last, I told myself, a little straightforwardness; at last you are what you were born to be. With what relief I abandoned my quest for an unattainable normality, and with what joy I revealed my super-nature to the world! (pp. 305–6)

The Moor describes his "delivery" of beatings as a quotidian event; the Mumbai Axis's "direct action" has become routine. As the Moor puts it later, "I am deep in blood." Moreover, the Moor is unabashed about the pleasure he takes in beating up people. It is not clear whether the violence itself is pleasurable, or the "simplicity" of his life in a world of straightforward truths. The fact that he is an amalgam of minorities, and marginalized because of his deformity, makes the ontological simplicity of his new existence all the more appealing. Rushdie points to the all too real appeal of fascism in a country that is as complex and polyvalent as India, and is made even more dizzyingly so by the contradictions of postcolonial modernity.

As a member of a powerful quasi-fascist organization, the Moor has the license to use his fist at will, or rather, at Mainduck's will. The Moor reflects upon the alienating effects of the Mumbai Axis's paramilitary violence:

> A man who is beaten seriously ... will be irreversibly changed. His relationship to his own body, to his mind, to the world beyond himself alters in ways both subtle and overt. A certain confidence, a certain idea of liberty is beaten out for good; always provided the beater knows his job. Often, what is beaten in is detachment. The victim—how often I saw this!—detaches himself from the event, and sends his consciousness to float in the air above. He seems to look down upon himself, on his own body as it convulses and perhaps breaks. Afterwards he will

never fully re-enter himself, and invitations to join any larger collectivity—a union, for example—are instantly rebuffed. (p. 307)

The Moor offers here a phenomenology of violence. In an impassive, quasi-scientific manner, the Moor notes the effect of his beatings on his victims: a detachment that precludes any future collective identification. At the same time, state violence makes him an automaton—"the hammer," perhaps an ironic distortion of the communist symbol. This fictional reflection on the effects of political violence on the victim has an interesting corollary in Arjun Appadurai's analysis of the effects of political violence on those who partake in it.[13] Appadurai argues that ethnic identification is forged through violence, and specifically a violence instigated by the modern nation-state. Bringing this argument to bear on Rushdie's novel, one could argue that state and paramilitary violence does not only terrorize and alienate its victims, it may in fact have a binding effect on its agents, making their ties "deep in blood." At the same time, it dehumanizes and objectifies them.

If, in the early part of the novel, Rushdie portrays violence in fanciful terms and celebrates its productive aspect, and in the second part of the novel uses simpler language to emphasize its reductive tendency when wielded by the state, in the last section of the novel violence becomes so extreme and spectacular that it takes on a farcical aspect. This spectacular violence begins in Mumbai with Nadia Wadia's defacement, the Moor's murder of Mainduck, and the bomb blasts. It is carried forward into the last segment of the novel, where the Moor travels beyond the realm of the nation-state to a hybrid and diasporic space in Andalusia—seat of Moorish Spain—in pursuit of Vasco Miranda and Aurora's remaining paintings. Within the logic of the narrative, the relatively contained, simplifying violence associated with the Mumbai Axis in the second part of the novel spawns an anarchic frenzy of violence that is retributive, cathartic, and in the instance of Aie Oue's death, entirely arbitrary. If Roy's novel is one of social detection, in which the continuities between the brutality of the state and civil society are exposed, Rushdie's takes on the character of a pulp thriller, in which violence overwhelms all structures and leads to their destruction.

I noted earlier with regard to Aurora's painting of Mother India that Rushdie aestheticizes violence. This tendency is at its most extreme in his account of the killing of Aoi Ue. In this instance, though, rather than naturalizing violence through the trope of the devouring mother, he dramatizes it in an intricate set piece:

Aoi screamed and ran uselessly across the room. There was a moment
when her upper half was hidden by the painting. Vasco fired, once. A
hole appeared in the canvas, over Aurora's heart; but it was Aoi Ue's
breast that had been pierced. She fell heavily against the easel, clutch-
ing at it; and for an instant—picture this—her blood pumped through
the wound in my mother's chest. Then the portrait fell forward, its top
right-hand corner hitting the floor, and somersaulted to lie face up-
wards, stained with Aoi's blood. Aoi Ue, however, lay face downwards,
and was still. (pp. 431–32)

The description calls attention with the words "picture this" to the
tableaux-like character of the scene. Rushdie creates the illusion of
Aurora's wounding and death by animating her painting with Aoi
Ue's blood. One might expect the moment to be depicted as traumatic,
graphically making reference as it does to the death of the mother. The
artificiality of the scene, however, gives the violence a surreal quality,
counteracting any experience of pain or loss on the part of the Moor
or the reader. Violence here is pure spectacle. The episode also marks
a retreat from the more political overtones one finds in the earlier part
of the novel. Vasco Miranda has become a mad megalomaniac, and
his victim Ue is such an unworldly character that the meaning of her
death has no obvious political relevance.

The political significance of Rushdie's vision is ambiguous in another way. The explosion of violence at the end of the novel has, on
the one hand, a cathartic quality, sweeping the board clean of corrupt
and vicious characters and institutions. In this vein, Vasco Miranda's
bloody implosion might be interpreted as the end of a European imperialism realized fully by the British in India, but inaugurated earlier
by the Portuguese, who indeed lingered after the British. The Moor's
last vision is that of the ruins of an earlier non-European Empire, a
vision that brings to mind the decayed edifices of the Mughal Empire.
At the same time, the devastation at the end of the novel marks a
flowing together of blood and an obliteration of boundaries.

And so I sit here in the last light, upon this stone, among these ol-
ive trees, gazing out across a valley towards a distant hill; and there
it stands, the glory of the Moors, their triumphant masterpiece and
their last redoubt. The Alhambra, Europe's red fort, sister to Delhi's
and Agra's—the palace of interlocking forms and secret wisdom, plea-
sure-courts and water-gardens, that monument to a lost possibility that

nevertheless has gone on standing, long after its conquerors have fallen; like a testament to lost but sweetest love, to the love that endures beyond defeat, beyond annihilation, beyond despair; to the defeated love that is greater than what defeats it, to that most profound of our needs, to our need for flowing together, for putting an end to frontiers, for the dropping of the boundaries of the self. (p. 433)

The "lost possibility" is that of a consummately hybrid culture, a fusion of East and West, Muslim and Catholic, that may now lie in ruins but whose remains bear witness to the fact that a culture and a self without constraining boundaries are realizable. Just as *The God of Small Things* points to a future in the face of its impossibility with the word "tomorrow," *The Moor's Last Sigh* ends with the Moor's wish to "hope to awaken, renewed and joyful, into a better time." In characterizing this "better time," Rushdie gestures toward a mode of being beyond the borders and in the interstices of the nation-state, of religion, of monolithically defined identity itself. Homi Bhabha's commentary "On Minorities: Cultural Rights," which argues that "in our times, 'partial cultural milieux' and 'non-state' social actors are increasingly relevant, nationally and internationally, in the fight for cultural rights and social justice," addresses precisely the significance of "a liminal, interstitial public sphere that emerges *in-between* the state and the non-state, *in-between* individual rights and group needs; not in the simpler dialectic between global and local."[14] In his final dislocation, the Moor embodies this in-betweenness.

CONCLUSION

In the liberal paradigm, the state guarantees law and order, and detects and punishes threats to these in the name of justice. Arundhati Roy poses the state's rationality as itself oppressive, as antithetical to the well-being of the small person; and the communist party, in so far as it is the ruling party, necessarily "sees like a state," to borrow from the title of James Scott's book. Roy imagines the postcolonial state as a unified construct that systematically pursues its goal—the preservation of the power of elites—through a bureaucratic logic and an efficient use of violence. In so doing, it reinforces gender, caste, class, and racial hierarchies, crushing the small beings in its way like a juggernaut. To capitulate to the rationality of the state is to betray these small beings. Roy's is ultimately a Romantic, anticapitalist critique of modernity. She looks to the domains of untamed nature and erotic love as spaces that are antithetical to the logic of modern governmentality in general and state rationality in particular.

The question remains: what kind of politics does such a critique enable? Roy certainly does not represent organized political resistance to the domination of the state, capital, and social elites in a sanguine way. Aijaz Ahmad has taken Roy to task for portraying communist party politics as negatively as she does: when Velutha turns for help to Comrade Pillai, the local party leader, Pillai tells him that he is powerless to help the laborer. Roy stresses the bankruptcy of left party politics, and represents the Communist Party of India (CPM) as yet another large, suspect organization that readily sacrifices the small person for whom it ostensibly stands. While Roy shows with all the imaginative power of her fiction how freedom and equality are denied to the subaltern by the state and social institutions, she does not spell out what an alternative to the state might be.

Roy's novel begs several questions: What kinds of institutional arrangements are truly liberatory? How does a liberatory politics of opposition avoid the pitfalls of institutionalization? To what extent does freedom necessitate the dismantling of oppressive structures and the building of alternative ones? How is one to keep these structures from being oppressive in turn? She might, on the one hand, urge a corrective to the state's abuses, but accept the existence of the state per se. Or, on the other hand, she might advance a more radical critique of the state itself. After all the subject of liberal political theory and practice is also the subject of modern disciplinary power and bureaucratic rationality, as Foucault so powerfully argued. That is, to act "freely" in acceptable ways, the subject must always already have been disciplined by state institutions and interpellated by state ideological apparatuses. In Roy's novel, those characters who are not "proper" subjects of governmentality—Ammu, her children, and Velutha—are all radically alienated or killed; no Shakespearean ending here with its glimmer of hope in a future world with different ruling powers and new kinds of subjects. Rather than clearly articulate a politics that would entail the transformation of institutions and the creation of new sorts of subjects, Roy espouses an ethic—an ethic of the small. She urges the need for a new kind of intersubjective relationship, a mode of relationship in which the fragile and the vulnerable are cherished. Of course, for such ethical relationships to exist, one has to have the right political conditions, and so to call for an ethic of the small is implicitly to urge a wholesale transformation of the status quo. The politics of the novel and Roy's political activism in grassroots social movements are not, then, as contradictory as they might seem.

While in her novel Roy focuses on the private and the realm of personal relationships, in her political writing and activism she confronts the workings of political power head-on. Roy has used her considerable rhetorical talent to mount a "scathing and passionate indictment of big government's disregard for the individual," to quote from the dust jacket of *The Cost of Living*.[15] Her targets have been varied: the testing and production of nuclear arms in South Asia, the effects of economic liberalization, the Prevention of Terrorism Act in India, the genocide in Gujarat, and the U.S. bombing of Afghanistan and the occupation of Iraq, to name but some. Her most passionate and concerted criticism, however, has been of the effects of World Bank–style development programs, and specifically the building of big dams. In "The Greater Common Good," Roy rehearses in passionate detail the human and environmental cost posed by the largest of the big dam projects in India, the damming of the Narmada. She notes the false estimates and practical inconsistencies associated with the project, the indebtedness to the World Bank that it would have entailed had the Bank not pulled out, the waterlogging and destruction of the habitat, and most devastating of all, the massive displacement and impoverishment of those who live in the Narmada valley and derive their living from the river. In the Narmada valley development scheme, it is the big things—the World Bank, the Indian state, the economic interests of the Indian bourgeoisie—that ride roughshod over the lives of the small things and people—the Adivasis who glean a livelihood from the forests, the poor who farm the land along the river, and the plants and animals that inhabit the valley. Roy's indictment in "The Greater Common Good" of the state's rationality and brutality is in this way continuous with her representation of the state, the bourgeoisie, and the course of liberalization and development in *The God of Small Things*. She suggests that the subject of liberal democracy and enlightenment progress has an "Other": what Spivak would term the subaltern, in this instance the Adivasi as well as poor lower-caste farmers whose existence is more or less discounted when the state formulates its plans for development.

Both novels contrast the state's mode of vision with other, more playful and less oppressive modes of experiencing the world. Whereas Roy's novel refuses to "see like a state," Rushdie's explores what it means to do just that. Rushdie's representation of violence is more ambiguous than Roy's, as I have suggested: he sees violence as not only destructive and reductive but also generative and cathartic, and in his view, it is not only the state that is violent but every element of society. Rushdie is less concerned by the inherent violence of the rationality of the state than he is by the rise of fascism as a monolithic political form that curbs multiplicity. Roy has been equally scathing in her indictment of the BJP's policies, and especially of its complicity in the killing of an estimated two thousand Muslims in Gujarat in 2002. What she emphasizes, however, is the failure of the Indian government to abide by the principles of liberalism and the protection of minorities. Rushdie, instead, explores the emergence of new kinds of hybrid political subjects.

We can look to Rushdie for a vision of what Duncan Ivison calls postcolonial liberalism, a liberalism that recognizes difference and hybridity. According to Ivison, "liberal governance presupposes that individuals are free, but free in the right way; free to exercise choice, to act rationally and reasonably and to subject themselves to certain kinds of social and political obligation."[16] By contrast, postcolonial liberalism directly addresses the question of how difference is to be negotiated. To do this is to dream up new political possibilities, as the dying Moor does at the end of *The Moor's Last Sigh*. Here the Moor invokes the principle of unbounded love to imagine new subjects and new civilizations that are hybrid and mongrel. Rushdie sees the rationality of the Hindutva state as a simplifying force that would silence the polyvocality of the nation. At the same time, Rushdie remains optimistic about the ability of India to survive the threat of the violent domination of one identity and one truth imposed by the Hindu right: his confidence in India's capacity to "accommodate one billion kinds of difference" was asserted in 1997, five years after the Bombay riots.

In May 2004, the Indian electorate voted the incumbent BJP out of power, replacing it with a coalition of the Congress and left parties, most importantly the CPM. Arundhati Roy's and Salman Rushdie's laudatory but very dissimilar responses, published as opinion pieces in the *Guardian* and the *Washington Post* respectively, exemplify the differences in their political visions. Both Roy and Rushdie note that the BJP has been voted out of power because of its neglect of, if not outright onslaught against, the poor and minority communities in India. Roy is much less sanguine than Rushdie about the political prospect: "But even as we celebrate, we know that on every major issue besides overt Hindu nationalism (nuclear bombs, big dams and privatization), the Congress and the BJP have no major ideological differences."[17] Roy proceeds to excoriate the Indian state for its human rights offenses, carried out under cover of the notorious Prevention of Terrorism Act. In the *Washington Post* op-ed piece, Rushdie uses the opportunity to voice two hopes: one, that the imputation of Sonia Gandhi's "foreignness" held no weight with the Indian electorate and might signal their rejection of racism; and two, that the rewriting of history by the Hindu right to fit "a narrow, revisionist, Hindu-nationalist vision of India's past" be rolled back.[18] Both wishes bespeak an overarching preoccupation in Rushdie's work with the celebration of a capacious, multivocal, hybrid understanding of "Indianness." Ultimately, this preoccupation supersedes a call for economic transformation or political accountability. Roy, by contrast, offers an impassioned indictment of postliberalization India: "You only have to close your ears to the sickening crunch of the policeman's boot on someone's ribs, you only have to raise your eyes from the squalor, the slums, the ragged broken people on the streets and seek a friendly TV monitor, and you will be in that other beautiful world. The singing, dancing world of Bollywoods' permanent pelvic thrusts, of permanently privileged, happy Indians waving the tricolour and Feeling Good."[19]

EIGHT

"The Unhistorical Dead"

Violence, History, and Narrative in
Michael Ondaatje's Anil's Ghost

In this chapter, I examine Michael Ondaatje's use of a narrative of intrigue to represent political violence in *Anil's Ghost*. Ondaatje writes
of a war-torn Sri Lanka where individuals have been stripped down
to an existence of bare life, as victims of a genocide that has become
a condition rather than an event. The writer fashions out of the political quagmire of Sri Lanka a novel that reads in many ways like a
detective story. He focuses on the effects of political violence on individual bodies. In a landscape replete with brutalized bodies—we read
of decapitated heads on stakes, bodies washed down rivers, corpses
dropped by helicopter into the sea, and cadavers dumped in fields—
Ondaatje makes a single body the object of a close investigation.

Anil Tessera, a forensic scientist, returns to Sri Lanka after an absence of many years, having been commissioned by the United Nations
to examine human remains for any evidence of political wrongdoing.
Anil is teamed with an archaeologist in Sri Lanka, Sarath Diyasena,
who uses his detective skills to reconstruct the ancient past. Soon the
two have a body—a skeleton of a recently dead man whom they nick-
name Sailor, and whose presence in an ancient Buddhist burial site to
which only the government has access is suspicious. Anil and Sarath's
quest to determine the body's identity, the cause of its death, and the
circumstances of its death takes them to a variety of characters, including Sarath's eccentric archaeology teacher, Palipana; Sarath's brother,
Gamini, a doctor; and Ananda, a painter of religious figures who is
employed to reconstruct "Sailor's" face. The "unhistorical" bodies
that inhabit the landscape become objects of various kinds of reconstruction in the novel: forensic, archaeological, medical, and artistic.

While Ondaatje uses the genre of intrigue to plot violence, the novel eschews a critical evaluation of violence: of what it is and what

its causes are. In fact, the narrator's comments on political violence, summed up in the epigram "the cause of war was war," are banal. The real intrigue of the novel concerns, on the one hand, the significance of history, and on the other, the problematic of reading. The novel draws the reader into an intrigue about the nature and place of history, an intrigue circling around questions of truth and causality. The protagonist, Anil, strives to identify "the unhistorical dead," as she puts it, a phrase that suggests a desire to restore these victims of violence to history, and to restore history to them. However, its formal and thematic aspects take the novel further and further away from historical explanations for the political violence in Sri Lanka. In fact, the novel expresses a suspicion of history, at times rejecting its worth altogether. Furthermore, the narrative involves the reader in an interpretive intrigue. The obvious mystery—"Sailor's" identity—turns out to be relatively insignificant. The novel plays a trick on us in terms of locating the ghost of the title. As we near the end, we find we must rethink the focus of the narrative. Looked at from this angle, the text itself is a body that must be deciphered. The novel embroils the reader in an ever-thickening plot about how to read.[1]

I begin by discussing the work of three anthropologists of the political violence in Sri Lanka: Stanley Tambiah, Pradeep Jeganathan, and E. Valentine Daniel. While Tambiah follows up his account of ethnic riots with an analysis of their antecedents and causes, Jeganathan's and Daniel's studies point to the very difficulty of representing violence in a way that is not positivist or reductive. Having considered the theoretical, ethnographic, and historical discussions of these anthropologists, I then turn to Ondaatje's use of the tropes and generic devices of fiction to grapple with the difficulty of apprehending and representing ethnic violence in Sri Lanka. I focus on different aspects of *Anil's Ghost:* the form of the narrative, its treatment of history, the representation of trauma, and finally, the redemptive possibilities of the aesthetic. Considering these in turn, I want to assess the novel's handling of history in a postmodern and postcolonial register. I conclude by suggesting that the suspicion toward historical explanation follows from an awareness of the limits of conventional modes of historical analysis in the context of Empire. Hardt and Negri's account of the new forms of Empire points to the need for new ways of understanding political violence and new ways of conceptualizing history.

After the linguistic turn in the humanities and social sciences, and the casting of suspicion upon "master narratives," historians have actively taken up the challenge of writing "the history of the frag- ment."[2] The Subaltern Studies historians of South Asia, for instance, have moved from more recognizably historical materialist analysis of marginalized groups to modes of history writing that are informed by poststructuralism. This shift in their work exemplifies the search for new modes of historiography that are sensitive to the discontinuous and fragmentary character of historical experience. Ondaatje's novel treats history in an analogous way; rather than the totalizing tropes of conventional historical fiction, he uses formal elements that con- vey disjointedness and immediacy. Not only does this mode of writing foreground the unintelligibility of the social and political landscape and the recognition that "positions are to be read as contingent, his- tories as local, subjects as constructed, and knowledge as enmeshed in power," it also heightens the emotional tone of the novel and com- municates the experience of living in the conditions of civil war.[3] At the same time, Ondaatje moves beyond an enunciation of the anti-es- sentialist position to an explicit consideration of what history is and how it is fashioned. The novel prompts the reader to puzzle over the nature of a dialectic of public and private history, of objective and subjective history, of history with a capital *H* and history with a small *h*. As one might expect, Ondaatje ultimately privileges the private and the subjective—history with a small *h*, but alongside an exploration of the power of history writ large.

ANTHROPOLOGIES OF VIOLENCE

The ethnic riots that exploded in 1983 were not the first to shake Sri Lanka. However, they were cataclysmic not only in their extent but in their demonstration of "organized mob violence at work."[4] Estimates of the dead ranged from 350 to 2,000. Tamils were systematically tar- geted with the help of voter lists and addresses of Tamil shop owners and residents, and killed in spectacularly brutal ways. The riots spread from Colombo to other parts of the country. Stanley Tambiah, in his book *Ethnic Fratricide and the Dismantling of Democracy*, notes that the riots had three aspects that made them uniquely atrocious: the use of organized mob violence; the destruction not only of homes but also of businesses; and the passive or active complicity of the police and army.

The 1983 riots inaugurated a civil war in which over 65,000 Sri Lankans have been killed. While historians and political scientists have explored the causes of the conflict in Sri Lanka, anthropologists such as

Tambiah, Jeganathan,[5] and Daniel[6] have done much of the most note-worthy scholarship on ethnic violence in Sri Lanka. These anthropologists have followed the turn away from a definition of *culture* as separate from politics and history, and as seamless and stable. They have emphasized the ways in which political violence calls for a complex analysis of shifting social forces and indeed demands new forms of ethnographic writing. At the same time, their approaches differ: Tambiah offers an analysis in the vein of classic social anthropology, whereas Jeganathan and Daniel engage in ethnography of a more reflexive, critical, experimental kind.

Tambiah poses the question, "How could such a people and such an island be capable of the horrendous riots that exploded in late July and early August 1983?"[7] In his attempt at an answer, Tambiah examines the dynamics of party politics, economic dislocations, social class, language, religion, colonialism, and ethnic identity. He provides a comprehensive, even masterful account of the circumstances in which the violence erupted. He identifies four principle causes for the violence: economic imbalances, increasing authoritarianism on the part of the government, the growth of political and social factions in the society at large, and the rise of a chauvinist, nationalist Buddhism. Jeganathan, also writing about the 1983 riots, calls into question such an explanatory mode. According to Jeganathan, Tambiah's analysis has two intellectual genealogies: the study of nationalism/ethnicity and of religion. With regard to the first, Tambiah provides a social history of two ethnicities, Sinhala and Tamil, with the object of mapping a breakdown in social relations between these. The riots are then explained: "Sinhalaness" + "Tamilness" = 1983. A second strand of his analysis emphasizes religion: Tambiah sees in the way Buddhists become politicized an explanation for the violence. Jeganathan's schematic summary of Tambiah's line of argument reads: history x (Buddhism + politics) = violence. The vision of political violence that emerges from his study is what one might call nominalist, in that its premise is that one can name the various aspects and causes of violence and thereby grasp its full meaning.

Rather than delineating the causes of ethnic violence, Jeganathan, who writes after the linguistic turn in anthropology, steps back and attempts to develop an analytic mode for the very phenomenon of violence, a category he considers far from transparent. According to Jeganathan, "'1983,' is a moment of incomprehensibility in the narration of Sri Lanka's modernity. Horror (agony/shame) is (are) the name(s) of that incomprehensibility, in both political science and anthropology.... Specially armed by its privileged access to culture, anthropology sets to work to transform its incomprehensibility into an analytical category. 'Violence' is the analytic of that incomprehensibility. The anthropology of violence, in other words, is a development of this analytic."[8] Jeganathan is wary of this discursive slide from "violence" to "horror," seeing in it a problematic reinforcement of humanism: "Consider: if horror, is a name for the destruction of the human that can not be apprehended politically, and violence is its analytic, a return to horror by way of 'violence' will also return to the problem of the human."[9] For Jeganathan, this move amounts to a recourse to the universals of humanism. Drawing on ethnographic research he conducted ten years after the riots, in an urban community near Colombo, Jeganathan proceeds to identify three specific conditions in which the violence of 1983 and its aftermath is produced: the practices of masculinity, moments of recollection, and the tactics of anticipation. Jeganathan's aim is to avoid taking the object of knowledge, "violence," as given and to detail the particular conditions of its emergence.

Daniel also moves away from the kind of social anthropology favored by Tambiah, and acknowledges rather the incomprehensibility that is at the very core of political violence. In his anthropological exploration of the 1983 riots, *Charred Lullabies*, Daniel foregrounds the difficulty of approaching violence as an object of interpretation. This difficulty attends a theoretical account no less than a more empirically descriptive one: "violence is such a reality that a theory which purports to inform it with significance must not merely 'stand under' but conspicuously 'stand apart' from it as a gesture of open admission to its inadequacy to measure up to its task."[10] Daniel uses a variety of discourses to fashion what he calls a "discordant" account "so as to echo the discordance of the phenomenon being studied—violence and its effects—albeit in a different register."[11] Interspersing historical information about estate Tamils (brought from India in the early nineteenth century by the British to work on tea plantations), interviews, a poem, archival documents, and theoretical speculation, Daniel fashions a contrapuntal, open-ended text around the 1983 riots.[12] In its form, his work avoids the conceit of a masterful perspective. At the end of *Charred Lullabies*, Daniel concludes, "Violence is an event in which there is a certain excess: an excess of passion, an excess of evil. The very attempt to label this excess (as indeed I have done) is condemned to fail; it employs what Georges Bataille (1988) called 'mots glissants' (slippery words)."[13] Ultimately, Daniel emphasizes the ineffability of violence, which he characterizes as a "counterpoint" to culture. However, he ends the book with a reported narrative of humane caring in an earlier anti-Tamil riot in 1977. An elderly Tamil man recounts how, when thugs mounted a train and began to pull out and beat Tamil passengers, a completely unknown Sinhala woman in a railway compartment came and sat next to him, possibly saving his life. Here the experience of a stranger's care in the face of violence is redemptive. At the same time, it is only momentarily and immanently so—no transcendent meaning is ascribed to the episode. Both Daniel and Jeganathan attempt to explore the phenomenon of political violence with considerable sensitivity to the pitfalls of reifying it as an object of knowledge.

NARRATIVE / KNOWLEDGE / HERMENEUTICS

Ondaatje, like Daniel and Jeganathan, is attentive to the difficulties of representing and interpreting political violence in Sri Lanka. Indeed, Ondaatje attempts to do in a literary register what Daniel and Jeganathan do in an anthropological one: explore the terms in which to apprehend political violence. He draws on the conventions of the literary genre of fiction of intrigue for this exploration. The novel begins as a story of forensic detection. Anil and Sarath have the body of a man who has apparently been killed, and their task is to identify the body and uncover the history of its death. This narrative form reinforces the operation of juridical power: the protagonists investigate a crime with the aim of bringing those who have violated the law to justice. Implicit in the operation of juridical power is the notion that "truth" can be determined through processes of inquiry and examination.[14] According to Foucault, the inquiry is a mode of analysis that arose in the medieval era specifically as a form of the search for truth within a judicial order. The examination emerged in the nineteenth century, also in the context of "juridical, judicial and penal problems," but "in direct conjunction with the formation of a certain number of political and social controls, during the forming of capitalist society in the late nineteenth century."[15] We see both these forms of analysis in *Anil's Ghost;* inquiry and examination frame Anil's quest for truth as part of a quest for justice whereby "wrongs and responsibilities are settled between men."[16] The processes of reconstruction and uncovering in the novel are carried on against the backdrop of a repressive, violent state. In this context, the knowledge that Anil and Sarath produce through inquiry and examination is a kind that is in the image of the state's rationality; at the same time, the knowledge has the power to discredit that rationality.

Anil's Ghost operates as a novel of intrigue at two levels. Superficially—and deceptively, we later realize—the novel follows Anil and Sarath's quest for "Sailor's" identity with the aim of exposing the crimes of the state. At the same time, the reader is positioned as a detective tackling the problem of how the novel plots history. In fact, these levels are folded together in that the examination of "Sailor's" body and the inquiry into his identity become attempts to reconstruct his personal history and his death. Ondaatje brings the domains of examination, reading and history together when, in describing Sarath's talents, he writes, "A good archeologist can read a bucket of soil as if it were a complex historical novel."[17] Sarath ascertains from the soil precisely what we might seek from a novel: an understanding of complex, geographically and historically shaped social relationships.

The novel also holds up another model of knowledge in the face of political violence: that of the empirical scientist. The scientific procedures that are used to examine the effects of violence are described in precise, logical, almost fetishistic detail in a manner that conveys a sense of masterful knowledge. In his descriptions of Anil and Sarath's detective work, Ondaatje displays his familiarity with the technical minutiae of forensic science—knowledge from palynology (the science of pollen and spores) and from the evidence of trace elements in bones; the way the skeleton is painted with plastic; the identification of bones and the damage done to them. When Anil attempts to delineate the facts of death by mapping the effects of violence on "Sailor's" body, Ondaatje emphasizes their universal quality—"same as for Colombo as for Troy." These facts are enumerated with the clinical dispassion of the scientist in a descriptive list that leaves little room for expression or interpretation. Anil is able to reconstruct from these facts the last moments of "Sailor's" life, which are again conveyed in a measured, neutral way. These details convey the sense that the evidence of violence done to the human body can be determined and interpreted with certainty. This emphasis on identifying marks bespeaks a sort of reification—the body takes on the status of an object and is known as such, stripped of its historical and social relations. At the same time, "Sailor's" body is more than a single body; it stands in for all those who have been brutalized by war: "Who was he? This representative of all those lost voices. To give him a name would name the rest" (p. 56). To know "Sailor's" body is to have objective knowledge of the effects of war on the social body.

While the detective plot of *Anil's Ghost* teasingly holds out the possibility of such knowledge, its form works against such an understanding. We have a looping and digressive narrative interspersed with decontextualized fragments on one hand, and detailed empirical descriptions of scientific technique on the other. Like many postmodern writers, Ondaatje favors a fragmentary, nonlinear narrative that shifts between the past and the present, and moves to different places, sketching episodes in the characters' lives. It also includes italicized segments that stand apart from the body of the text. The structure of the narrative reinforces the sense of bodily fragmentation that the novel elaborates at a thematic level. For example, several of the italicized segments are third-person descriptions of particularly brutal episodes that are not contextualized in any way, including that of a man strangling a government official and throwing his body from a moving train as it passes through a tunnel and becomes dark. None of the other passengers are aware of what is happening. We the readers are interpellated as the sole witnesses of this act of violence and are implicitly charged with the responsibility of making sense of it. Yet the novel presents this incident to us in so fragmentary and disjointed a form that it seems meaningless. Similarly, in another instance, a young woman (who we later learn is the painter Ananda's wife) walks toward her place of work to be faced with a Conradian vista of heads mounted on stakes in a field along the way. These free-standing descriptions are not integrated into the movement of the plot, but rather stand apart and thereby accentuate the sense that political violence defies assimilation into a coherent, historical narrative.

Not only does the novel resist the kind of diagnostic reading of the detective, it actually teaches readers to be suspicious of modes of reading in characteristically postmodern fashion. The novel problematizes the process of reading in several instances. The narrator recounts Gamini's sojourn in the north, where his fellow doctors have distinguished themselves as "marginalia criminals" who express their dissatisfaction with the books they read and share their own attempts to make meaning. A sense of the trickiness of reading is also conveyed by the novel's emphasis on quotations that take on the status of epigrams and are italicized. We don't know the full significance of these

epigrams; nor do we know which ones to trust when they have contradictory implications. For instance, Anil repeats in various forms
the sentiment that "Sailor's" body stands for those of all the victims
of the war: "One village can speak for many villages. One victim can
speak for many victims." Here Ondaatje ascribes to Anil a firm belief
in the possibilities of metonymic connection. However, another sentence that Gamini has read in a hospital text and that also becomes
epigrammatic—"In diagnosing a vascular injury a high index of suspicion is necessary"—has decidedly different implications. This epigram
cautions against an unreflective interpretation of interconnections. In
fact, this statement could be read as the maxim of the novel, for it dis-
tills the novel's suspicion of connectivity. The evidence of "Sailor's"
body can't be made to express unproblematically the victimization of
a larger polity. This epigram calls the very connectivity of narrative,
and of the social, into question. As a result, the novel conveys little
sense of a social totality.[18]

While the novel casts suspicion on certain paradigms of interpretation, it does, I would suggest, offer a model of reading in its references
to interlinearity. Palipana, the aging epigraphist, we learn, is an interlinear reader, one who is able to read inventively and learn truths that
have been hidden:

> Most of his life he had found history in stones and carvings. In the
> last few years he had found the hidden histories, intentionally lost, that
> altered the perspective and knowledge of earlier times.... The dialogue
> between old and hidden lines, the back-and-forth between what was
> official and unofficial during solitary field trips, when he spoke to no
> one for weeks, when they became his only conversations—an epigra-
> phist studying the specific style of a chisel-cut from the fourth century,
> then coming across an illegal story, one banned by kings and state and
> priests, in the interlinear texts. (p. 105)

Merriam Webster's Collegiate Dictionary defines interlinear as "inserted between lines already written or printed"; also, "written or
printed in different languages or texts in alternate lines."[19] Ondaatje
advances a mode of interpretation that gets at what is obscure not
through a process of metonymic substitution or logical deduction,
but rather, through a "dialogue between old and hidden lines" and a
"back-and-forth between what was official and unofficial." We might
take from this a lesson in reading between the lines, not to grasp a

whole social totality or to make sense of a shattered totality, but to discover meaning in the interstices of the known. In this privileging of the interlinear, the novel also reflects on its own interlining of different domains: the sacred and the profane, the public and the private, and narrative and history.

HISTORY

I want now to focus more closely on the question of history that I have alluded to earlier—that is, on what kind of historical vision is efficacious in contemporary Sri Lanka, if any. As I suggested, the novel makes little attempt to explain the civil war. Ondaatje repeatedly makes equivalences between the carnage of the various groups. This has the rhetorical effect of flattening historical difference and essentializing violence:

> There had been continual emergency from 1983 onwards, racial attacks and political killings. The terrorism of the separatist guerilla groups, who were fighting for a homeland in the north. The insurrection of the insurgents in the south, against the government. The counterterrorism of the special forces against both of them. The disposal of bodies by fire. The disposal of bodies in rivers or the sea. The hiding and then reburial of corpses.
>
> It was a Hundred Years' War with modern weaponry, and backers on the sidelines in safe countries, a war sponsored by gun-and drug-runners. It became evident that political enemies were secretly joined in financial arms deals. "The reason for war was war." (pp. 42–43)

This passage is written in the third person and reflects the conclusions Anil draws from newspapers and reports. It emphasize that all the factions are culpable. Moreover, by listing the groups in such schematic fashion, Ondaatje suggests they are interchangeable in character. Insofar as there is any material context provided, it is again completely schematic: foreign arms dealers and drug runners, with absolutely no account of the character of Tamil nationalism, the JVP, or the political makeup of the government. We are left with a sort of Hobbesian "state of nature" in which no power is able to establish itself as sovereign.

This condition is implicitly contrasted with the case of Guatemala, which has a phantasmatic presence in the novel. *Anil's Ghost* in fact begins with the description of a scene in Guatemala where Anil has been working with a forensic team, excavating the remains of victims of war. As in other parts of *Anil's Ghost*, the lyrical language emphasizes the poignancy of personal loss rather than the enormity of the political crime at hand; it foregrounds subjective emotion rather than objective historical fact. However, Ondaatje is unequivocal in his view that it is the government that has massacred indigenous peoples in Guatemala. In Sri Lanka, by contrast, "The government was not the only one doing the killing." Not that Ondaatje is wrong in his view that "every side was killing and hiding the evidence. Every side." Rather, it is the implication that violence in Sri Lanka cannot be historicized that leaves the reader with the sense that the carnage there is inexplicable and unavoidable. Ultimately, Anil and Sarath identify the body and Anil publicly implicates the government in his murder. The novel veers away from an exposé of ethnic violence, and inculpates the government in the repression of Marxist insurgents.[20] However, by this point the actual cause of "Sailor's" murder hardly seems relevant. Anil is now so convinced of the pervasiveness of violence and the impossibility of its resolution that the novel abandons the generic logic of intrigue. A novel that begins as a quest for the truth about political violence in the interests of its resolution ends up advancing the view that this violence is a truth in itself; as the novel puts it, "the cause of war was war." As a consequence the dead remain unhistorical in *Anil's Ghost*. Ondaatje's mode of representing political violence makes it appear to be endemic and intractable.

While Ondaatje appears to disavow history as a lens through which one can make sense of the violence in Sri Lanka, a preoccupation with historical knowledge runs through the novel in a submerged and displaced form. This preoccupation is evident in the novel's emphasis on ancient history and on natural history. Sarath's ambition, we learn, is to write "about a city in the south of the island that no longer existed. Not a wall of it remained, but he wanted to tell the story of that place. It would emerge out of this dark trade with the earth, his knowledge of the region in chronicles—its medieval business routes, its presence as a favourite monsoon town of a certain king, as revealed in poems that celebrated the city's daily life" (p. 29). In this briefest of sketches, we have the sense of a living community, knit together by commerce and social institutions—but it is relegated firmly to the past: "Not a wall of it remained." Later, Sarath explains to Anil, "I love history, the intimacy of entering all those landscapes. Like entering a dream. Someone nudges a stone away and there's a story" (p. 259). Insofar as Ondaatje valorizes history, it is that of a mysterious and magical "other world," remote in sensibility and time.

The novel's most vivid representation of history is in the domain of the natural world—a world that is posed in contradistinction to the human world in *Anil's Ghost*. It is only in the lyrical descriptions of landscape and nature that Ondaatje imagines a contemporary history that is not dark and meaningless. In an italicized excerpt that is inserted into the narrative, Ondaatje suggests that natural history is more significant than human history when he describes the *National Atlas of Sri Lanka,* and notes that while the atlas includes templates of birds, bodies of water, and minerals, none of the seventy-three pages bear witness to human life. He similarly valorizes natural history in his portrayal of Palipana, Sarath's teacher, who lives with his niece in the shelter of an ancient ruined forest monastery, with the barest evidence of human contrivance. In the description of this retreat from the world of war, the vestiges of an ancient civilization blend harmoniously with forest, rock, and lake—and are distinguished sharply from the contemporary political landscape, which is by contrast, a space of senseless and meaningless violence. As in *The God of Small Things,* the natural world is an antithesis to the built, historical, human world.

Anil's Ghost, then, in its tendency to flatten and displace the historical, disappoints if one seeks the insights of a historical novel. What it does do successfully is stage a problematic of history and this refocuses the critical vision of the novel. In an important passage in which Sarath, Gamini, and Anil speak of Palipana, the novel likens history to a body:

"What did he call himself?"

"An epigraphist," Sarath said.

"A skill ... to decipher inscriptions. Wonderful! To study history as if it were a body."

"Of course your brother does that too."

"Of course. And then Palipana went mad. What do you say, Sarath?"

"Hallucinations, perhaps."

"He went mad. Those over-interpretations, what we must call lies, over the interlinear stuff."

"He isn't mad."

"Okay, then. Same as you and me. But no one in his clique supported him when it was revealed. He was certainly the only great man I ever

met, but he was just never a 'sacred' guy for me. You see, in the heart of
any faith is a history that teaches us not to trust—" (p. 193)

This rich passage brings together the preoccupations that I have un-
derscored—interlinearity and the difficulties of interpretation, the
study of history, and finally, the caution against trust, a lesson taught
by history itself. When Sarath defends his teacher Palipana's advo-
cacy of interlinearity, Gamini insists that any system of belief, any
faith, has questionable antecedents. If history is like a body, the novel
warns, we must exercise skepticism when deciphering its wounds. "In
diagnosing a vascular injury, a high index of suspicion is necessary."
The novel emphasizes a basic principle of historiography: a constant
circumspection about what really happened and why.

TRAUMA

In likening history to a body—and implicitly, to a wounded body—is
Ondaatje writing history as trauma? This would certainly be one way
to interpret his apparent reluctance to offer a historical account of
the present. Anil clearly recognizes that the traumatic nature of political violence makes it difficult to apprehend: "She used to believe that
meaning allowed a person to escape grief and fear. But she saw that
those who were slammed and stained by violence lost the power of
language and logic" (p. 55). In other words, the traumatic violence
that civilians have suffered in the conflict in Sri Lanka has made their
experience inaccessible to language and logic, and hence inimical to
historical narration. Rather than attempting to provide a historical
narrative, the novel dwells on the repercussions of violence as a private, emotional experience. Anil's return to Sri Lanka is not only a
journey to a scene of political carnage but also a return to the scene
of past personal trauma. Anil, we are told, gained her name in a sexual exchange with her brother, though the novel urbanely skims over
the possible violence of such an exchange. And her departure from
Sri Lanka was followed by the death of her parents in a traffic ac-
cident—her only previous return was to attend their last rites. Other
principal characters are similarly sketched with reference to traumatic
events—Gamini's wife killed herself by swallowing lye, and Anil's
closest friend Leaf is dying of Alzheimer's. The novel concerns itself
with articulating these "private woes" and to the extent that healing
takes place, it happens at an individual level.

The most poignant instance of trauma and healing comes toward the end of the novel, when Gamini is faced with Sarath's brutalized body. "He began washing the body's dark-brown markings with scrub lotion. He could heal his brother, set the left leg, deal with every wound as if he were alive, as if treating the hundred small traumas would eventually bring him back into his life" (p. 287). As Gamini sits with his murdered brother's body, he recounts the moments that the brothers have shared and the divergence of their paths. The scene is one of painful loss, but also of a reconciliation and confraternity. Gamini is able to translate the trauma of his brother's death into the register of history, albeit a highly personal and impressionistic history—and he does this via medical science.

At the same time, the novel resists rendering historical trauma in a narrative that is in any way teleological or redemptive. Dominick LaCapra's remarks on the pitfalls of transference in writing a history of the Holocaust are helpful in exploring the question of how the novel addresses the problem of representing trauma.[21] Recognizing all the difficulties of such an endeavor, LaCapra argues that it is possible to write a history that is a "working through" rather than an unreflectively "acting out." The crucial challenge in doing so is negotiating the problem of transference: "Working through requires the recognition that we are involved in transferential relations to the past in ways that vary according to the subject positions we find ourselves in, rework, and invent. It also involves the attempt to counteract the projective reprocessing of the past through which we deny certain of its features and act out our own desires for self-confirming or identity-forming meaning."[22] A narrative of trauma that "works through" it is one that recognizes the transferential relations that obtain as one represents the traumatic event. A failure to recognize transference can lead to "acting out" via the construction of redemptive narratives.

The pitfalls of transference are dramatized in the novel vis-à-vis "Sailor," the representative of the "unhistorical dead." Anil's mission is to give these dead a history. That Anil engages in transference is suggested by her strong attachment to "Sailor," and her project of constructing an identity for him by reading the marks of his vocation. Not only does she feel compelled to fashion a history for him that is mediated by her own libidinal investments, she wants to extrapolate from this act of projection a larger history—"to name him would name the rest." In her public indictment of the government, she acknowledges this investment, identifying herself with "Sailor":

"I think you murdered hundreds of us" (p. 272). Ananda's attempt to reconstruct "Sailor's" face with rubber and plasticine is similarly cathected and he transfers to Sailor the expression he desires for his wife, Sirissa, who has disappeared in the convulsions of war. An attempt to reconstruct the history of violence, the novel suggests, is bedeviled by the tendency to rewrite this history as one's own.

The novel offers a counterpoint to "Sailor" in the figure of Sarath Diyasena—a man who is repeatedly characterized as remote, private, detached, and not a viable object of transference. The novel's answer to the problem of transference is also the solution to an implicit riddle: who is Anil's ghost? It is in fact Sarath, and not "Sailor," who is the ghost of the novel's title. This is announced explicitly at the end: "He [Ananda] and the woman Anil would always carry the ghost of Sarath Diyasena" (p. 305). If Anil's public denunciation of the government, and implicitly of Sarath, is an acting out, Sarath's murder will force her to work through the implications of his violent death. The novel, by refusing the possibility of transference at this crucial juncture, asserts the local, the personal, and the present over any larger totalizing history. A working-out results in an insistence on the importance of the private. The novel announces this privileging in another epigrammatic moment: "One can die from private woes as easily as from public ones" (p. 202).

While one might agree with Ondaatje's suggestion that the traumatic and immediate nature of ethnic violence might render any explanation, including historical explanation, difficult, the imperative to claim experience, to reassert the power of language and logic, surely remains in the face of a discursive vacuum that could otherwise be filled by reactionary histories. The novel does not abdicate this responsibility entirely, offering as it does a vision of individual care and healing, but it repudiates a mode of historicism that makes sense of the past or offers a vision of the future. In a recent essay in which he assesses the postmodern turn in historiography of the last twenty years, Arif Dirlik concludes, "However welcome may be the abolition of the earlier hierarchies of history, there is a price to be paid for the liberation from the hegemony of history: loss of a vision of the future that may help make sense of the present, and the past as well."[23] The cultural critic who has taken on board the poststructuralist critique of grand, recuperative historical narratives and appreciated the value of postmodern modes of representation, yet is convinced of the efficacy of history as a hermeneutic discourse, is faced with the challenge of how to fashion history. This is a challenge that Ondaatje himself sidesteps.

To recapitulate, then, we find in *Anil's Ghost* not only the absence of a historical vision of political violence, but an outright suspicion if not rejection of historicism. To the extent that the novel does give credence to a historical perspective, it privileges a traumatic, highly personal discourse of history. Ondaatje's literary mode involves a radical retreat to the individual and the private, albeit in the most sophisticated and self-conscious way. Ondaatje is quite explicit in his rejection of a political commentary on circumstances in Sri Lanka. In an interview, Ondaatje comments on his suspicion of the terms "human rights" and "politics": "Certain words, certain phrases are said so often that they come to have no reverberation. 'Human rights,' the phrase is indivisible, but the words mean nothing to me. When I hear the word 'politics' I roll my eyes, or if I hear a political speech I can't listen to it. And so in a way I burrow underneath these words, I try not to refer to them. The words are like old coins. They just don't feel real."[24] Ondaatje emphasizes his sense of the inadequacy and tiredness of language in the face of ongoing, extreme, and seemingly insoluble violence. While one might agree with Ondaatje's suggestion that the traumatic and immediate nature of ethnic violence might render any explanation, including historical explanation, difficult, many would argue that the imperative to claim experience, to reassert the power of language and logic, remains in the face of a discursive vacuum that could otherwise be filled by reactionary histories.

POSTCOLONIAL VIOLENCE AND *HOMO SACER*

Rather than view Ondaatje's repudiation of historical representation as an abdication of political responsibility, one can understand his vision as symptomatic of a new postcolonial moment. Specifically, the way that Ondaatje represents the political landscape of Sri Lanka is symptomatic of new kinds of sovereignty and new conditions of subjectivity. I want to characterize this moment by drawing selectively on the work of three political theorists, Giorgio Agamben, Michael Hardt, and Antonio Negri, all of whom conceptualize the operation of modern forms of power.

In *Homo Sacer*, Agamben argues that the concentration camp (and not the carceral, as Foucault suggests) best exemplifies the way modern power operates, even in liberal democracies.[25] To support this provocative claim, Agamben explores the significance of a figure of ancient Roman law: *homo sacer* or "sacred man." *Homo sacer* is a criminal who may neither be legally executed nor sacrificed; rather, anyone may kill him with impunity.[26] This places *homo sacer* at the limits of the human and the divine order. In an inclusionary exclusion, this figure is outside the polis, and yet negatively defines life within the polis. Agamben proceeds to argue that the sovereign exception that places the sovereign both beyond the law and defines its domain is not merely analogously situated in an exclusion that is at the same time an inclusion; sovereign power is actually constituted in relation to *homo sacer* or sacred life: "The sovereign sphere is the sphere in which it is permitted to kill without committing homicide and without celebrating a sacrifice, and sacred life—that is, life that may be killed but not sacrificed—is the life that has been captured in this sphere."[27] The figure of *homo sacer* stands as a placeholder for the domain of sovereign power. Absolute power over life and death becomes the hallmark of sovereignty. The concentration camp is the space where bare life is the norm—and the structure of political power that relegates bare life to the threshold and at the same time is defined by this threshold is manifest in its starkest form.

This figure of *homo sacer* in many ways captures the predicament of "Sailor" in *Anil's Ghost*. "Sailor" has seemingly been killed with impunity, and exists at the threshold of the social order: he has no identity, no history, and no home. He is simply a body, stripped of all humanity. This denuded state is emphasized in the novel in the descriptions of him as an object of scientific investigation. "Sailor" stands in for the many victims of war who are similarly marginal in the Sri Lankan landscape that Ondaatje presents. These "unhistorical dead" are people who may be killed with impunity, relegated as they are to the extreme periphery of social life. These are people who are outside the polis and outside history. Hence the absence of a historical account for the violence that marks the "lives that meet in the wasteland between exile and belonging, between life and death" in the landscape of *Anil's Ghost*.[28] If we accept Agamben's account, then the sovereign power of the state is asserted via these "unhistorical dead."

Ondaatje represents political power as totalizing, as reducing humans literally to their bare bones, biopolitical objects without history. "Sailor's" status as bare life necessarily places him outside history and outside the legal order, and at the same time throws into relief the contours of the political order. Anil tries to fashion for "Sailor" an identity and a history, and to inscribe him within a juridical narrative, but even though he is finally identified and his death "explained," the kind of detective narrative and its corresponding juridico-institutional logic that we see in the other fictions of intrigue that I have discussed is never fully elaborated. We are left with a scenario in which violence has become generalized, and the state omniscient.

If Agamben's analysis helps us to understand the condition of "naked life" and the operation of biopolitics represented in *Anil's Ghost*, Hardt and Negri's account of a postmodern, global political terrain in *Empire* resonates strongly with Ondaatje's depiction of the political landscape in *Anil's Ghost*. Anil herself works for an international human rights organization, one of the organs of global governance to which Hardt and Negri refer. The novel depicts this transnational regime as at odds with the seemingly rogue activities of the nation-state. At the same time, in contrast with Guatemala, which I have suggested has a phantasmatic presence in the novel and where violence is attributed to the state, in the case of Sri Lanka violence extends beyond the apparatuses of the state.

The power of the state is itself amorphous and extensive: governmental power is concentrated in the city, but its reach is unpredictable. Sarath repeatedly warns Anil that she is under continual surveillance. Empire produces new kinds of subjectivities as well: Anil's own work and her identity are deterritorialized. She has lived in Sri Lanka as a child, been educated in Britain, works for an international organization (the Center for Human Rights in Geneva), and travels all over the world on a British passport. She has no ties to any family; her fleeting encounters with her lover, Cullis, are in strange hotel rooms at scientific meetings. Her community, such as it is, is a group of forensic scientists like her who exercise their highly specialized scientific expertise outside the conventional moorings of space and time, working at all hours and in places with which they have no connection. Her movements even within Sri Lanka are erratic, reflecting her own lack of territorial location as well as the decentered nature of the political field that she and Sarath traverse in their detective quest. That is, the fragmentary quality of the novel extends not only to its temporality but also to its spatial sense. This representation marks a shift away from a modern understanding of power, where there is an outside/inside as well as distinct centers of power, to the kind of decentered, unbounded vision of power outlined in *Empire*. Hardt and

Negri's account of the increasingly postmodern modalities of political power, the novel institutions through which these are exercised, and the new forms of identity that these produce throw light on the characterization of Anil and the political landscape she traverses.

While the novel sketches a postmodern vision of power à la Hardt and Negri, at its end Anil asserts a modern understanding of power to which she ascribes an outside/inside when she makes it her mission to smuggle evidence of state-sponsored violence out of the country.[29] She believes that she can find an "outside" to the political machinations of the nation-state in some supposed international realm where justice may be guaranteed. At the same time, the novel suggests that the postcolonial nation-state exists in a context of generalized and globalized violence, as in the references to Anil's stints as a forensic investigator at sites of political violence all over the world. One might interpret Anil's impulse as a romantic recuperation that goes against the grain of the novel, which for the most part shows power to operate in the terms that Hardt and Negri describe in *Empire:* in a decentered, deterritorialized, globalized way. Or, at the risk of stretching Agamben's terms, one might read the Sri Lankan nation-state as a criminal, a sort of *homo sacer* or example of "bare life" that may be killed but not sacrificed, and to whom the codes of civil international conduct do not apply: this certainly seems to be the attitude to pariah "failed states" such as Iraq in the discourse of the New Empire at the present moment. Happily, perhaps because of its relative economic and political inconsequentiality, Sri Lanka has not in fact been reduced to this condition. In any case, rather than forcibly try to reconcile the visions of Agamben on the one hand, and of Hardt and Negri on the other, one might acknowledge the simultaneous existence in postcolonial societies of modern and postmodern forms of power.

THE DEMAND OF INTERPRETATION

The move away from a narrative of detection in the novel can, then, be explained in two ways. On the one hand, it represents an acknowledgment of the limitations of a juridico-political narrative in a world where "Sailor" has become, like *homo sacer*, a man who exists at the limit of sovereign power, a man beyond the law. On the other hand, the novel's repudiation of a logic of detection corresponds to its vision of a new form of sovereignty, one that is not delimited and centered by the structures of the nation. In this new context of Empire, the tropes of detective fiction no longer serve to express the juridical logic of sovereignty, the rationalities whereby people's mutual relations are governed and adjudicated. The novel's shift away from a juridical logic does not entirely void the position of the detective; rather, it shifts the role of the detective onto the reader, who must piece the fragments of the text together to come up with its meaning. In other words, the novel moves from a juridical narrative to a narrative about the political demands of hermeneutics. The "who done what" logic gives way to one in which the primary question is, How do we interpret the novel and what political demands does our interpretation place on us?

To ask this question is to ask how the novel positions the reader. As Anil's quest becomes more meandering and loses its centrality in the novel, the reader becomes less engaged in the project of uncovering a crime and more attentive to the process of making sense of a politically complex, heterogeneous text. The novel gives the reader little historical anchorage, for, as I have suggested, it refers to history only in relation to the ancient past, and to the natural world, not the political situation, in the present. I have suggested that the novel's disavowal of historical narrative bespeaks a wariness of totalizing claims. In this context, *unhistorical* might refer to what is not reduced and made part of a grand narrative. I have earlier pointed to the imperative voiced in the novel to restore the "unhistorical dead" to history, and history to them. One could argue the contrary: that the "unhistorical dead" must be preserved from the reductive moment of historical discourse. The novel poses the problem of how one might render historical events into narrative without being reductive. I want to suggest that the novel gestures toward a third possibility that entails neither the postmodern repudiation of grand narratives nor the positivist assertion of historicism—the novel makes a political demand of the reader to imagine such a possibility.

As the novel makes this interpretive demand, it suggests two possible ways to proceed. On one hand, the novel advances a principle that I have already discussed: that of interlinearity. It urges an experimental mode of hermeneutics that involves sensitivity to gaps, fissures, and ambiguities, and a wariness of masterful and seamless narratives. Though the reader is at first invited to see through the eyes of the forensic detective and to share her pleasure in a penetrating gaze, the detective has increasingly less agency in the novel. By its end, Anil, and by identification the reader, view contemporary Sri Lanka with a scattered, tentative apprehension. On the other hand, the novel veers away from an attempt to represent and to interpret historical events altogether, emphasizing instead the domain of affect. In other words, the novel does not purport to index the "real" of history via representation; instead, it locates the "real" in the realm of affect. Brian Massumi, in his introduction to *Parables for the Virtual*, argues that most recent social theorists have seen the body or subject as positioned within signifying structures, and as themselves inert.[30] This certainly has been the tendency among the many of us who engage in ideology critique and examine the politics of representation, as has been my object in this book.

Massumi argues that for those who think along these lines, meaning is already bounded and delimited by the possibilities of systemic structuring, "positioning on a grid." Turning to the domain of affect to understand the body as "more than a local embodiment of ideology," Massumi suggests that there "seems to be a growing feeling within media, literary and art theory that affect is central to an understanding of our information- and image-based late capitalist culture, in which so-called master narratives are perceived to have foundered."[31] I want to suggest that Ondaatje appeals precisely to the realm of affect to imagine new possibilities of meaning. In a book that is overwhelmingly about violence done to bodies, and that searches for ways of making sense of this violence, the workings of affect offer a distinctive and important way to make sense of this violence.

I referred earlier to two episodes in the novel that strikingly show Ondaatje's attempt to view political violence through the prism of affect: the painter Ananda's reconstruction of "Sailor's" expression, and Gamini's discovery of Sarath's body. When Ananda finally completes his reconstruction of "Sailor's" face, Sarath and Anil discover that it has a serene expression. Sarath explains to Anil that Ananda has given "Sailor" the expression he would want for the faces of the dead and the disappeared, especially for his vanished wife, Sirissa, in a moment of transference. As a historical reconstruction, the painting is a failure, but it has the effect of making Anil weep uncontrollably. When Sarath proposes to show the head to local villagers, she protests, "Sarath, you can't do this. You said...these are communities that lost people. They've had to deal with beheaded bodies." Sarath insists, "What's our purpose here? We're trying to identify him. We have to start somewhere" (p. 186). Anil repudiates an instrumental view of bodies that have been subjected to violence and asserts instead their affective moment. When Gamini cradles Sarath's battered body, he too reads the body in the language of shared memory and affect: "This scar I gave you hitting you with a cricket stump. As brothers we ended up never turning our backs on each other" (pp. 287–88). By privileging these moments, the novel describes the bodily victims of political violence not in relation to an ideological grid or historical discourse, but rather in terms of the power they have to move.

ENDINGS

I began by arguing that the novel is concerned on the one hand with the efficacy of historical discourse and on the other with the problem of reading. I want to trace through the different movements at the end of *Anil's Ghost* because these stage the complex arguments about violence, history, and narrative that run through the novel. In fact, the book has two endings. It could have ended with the penultimate section, titled "The Lifewheel," but this is followed by a section called "Distance," which functions as an epilogue. The title of the first ending, "The Lifewheel," has a double meaning. First, it refers to the lifewheel of the miner's song that serves as an epigraph to the novel: "Blessed be the lifewheel on the mine's pithead." I want to suggest that it also refers to Sarath himself. After her public statement, Anil finds Sarath's tape in "Sailor's" skeleton and listens to his last words to her, which are also his last words in the novel. The episode ends with the line "Listening to everything again"—a clause that is set apart and not only describes what Anil does, but also functions as an enjoinment to the reader to rethink the narrative.

At this point the lifewheel begins to turn and we/she review events, this time trusting Sarath. The miner's descent then is a metaphor for Anil's journey into Sri Lanka—Sarath turns out to be her lifewheel, guaranteeing (with his life) her safe ascent and departure. At the same time, she departs carrying his ghost with her—so that she cannot be the visiting Western political writer lampooned in the following section who is able to "go home. Write a book. Hit the circuit"—that is, facilely recycle his or her experience for commercial consumption. Sarath's history is private, traced painfully by his brother Gamini in the next section, which I have quoted earlier, when the doctor recognizes Sarath's broken and lifeless body by the marks of a shared personal history: "The gash of scar on the side of your elbow you got crashing a bike on the Kandy Hill. This scar I gave you hitting you with a cricket stump." In the ensuing passages, Gamini holds his brother in an intensely private pietà, a last chance at communication, and as I have suggested, of intense affect.

From the state's point of view, Sarath is the ghost of *homo sacer*, the man who may be killed but not sacrificed; Gamini's ritual incantation of his brother's bodily wounds brings him back into the domain of the polis, into the realm of a shared history. Then we have a section that describes a highly public act of violence, the blowing up of President Katugala. Of these three episodes, none is given hermeneutic priority; each must be understood as contiguous to but not explained by the others. In these lyrically crafted and skillfully interwoven sections, one has an interlinearity of public and private experiences of political violence that stand adjacent to one another.

The last section offers a pedagogical statement about how to view the whole novel, giving us distance from the core narrative. In fact, the novel has been preoccupied with questions of closeness and distance throughout. For example, at the beginning, Ondaatje suggests that both temporal and spatial distance is vital to the remaking of meaning. The narrator tells us, "Anil had read documents and news reports, full of tragedy, and she had now lived abroad long enough to interpret Sri Lanka with a long-distance gaze. But here it was a more complicated world morally." And later he writes of Anil that "in the midst of such violence, she realized, there could never be any logic to the human violence without the distance of time." We are given this distance as we move to the final description of the two Buddhas. We have, in tandem with a cautious reflection on what might be the best interpretive stance, a staging of two possibilities of representation. At the very end of *Anil's Ghost*, Ananda reconstructs a Buddha that has been blown apart by thieves, and fashions an identical replica at the same time. Ananda's decision not to hide the imperfections in the Buddha represents the artist's compromise:

> Now sunlight hit the seams of its face, as if it were sewn roughly together. He wouldn't hide that. He saw the lidded grey eyes someone had cut another century, that torn look in its great acceptance; he was close against the eyes now, with no distance, like an animal in a stone garden, some old man in the future.... He looked at the eyes that had once belonged to a god. As an artificer now he did not celebrate the greatness of a faith. But he knew that if he did not remain an artificer, he would become a demon. The war around him was to do with demons, specters of retaliation. (p. 305)

Here we have a disenchanted vision of creation. From close, the artist Ananda sees a god who has been shattered, who cannot guarantee the plenitude of the world. The passage ends, however, with Ananda's own acceptance of a responsibility of an artificer: to create through art the possibility of a world where enchantment remains—a world that is the antitheses of the demonic war around him. We then have a description of Ananda ceremonially painting the new Buddha's eyes and thus bringing him to life. Ananda for a moment sees the world through these eyes.

> And now with human sight he was seeing all the fibres of natural history around him. He could witness the smallest approach of a bird, every flick of its wing, or a hundred-mile storm coming down off the mountains near Gonagola and skirting to the plains. He could feel each current of wind, every lattice-like green shadow created by cloud. There was a girl moving in the forest. The rain miles away rolling like blue dust towards him. Grasses being burned, bamboo, the smell of petrol and grenade. The crack of noise as a layer of a rock on his arm exfoliated in heat. The face open-eyed in the great rainstorms of May and June. (p. 307)

This vision is of an enchanted world. In this description of an uncanny moment, the newborn Buddha surveys the natural world and contemplates its beauty and dynamic quality. This Buddha can see the proximate and the distant. Human action, even destructive human action, is subsumed by this redemptive vision. In twinning the two Buddhas, the novel suggests that the enchanted and disenchanted exist side by side in this historical moment.

I want finally to return to the question of how postcolonial fiction represents political violence. As a genre, fiction of intrigue pivots upon a logic of causality. When it takes the form of counterinsurgent discourse, fiction of intrigue flattens social and historical causality by rewriting political violence as crime and locating criminality in the "native." Postcolonial fiction of intrigue, as I have shown in the latter half of this book, experiments with generic expectations in order to critique the violence of the nation-state. *Anil's Ghost* takes us one step further and points to the limits of a critique of state violence. One might argue that Ondaatje, by depicting political violence in Sri Lanka as ahistorical and inexplicable, essentializes violence, that is, imputes to it a fixed and inexorable quality. Violence in this view confounds historical explanation. One could well argue that a retreat from the terms of political discourse is, in the circumstances, questionable.

But is it a retreat, or does new political terrain call for new terms of political discourse? In spite of himself, Ondaatje may be, if not offering us new terms, showing us the limits of the old ones. One could read *Anil's Ghost* not as an inadequate response to the historical exigencies of the moment, but rather as symptomatic of these exigencies. *Anil's Ghost*, in this reading, maps a new postcolonial order. The novel begins as a narrative of forensic detection in which the state is seemingly culpable of murder, but by the end of the novel violence is so widespread and the state itself so decentered that the detective narrative loses its juridical logic. I have suggested that the object of violence is no longer, in this wartime landscape, the liberal subject of juridico-political discourse, but rather, the subject of biopolitics, stripped down in *Anil's Ghost* to a condition of "unhistorical death." If we are to accept Agamben's analysis, this threshold figure is a placeholder for sovereign power. Sovereignty, as it is depicted in relation to the postmodern, globalized, war-riven terrain of *Anil's Ghost*, has distinctive features: it is decentered and deterritorialized, with no clear boundaries. The lack of a critique of nationalism and state violence in the novel is in this reading symptomatic of political conditions in Sri Lanka and the logic of Empire. Both Hardt and Negri and Agamben speak at a broad conceptual level—Agamben about the production of bare life, the subjects of biopolitics, Hardt and Negri about new forms of sovereignty in a globalized, postmodern world. While their work sheds light on the geopolitical terrain of *Anil's Ghost*, Ondaatje writes in a very different register, addressing these transformations but bringing them to a personal level. Arguably, this attempt to connect with the homeland on the terrain of the aesthetic is characteristic of a diasporic sensibility.[32] The novel repudiates a mode of historicism that makes sense of the past or offers a vision of the future. Instead, it privileges a personal aesthetic response to political violence, and asserts the redemptive role of the aesthetic.

"Power Smashes Into Private Lives"

Cultural Politics in the New Empire

In a poor country, power smashes into private lives every single day.
Survival is such a big issue. And I have to think about what one can
do with that as a writer. I think there is something in the form of the
novel that wants to be provincial. The novel wants to be about a small
town in which Madame Bovary has an affair. There is something
intrinsic to the novel about that. One place, one time, three or four
characters, and the interaction between those characters—and that is
the story of the novel. I think you can't write like that now, and so the
problem of how you do write becomes very difficult.
—Salman Rushdie[1]

In this book, I have explored how fiction of intrigue reveals and critiques
the rationalities of power in an imperial world. In the first part, I traced
the workings of a will to maintain imperial power by analyzing British detective and spy fiction by Arthur Conan Doyle and John Buchan
from the turn of the twentieth century. This fiction displays the imperial
regime's anxieties about control while simultaneously affirming imperial
order; resolution comes when the criminal is unmasked and captured.
I have mapped the ways in which colonial fiction of intrigue expresses
anxieties about how natives are to be governed, about imperial class
formations, and about insurgency. Novels of detection and espionage
allay these anxieties by establishing order both in the judicial and the
cognitive sense. In the British Empire, power is maintained not so much
through the elaboration of a norm and the invisible policing of deviance,
as Foucault writes of Europe and North America, but rather through
the proliferation of categories of difference and their rationalization and
hardening. In making its central concern the imposition of cognitive and

judicial order through the rationalization of difference, fiction of intrigue exemplifies for readers a key modality of imperial domination.

In the second part of this work, I have argued that in the late twentieth century, many writers turned the conventions of detective and spy fiction inside out or used them in creative ways to explore the power dynamics of a postcolonial New Empire. The novels I've examined by Amitav Ghosh, Michael Ondaatje, Arundhati Roy, and Salman Rushdie exemplify a preoccupation in South Asian Anglophone writing: the anxieties and coercive actions of the postcolonial state. I suggest that these postcolonial writers turn the generic conventions and topography of fiction of intrigue topsy-turvy so as to make both the repressive and emancipatory impulses of postcolonial modernity visible. The late twentieth-century South Asian writers whose work I discuss explore the state's anxieties, but unlike British imperial writers, they take a critical view of the state's rationalities and deplore the state's authoritarian tendencies. In their work, the detective function shifts from an individual's shoring up of social and political order to social detection, and an exposé of the corrupt and oppressive operation of "big" things: the institutions of civil society, the postcolonial state, and global forces. These writers point to the emergence of new kinds of subjectivity and new forms of sovereignty. They express the paradoxes of postcolonial modernity and trace the ruses and uses of reason in a world where the modern marks the horizon of hope as well as of economic, military, and ecological disaster.

Postcolonial writers are faced with a rapidly changing world in the early twenty-first century. The nation is still the dominant form of political organization in the landscape of the New Empire, and conflicts continue to take the form of struggles for self-determination within nations and for power between nations. At the same time, we have seen the emergence of regional and global geopolitical formations with new structures of governance as well as economic production and regulation. In this brave new world, migration has become a major index and force of geopolitical change. A United Nations report published in 2004 estimated that between 1990 and 2000, a net average of 2.569 million people migrated every year from more developed regions to less developed regions (the report's terms).[2] This says nothing of regional migration and movements within nations. Whether in search of better economic opportunity or in flight from oppressive political regimes, or both, migrants are engaged in new kinds of struggles, and states and international organizations are developing new ways of managing and policing them.

Conclusion

I've explored the ways in which postcolonial writers use the genre of intrigue to portray some of the global transformations that have taken place at the end of the twentieth century. Ghosh ends *The Circle of Reason* by sketching the divergent lives and trajectories of poor and middle-class migrants from India. Roy is scathing in her depiction of the effects of international tourism and global media on small-town life in India. Rushdie sets the last part of *The Moor's Last Sigh* in a fictional place where everyone is rootless and homeless. Ondaatje depicts the violence and displacement caused by the internationally financed ethnic conflict in Sri Lanka, and casts a deracinated U.N. employee as his protagonist.

In this conclusion, I further explore the cultural landscape of globalization by examining Rushdie's novel *Shalimar the Clown* and Stephen Frears' film "Dirty Pretty Things." In the quotation above, taken from an interview, about *Shalimar the Clown*, Rushdie speaks of the challenge that a writer faces in finding an appropriate form to express the situation of ordinary people in areas of the Third World such as India. In *Shalimar the Clown*, Rushdie uses elements of intrigue to explore Kashmiri nationalism, terrorism, and the Indian army's military action in Kashmir. He links this narrative to a love triangle that spans the globe and allegorically represents geopolitical relationships. Using elements of the crime thriller, sensation fiction, and noir, Rushdie explores the bloodier dimensions of globalization: neoimperialism, geopolitical violence, Islamic militancy, and global discourses and practices of terrorism and antiterrorism. Ultimately, I argue, Rushdie posits diasporic location and cosmopolitan identity as a point of departure for a "solution" to ethnic and state violence. Stephen Frears's film, by contrast, emphasizes the vulnerability of migrants who are excluded from the borders of legality demarcated by the nation-state. The film uses elements of a detective plot to expose a trade in the bodies of migrants, who form a global subaltern class that is excluded from the structures of civil and political society but is inserted into different kinds of economic traffic. The novel and the film present very different views of the social, political, and economic conditions engendered by the New Empire.

TEARS OF A CLOWN:
RUSHDIE, STATE VIOLENCE, AND GLOBAL TERRORISM

Through a story of intrigue, *Shalimar the Clown* poses the large and pressing question of how we are to understand the plight of Kashmir, the emergence of Islamic terrorism, and the United States' exercise of global power. The eponymous Shalimar the Clown is the central character in the novel, and in tracing how he becomes a killer, Rushdie attempts to understand the contemporary experience of Kashmir. As he puts it in the interview, "How, in an individual life, can someone begin as a person who would not hurt a fly and end up being someone who cheerfully slits people's throats and cuts their heads off?"[3] He tries to make sense of how "this beautiful place, famously peaceful, with its almost comically peaceful people," has been so unhappily transformed into a region ravaged by violent conflict.[4]

The ideal of Kashmiriyat—of a regional spirit of communal harmony and cultural syncretism—is key to Rushdie's representation of the region and especially the villagers of Pachigam. As Mridu Rai argues in her longue-durée history of Kashmir, the term is vague and adaptable, but nonetheless resonant.[5] Rushdie invokes this ideal most obviously in his description of the romance between Shalimar the Clown and Boonyi. Though Shalimar the Clown is Muslim and Boonyi is Hindu, their youthful affair is condoned and they are married in the name of Kashmiriyat: "Abdullah then mentioned Kashmiriyat, Kashmiriness, that belief that at the heart of Kashmiri culture there was a common bond that transcended all differences.... 'We are all brothers and sisters here,' said Abdullah. 'There is no Hindu-Muslim issue. Two Kashmiri—two Pachigami—youngsters wish to marry, that's all. A love match is acceptable to both families and so a marriage there will be; both Hindu and Muslim customs will be observed.'"[6] This affirmation of cross-religious kinship through marriage is the most pointed way in which Rushdie represents the ideal of Kashmiriyat. Such a union is akin to what Doris Sommer, writing about nineteenth-century Latin American novels, calls national romance: ethnic, religious, or class differences are bridged via a narrative of romance to create a syncretic nation.[7]

While the romance between Shalimar the Clown and Boonyi serves to show how strong the spirit of Kashmiriyat is, this ideal is actualized in a more ongoing way in the novel through the medium of culture. People of all religions jointly participate in the arts that are the basis of the village's sustenance: acting, and more recently, cookery. Rushdie suggests that it is in and through the sharing of everyday cultural activities that the principle of Kashmiriyat is sustained as well as trumps putative differences of religion and politics. Rushdie returns to the motif of arts and crafts as a key but threatened economic resource at the end of the novel, asserting once again the cultural patrimony that, in his view, underpins Kashmiri identity.

In Rushdie's writing, a crucial signifier of Kashmiriyat has been the propensity to share stories. It is the failure of syncretic storytelling that presents a crisis in the Valley of K in *Haroun and the Sea of Stories*. In *Shalimar,* when Pyarelal, Boonyi's Pandit father, questions the viability of communal harmony, he thinks, "Maybe Kashmiriyat was an illusion. Maybe all those children learning one another's stories in the panchayat room in winter, all those children becoming a single family, was an illusion"(p. 239). Pyarelal voices his misgivings by wondering whether the project of joint storytelling has been illusory. The narrative also loses the elements of magical realism that have marked Pachigam out as a charmed place. The magical moments in the early part of the novel are a residue, a vestige of an earlier enchanted Kashmir. They have been part of a possibility of storytelling that becomes more and more limited. A breakdown or degradation of narrative parallels a cessation of magical realism.

The project of creating an "azad Kashmir" is destroyed by the mutually opposed yet combined forces of Islamic militants and the Indian army. The secular, nationalist JKLF is gradually outflanked by different Islamic groups. These groups make forays into the Valley, where, Rushdie makes it clear, they are not particularly welcome; it is only under brutal threats from the Lashkar that women in Shirmal and Pachigam adopt the veil. In depicting the rise of communal violence in Kashmir, Rushdie emphasizes that communal identities in Kashmir are not "natural" or "given" but are produced when resources grow scarce and when outside forces intervene in local spaces. These outside forces are global in scope; Rushdie alludes to the workings of an international network of Islamic terrorism, extending to the Philippines and the Middle East, and backed with Saudi cash.

Rushdie again comments on and makes use of language to convey the nature of the forces that destroy Kashmir. In a scathing satire of the Indian general Kachhawa, nicknamed General Turtle, Rushdie blasts the Indian armed forces for their brutal and unremitting campaign against both civilians and militants. In his portrait of General Kachhawa, Rushdie lampoons the rationale of the Indian army for so called "crack downs":

Kashmir was an integral part of India. An integer was a whole and India was an integer and fractions were illegal. Fractions caused fractures in the integer and were thus not integral. Not to accept this was to lack integrity and implicitly or explicitly to question the unquestionable integrity of those who did accept it. Not to accept this was latently or patently to favour disintegration. This was subversive. Subversion led to disintegration and was not to be tolerated and it was right to come down on it heavily whether it was of the overt or covert kind. (p. 96)

In this highly tautological and paratactic passage, Rushdie mocks the kind of reasoning or pseudoreasoning that the army uses to justify its violence. The repetition of words, the circularity of the sentences, and the mock-mathematical logic that Kachhawa invokes bespeak a corruption of language of exactly the sort that George Orwell warns against in "Politics and the English Language." Rushdie implies that fascism brings with it the decay of language itself.

The decay of language that Rushdie associates with the military aggression of the state contrasts sharply with the breakdown of language we see in the narrator's account of the army's destruction of Pachigam, and the ideal of Kashmiriyat that they have lived by and stand for. In the two pages where he recounts this cataclysm, Rushdie emphasizes the limits of the representational possibilities of language. The narrator first poses a series of questions: "What was that cry? Was it a man, a woman, an angel or a god who keened thus, who howled just so? Could any human voice make such a desolate noise?" (p. 308). He invokes the structuralist oppositions of man/woman and human/divine, questioning its intelligibility in terms of these linguistic structures. He then presents a series of measured, simple sentences as if to bring his attempt to find meaning back to the ground: "There was the earth and there were the planets. The earth was not a planet. The planets were the grabbers. They were called this because they could seize hold of the earth and bend its destiny to their will. The earth was never of their kind. The earth was the subject. The earth was the grabbee." Recalling the verbal gymnastics of General Kachhawa, these sentences convey an attempt to establish a linguistic paradigm that will be clear and precise, yet adequate to describing what has happened in the village. In the following paragraph, these sentences comprise the vehicles of an extended, complexly phrased metaphor: "Pachigam was the earth, the grabbee, helpless, and powerful uncaring planets stooped low, extending their celestial and merciless tentacles and grabbed." In a Blakean moment of sublime lyricism, Rushdie paradoxically uses a celestial metaphor to attempt to communicate once again the full horror of what has happened. This again is inadequate, the narrator implies, and the following paragraph consists of a series of very simple literal questions all beginning with "who": "Who lit that fire? Who burned that orchard? Who shot those brothers who laughed their whole lives long?" and so on, providing an inventory of specific acts of violence, and incrementally building an account of culpability. The mode in these lines is questioning, and speaks to the necessity of bearing witness in the event of a genocide; even though the narrator's testimony is necessarily partial and incomplete, it is vital.

This act of bearing witness to ethnic violence is one that we have seen in relation to Ondaatje's *Anil's Ghost*. Three final paragraphs follow this list of questions, each attempting to locate the village of Pachigam on official maps, in memory, and in the imagination, and all raising the ontological question of its existence. Deftly moving between linguistic registers, Rushdie probes the representational challenges, the ethical demands, and the ontological exigencies of chronicling genocide.

In his account of Pachigam, Rushdie represents Kashmir through the lens of bourgeois nationalism, as an organic community, along Leavisite lines. This notion of community breaks down and is replaced by a classic ethnic nationalism. But the novel does not only tell the story of Pachigam; as I have suggested, it begins in and returns at the end to Los Angeles, moves to Kashmir, but also traverses continental Europe and England. In *Shalimar the Clown*, Rushdie gives an allegorical cast to the main characters of the novel—Shalimar the Clown, Boonyi, Max, and India/Kashmira—but, unlike in his earlier national allegories such as *Midnight's Children* and *Shame*, he projects his characters' lives onto a global landscape.[8]

What kind of political and cultural imaginary, then, is asserted at the end of the novel? I want to suggest that in the final instance, Rushdie validates the deterritorialized, diasporic cultural nationalism of migrants. The Los Angeles of the novel is characterized as an urban landscape peopled by immigrants who live in a sort of limbo. As India's neighbor Olga Volga puts it, "I live today neither in this world nor the last, neither in America nor in Astrakhan. Also I would add neither in this world nor the next. A woman like me, she lives some place in between. Between the memories and the daily stuff. Between yesterday and tomorrow, in the country of lost happiness and peace, the place of mislaid calm." While a character such as Olga is tragic-comic, she is also heroic in her resilience. For Rushdie, I want to suggest, the most efficacious subject of this new political landscape is a cosmopolitan, postnational subject. I use the word *postnational* following Jurgen

Habermas, who argues for a nationalism that eschews ethnic and racial identification and is conceived purely in civic terms. And for Rushdie, the privileged space wherein to conceive such a subject is a space outside the nation, a space of diaspora or exile.

We see this privileging of cosmopolitanism clearly at the end of the novel. As the triangle between Max, Boonyi and Shalimar moves the story to its bloody end, another romance emerges—that between Max and Boonyi's daughter Kashmira and a young Kashmiri merchant who exports crafts. Kashmira and Yuvraj's relationship represents a transformed Kashmiriyat that is deterritorialized: the largely deracinated Kashmira lives in Los Angeles, a city of rootless people, and they maintain their ties across the globe. In the romance between these characters, Rushdie gestures toward diasporic sensibilities and location as an answer to a narrow ethnic or national chauvinism. Rushdie looks beyond the nation, and projects the ideal of Kashmiriyat across the globe.

In the narrative of India/Kashmira, Rushdie uses elements of the genre of crime thriller to explore Shalimar's murder of Max and his pursuit of Max's daughter, and the political and personal implications of this quest for vengeance. Unlike in *The Moor's Last Sigh*, where he attempts to probe the psyche of the fascist recruit, Shalimar joins a network of Islamic terrorists entirely for reasons of expediency. He is motivated neither by nationalist fervor nor by religious zeal; his single-minded quest is ultimately to avenge his betrayal by Boonyi and Max.

The last section of the novel, called "Kashmira," focuses on the trial, imprisonment, and escape of Shalimar the Clown, and who now stalks Max and Boonyi's daughter. This part of the novel witnesses the transformation of India into Kashmira, when she returns east, seeking to learn the truth of her mother's death. It is her words that convict Shalimar the Clown: "My mother died because that man, who also killed my father, cut off her beautiful head." Six years later, at the close of the novel, Kashmira, crack shot and expert archer, awaits Shalimar's arrival. Through this final confrontation, Rushdie asserts that it is a reborn, cosmopolitan, and deterritorialized Kashmir that will replace the wounded and monstrous Kashmir that Shalimar the Clown represents.

While Rushdie's vision of a transnational cosmopolitan identity that can transcend narrow ethnic particularism is appealing, it is problematic on two fronts. First, Rushdie does not address the phenomenon of the diasporic long-distance nationalism of, for instance, Hindutva organizations in the United States.[9] Rather, he characterizes the space beyond the nation as a space where a liberal cosmopolitanism will flourish.[10] Second, Rushdie's vision is predicated on the experience of a transnational bourgeoisie.[11] As I have argued in relation to Amitav Ghosh's *The Circle of Reason*, bourgeois and subaltern migrants have completely different trajectories and experiences.

"WE ARE THE PEOPLE YOU DO NOT SEE":
FREARS'S *DIRTY PRETTY THINGS*

Stephen Frears's 2002 film *Dirty Pretty Things* explores the predicament of a current generation of illegal immigrants in London who are crucial to its economy, but exist at the margins of civil society. Frears has visited the postcolonial landscape of London before in *My Beautiful Laundrette* (1985) and *Sammy and Rosie Get Laid* (1987), where the focus is on South Asians' negotiation of queer and immigrant identity against the backdrop of a rapacious, unevenly decaying Thatcherite metropolis. In *Dirty Pretty Things,* Frears uses the genre of thriller to expose the ugly underbelly of immigrant life in contemporary Britain. The kind of liberal cosmopolitanism that Rushdie validates may have some value as an aspirational end, but Frears's film reminds us that class divisions and nation-state borders pose an immense obstacle to actualizing cosmopolitanism on the ground.

Frears uses the genre of the thriller to reveal the predicament of illegal immigrants who have no recourse to the apparatus of the law and are consequently the most vulnerable victims of criminal intrigues; Empire marks out new domains of illegality, of exploitation—and of resilience. *Dirty Pretty Things* explores a seam of criminal intrigue in an expensive London hotel, serviced by an array of immigrants, including Nigerian exile Okwe (played by Chiwetel Ejiofor) and Turkish asylum seeker Senay (played by Audrey Tautou).

One morning, Okwe discovers while cleaning a room that a blockage in the lavatory has been caused by an excised human heart. We gradually discover with Okwe that the hotel is used to traffic the kidneys of immigrants who in exchange obtain fake or real passports and immigration papers. Senor Juan, the manager of the hotel, who runs this trade in immigrants' body parts, puts pressure on Okwe, who has been a doctor in Nigeria, to operate on hapless donors, but Okwe refuses. Senay finally agrees to trade her kidney to Senor Juan for a new passport—her passport to a new and legitimate life in New York. In an ironic twist that forms the dramatic climax of the film, Okwe, having recruited a gleeful Senor Juan to assist him in removing Senay's kidney in exchange for a passport, drugs the hotel manager and applies his scalpel to Senor Juan. He then hands over Senor Juan's kidney to a waiting middleman in exchange for a packet of money. Equipped with a new passport and this cash, Senay leaves for New York, and Okwe returns to his daughter in Nigeria. The scene of their departure from the airport is both tragic—they part as they acknowledge they love each other—as well as hopeful—each looks forward to the next journey. The film promises no easy resting place for subaltern migrants, only new horizons.

Frears presents a very different experiential geography of London than one gets from the eyes of the tourist or legitimate resident. We are given views of interiors rather than expansive vistas; and when we do see street life, it is that of markets and cheap corner shops. We see none of the familiar landmarks of the city. The upscale hotel is seen from the point of view of its staff, one of whom lives illicitly in its subterranean passages. Not only do immigrants see a different London; they are invisible to the mainstream of Londoners. When one of the traffickers in organs remarks that he has never seen Okwe before, the latter responds, "We are the people you do not see. We drive your cars and clean your rooms and suck your cocks." Indeed, the immigrants who are portrayed in the film are always engaged in menial work of one sort or another. The film brings home the point that the labor of immigrants is vital to Western economies, and particularly in so-called "global cities," as Saskia Sassen points out.[12] *Dirty Pretty Things* maps a social, economic, and experiential reterritorialization of the metropolis that is an essential aspect of Empire, and is profoundly exclusionary.

Frears's film is both a classic mystery and a narrative of social detection in that it suggests that corrupt individuals pose a threat to social order, and at the same time implies that this social order is itself problematic in being sustained by the labor of exploited immigrants whose existence it scarcely recognizes. As Senor Juan points out to Okwe, his scheme is one that makes everyone happy: the kidney donor gets a passport and a legal life, the recipient gets a new lease on life, and Senor Juan gets three thousand pounds. It is the social, economic, and political exclusion of immigrants that underpins this seemingly felicitous contract. Like the *homo sacer* whom Agamben discusses, the immigrant has a biological life but no political life. In the film, illegal immigrants gamble their bare lives in order to stake a claim to a life in the polis. A migrant may be killed but not sacrificed; though someone dies from a botched operation and is dismembered and flushed down the toilet, his death has no public or political repercussions whatsoever.

The terms in which Frears stages this social and political exclusion are unambiguous with regard to class and especially gender; women are particularly vulnerable to sexual exploitation. In one particularly grim scene, a South Asian sweatshop supervisor forces Senay, on the run from immigration officers and desperate for work, to fellate him, while claiming to make a concession to preserve her virginity. And Senay is finally asked to trade not only her kidney but also sex with Senor Juan to obtain a passport. She is willing to doubly commodify and abject her body in the hope of entering into a circuit of bourgeois migration, such is its allure and so dire are her circumstances. At the same time, Frears is somewhat ambiguous about the significance of race in the film. Senor Juan is ambiguously swarthy and speaks Spanish when he is drugged, and the man who demands oral sex of Senay is clearly South Asian. Immigrant entrepreneurs, whether white or not, are grossly rapacious in their dealings with the subaltern migrants who work for them. And we know nothing of the faceless elites who buy the organs. One might question the politics of this characterization of migrants, both prosperous and subaltern ones, as a "problem," and the film for a failure to indict the mainstream of British society. Frears's point, suggested by the title and by Okwe's words, is precisely that the good citizens of Britain are able to enjoy their pretty lives because of the invisible labor and moral compromises of the immigrants who launder their dirt.

Faced with bleak circumstances, the subaltern migrants in the film demonstrate forms of solidarity that help them navigate the bounded and policed spaces of the city and the nation-state. Shorn of family and nation, they forge ties of affiliation in their places of work and makeshift resting places. Okwe snatches spells of sleep first on Senay's sofa, then in a hospital morgue where his friend and chess partner, Guo Yi, works. He treats his fellow drivers and boss for a sexually transmitted infection, although he is not legally licensed to practice in Britain. The doorman Ivan helps Senay evade discovery by immigration officials even though he must cut short a sexual tryst to intercept her.

Senay, Okwe, and their fellow migrants are inhabitants of a shadowy netherworld where their humanity and friendship is all that staves off the abyss of deportation. It is the difficulty of this solidarity that gives the otherwise maudlin ending a certain poignancy and political significance. The last scene of *Dirty Pretty Things* takes place at the airport, where we have a rare view of open sky, signifying the opening up of Senay's and Okwe's horizons. As Senay moves away from Okwe and toward the departure lounge, she silently mouths to Okwe, "I love you." Okwe silently repeats her words as they exchange a parting look. Their love is romantic, but it is not the romance of a migrant bourgeoisie that will forge diasporic families. Rather, it is the fragile love of subaltern migrants, a love engendered by necessity but also freely given.

Experimentation with the genre of intrigue marks an attempt to think new narrative and conceptual possibilities and yet ground these in the contemporary political moment, rather than moving away from political "truths" as one sees in some kinds of postmodern writing, or conversely, resuscitating old Orientalist logic in the face of the anxieties of the New Empire. The fiction that I have examined poses the demand for new ways of reading. Both *Anil's Ghost* and *The God of Small Things* validate the small, the personal, and the interstitial, as we have seen. In each, the small is juxtaposed with the larger theaters of state drama. In *Anil's Ghost*, however, this privileging of the personal, which goes hand in hand with a turn to the aesthetic, constitutes a "disavowal of the historical and political coordinates of the violence on which the novel is premised."[13] Whereas turn-of-the-century colonial fiction of intrigue provides a characteristically modern aesthetic resolution to the literary and cultural problems explored in the novel, in that fragments are reconstituted into a coherent whole, *Anil's Ghost* provides a typically postmodern aesthetic "solution" to the narrative and cultural challenges that it sketches. This tension between the novel's foregrounding of political violence and the operation of the security state and its move to pose the aesthetic as a "solution" to this violence in fact replicates "the conflicting interpretive imperatives at the heart of detective and spy fiction: to expose the violence of state power, or to will it away, so to speak, by making it aesthetically and entertainingly intriguing." In the final analysis, I would argue, Ondaatje's privileging of the aesthetic is not a satisfactory resolution of the questions about political violence that the novel raises. At the same time, the novel provides a valuable model for postcolonial reading in its self-reflexive concern for the process of interpretation. It urges the merits of reading between the lines, of paying attention to traces and old scars, in order to recover and acknowledge other temporalities and other stories. For Roy, this alternative mode of reading makes possible an alternative mode of politics, a politics that honors the diminutive and the fragile. Frears's film also asks us to "read" the postcolonial landscape, taking as its focus the lives of subaltern migrants in the global city. It bears witness to the occluded violence that scars their lives, as well as to the cosmopolitan ties of friendship that their predicament fosters. The brave new postcolonial world that is represented in contemporary fiction and film demands new ways of thinking and seeing to engender new political possibilities.

Notes

INTRODUCTION

1. Bernard Cohn, *Colonialism and Its Forms of Knowledge* (Princeton: Princeton University Press, 1996), p. 5.

2. Michael Denning, in *Cover Stories*, citing Martin Green, sees the exhaustion of the adventure tale and the rise of the spy thriller as evidence of a crisis in imperialist culture. See Michael Denning, *Cover Stories: Narrative and Ideology in the British Spy Thriller* (London: Routledge and Kegan Paul, 1987), p. 39.

3. As Timothy Mitchell shows in his Foucauldian analysis of colonial Egypt, this concern with order marked the ways in which Britain "reformed" Egypt, focusing on military control, architectural and urban planning, schooling, policing, and sanitation. See Timothy Mitchell, *Colonizing Egypt* (Cambridge: Cambridge University Press, 1988).

4. Samuel Huntington's article in *Foreign Affairs*, "The Clash of Civilizations?" makes the argument that discourse about the instability of the South and the threat of, for instance, Islamic fundamentalism, has accelerated since the end of the Cold War. Samuel P. Huntington, "The Clash of Civilizations?," *Foreign Affairs* 72, no. 3 (Summer 1993): 22–49.

5. David Harvey, *The New Imperialism* (Oxford: Oxford University Press, 2003); Ellen Meiksins Wood, *The Empire of Capital* (New York: Verso, 2003).

6. Michael Hardt and Antonio Negri, *Empire* (Cambridge, Mass.: Harvard University Press, 2000).

7. Some other critics who emphasize the triumphalist elements in colonial discourse are Abdul JanMohamed, *Manichean Aesthetics: The Politics of Literature in Colonial Africa* (Amherst: University of Massachusetts Press, 1983), and Gauri Vishwanathan, *Masks of Conquest: Literary Study and British Rule in India* (New York: Columbia University Press, 1989).

8. Frederick Cooper and Ann L. Stoler, "Tensions of Empire: Colonial Control and Visions of Rule," *American Ethnologist* 16 (1989): 609.

9. For example, with the reassertion of British hegemony after the Revolt of 1857 came an increase in militarization. See David Arnold, "European Orphans and Vagrants in India in the Nineteenth Century," *Journal of Imperial and Commonwealth History* 7, no. 2 (January 1979): 104–27.

10. Other critics who do focus on anxieties in the literature of Empire are Nigel Leask, *British Romantic Writers and the East: Anxieties of Empire* (Cambridge: Cambridge University Press, 1992), and Ali Behdad, *Belated Travelers: Orientalism in the Age of Colonial Dissolution* (Durham: Duke University Press, 1994). Patrick Brantlinger points to the anxious elements in late Victorian imperial culture in *The Rule of Darkness: British Literature and Imperialism, 1830–1940* (Ithaca: Cornell University Press, 1988). Ann Stoler and Frederick Cooper argue for the salience of colonial tensions and contradictions, and Stoler demonstrates the complexities of imperial formations in her studies of Dutch rule in Indonesia. See Cooper and Stoler, "Tensions of Empire," pp. 609–21. Homi Bhabha and Sara Suleri are two postcolonial critics who accentuate and offer theoretical accounts of the troubled moments in colonial discourse. See Homi K. Bhabha, *The Location of Culture* (London: Routledge, 1990); Sara Suleri, *The Rhetoric of English India* (Chicago: University of Chicago Press, 1992).

11. Edward Said, *Culture and Imperialism* (New York: Vintage, 1994).

12. Partha Chatterjee, *The Nation and Its Fragments: Colonial and Postcolonial Histories* (Princeton: Princeton University Press, 1993).

13. Hamza Alavi, "The State in Post-Colonial Societies: Pakistan and Bangladesh," *New Left Review* 74 (July–August 1972): 59–80.

14. Scholars and critics have tended to conceive of British culture as self-constituting, as existing prior to and responding to Empire. This bias has been challenged by scholars such as Edward Said and Gauri Vishwanathan. In a recent essay, "Raymond Williams and British Colonialism," Vishwanathan argues against the "assumption that what makes an imperial culture possible is a fully formed national culture shaped by internal social developments." In the vein of her work, this essay constitutes an attempt to "reinsert 'imperial' into 'national' without reducing the two terms to a single category." I argue that the terrain of Empire was perceived as an unsafe "outside" that threatened to permeate and destabilize a national culture and that this sense shaped conceptions of Englishness.

15. Pierre Macherey, *A Theory of Literary Production*, trans. Geoffrey Wall (London: Routledge and Kegan Paul, 1978). For a helpful exposition of Macherey's thought see Tony Bennett, *Formalism and Marxism* (New York: Routledge, 1979, 2003), pp. 86–89.

16. Carlo Ginzburg, *Clues, Myths and the Historical Method*, trans. John and Anne Tedeschi (Baltimore: Johns Hopkins University Press, 1989), pp. 96–125.

17. Ginzburg, *Clues, Myths and Historical Method,* p. 123.

18. See the definition of *subaltern* in the *Oxford English Dictionary.*

19. This sense of the subaltern is, of course, implicit in Gramsci's usage, and accords with his theory of hegemony, which holds that subordinated groups, such as subalterns in the army, consent to being led.

20. Guha's note on the use of *subaltern* in his introduction to the Subaltern Studies project acknowledges the heterogeneous and discontinuous nature of subaltern experience: "The same class or element which was dominant in one area according to the definition given above, could be among the dominated in another. This could and did create many ambiguities and contradictions in attitudes and alliances, especially among the lowest strata of the rural gentry, impoverished landlords, rich peasants and upper-middle peasants, all of whom belonged, ideally speaking, to the category of 'people' or 'subaltern classes.'" It is hard to determine what criteria would "ideally" bespeak the subaltern status of the groups Guha enumerates: the rationale for his classification is not clear. However, what is helpful here is Guha's contention that subaltern consciousness is historically contingent and often contradictory, and that the allegiances and attitudes of both dominant and subordinate groups are multiple and shifting. See Ranajit Guha, "On Some Aspects of the Historiography of Colonial India," *Subaltern Studies I* (1982): 1-8

21. Fredric Jameson, *The Geopolitical Aesthetic* (Bloomington: Indiana University Press, 1992), p. 1.

22. Jameson, *The Geopolitical Aesthetic,* p. 3.

23. Jameson, *The Geopolitical Aesthetic,* p. 37.

24. Peter Stallybrass and Allon White, *The Politics and Poetics of Transgression* (Ithaca: Cornell University Press, 1986).

1. COLONIAL ANXIETIES AND THE FICTION OF INTRIGUE

1. Britain was one of a handful of Western powers that effectively dominated the world. "The economic and military supremacy of the capitalist countries had long been beyond serious challenge, but no systematic attempt to translate it into formal conquest, annexation and administration had been made between the end of the eighteenth and the last quarter of the nineteenth century. Between 1880 and 1914 it was made, and most of the world outside Europe and the Americas was formally partitioned into territories under the formal rule or informal political domination of a handful of states: mainly Great Britain, France, Germany, Italy, the Netherlands, Belgium, the USA and Japan." E. J. Hobsbawn, *The Age of Empire 1875–1914* (London: Cardinal, 1987), p. 57. In 1914, Europeans occupied or controlled 84.4 percent of the

world's land surface. D.K. Fieldhouse, *Economics and Empire 1830–1914* (London: Weidenfeld and Nicolson, 1973), p. 3.

2. J. R. Seeley argues in *The Expansion of England* that the very tendency of England's history is imperial expansion, although the significance of this fact, he claims, is often neglected. As he famously observes, "We seem, as it were, to have conquered and peopled half the world in a fit of absence of mind. While we were doing it, that is in the eighteenth century, we did not allow it to affect our imaginations or in any degree to change our ways of thinking; nor have we even now ceased to think of ourselves as simply a race inhabiting an Island off the northern coast of the Continent of Europe." John Robert Seeley, *The Expansion of England* (Chicago: University of Chicago Press, 1971), pp. 12–13. Robert MacDonald notes that Seeley put his intellectual weight as a historian behind his claims. "As a practitioner of the new 'scientific' history, Seeley provided imperialists with a more rational justification of empire, and carefully dissociating himself from stories of heroes and the excesses of the 'bombastic' school, announced that history was a moral force that, properly appreciated, would give the nation purpose and conviction." Robert MacDonald, *The Language of Empire: Myths and Metaphors of Popular Imperialsim, 1880–1918* (Manchester, Eng.: Manchester University Press), p. 55.

3. Antoinette Burton sums up the importance of imperial experience to British culture: "Even after the abolition of the slave trade, colonial peoples came to Britain, taking up permanent or semi-permanent residence; manufactures based on the raw materials produced from colonial plantations filled the marketplaces of the "nation of shopkeepers"; and displays of Britain's colonial experience and power were everywhere on offer in Britain at home—whether it was through the medium of political debates, missionary activities, consumer capitalism, novels, children's books, regional exhibitions, the decorative arts, or popular entertainments." Antoinette Burton, *At the Heart of the Empire: Indians and the Colonial Encounter in Late-Victorian Britain* (Berkeley: University of California Press, 1998), p. 7.

4. Denis Judd discusses the Golden Jubilee celebrations in *Empire: The British Imperial Experience, 1765 to the Present.* "For the populace as a whole, both rich and poor, the climax of the Jubilee celebrations was the great royal procession to and from St Paul's Cathedral on 22 June.... Over 50,000 troops in wave after glittering wave made up the procession: Hussars from Canada, the Royal Nigerian Constabulary, the Cape Mounted Rifles, the Trinidad Light Horse, Zaptiehs from Cyprus (whose fezzes caused some in the crowd to hiss them as Turkish interlopers), headhunters from the dyak police of Borneo, 'upstanding Sikhs, tiny little Malays, Chinese with the white basin

turned upside down on their heads,' Hausas from northern Nigeria, Jamaicans in white gaiters, and turbaned and bearded Lancers of the Indian Empire 'terrible and beautiful to behold.'" Denis Judd, *Empire: The British Imperial Experience, 1765 to the Present* (New York: Basic, 1996), p. 131.

5. See P. J. Marshall, ed., *Cambridge Illustrated History of the British Empire* (Cambridge: Cambridge University Press, 1996), p. 60. Although Marshall ascribes this view to Chamberlain here, it was widely held. One of the aims of imperial societies such as the Legion of Frontiersmen and the Imperial Federation League, to which Doyle belonged, was to rejuvenate English manhood. Also see John M. MacKenzie, *Propaganda and Empire: The Manipulation of British Public Opinion, 1880–1960* (Manchester, U.K.: Manchester University Press, 1985).

6. John MacKenzie describes the role of popular culture in shaping imperial sentiments in *Propaganda and Empire*. Imperialist sentiments were expressed and disseminated in "the theatre, the cinema, education, juvenile literature, imperial exhibitions, youth movements and a variety of imperial propaganda bodies between the mid-nineteenth and mid-twentieth centuries" (p. 11). As Bernard Porter observes, "the fundamental solidity of popular imperialism was reckoned to be amply demonstrated when the patriotic working classes took to streets during the Boer War—or seemed to. On the night of 18 May 1900 vast crowds all over Britain rowdily celebrated the relief of Mafeking after a seven-month siege. On innumerable occasions thereafter mobs attacked houses of suspected anti-imperialists and broke up 'pro-Boer' meetings." Bernard Porter suggests that although the working classes were probably less enthusiastic about imperialism than the middle classes, "imperialists were able to claim convincingly that they represented the mood of the nation." Bernard Porter, *The Lion's Share: A Short History of British Imperialism, 1850–1995* (London: Longman, 1996), p. 138.

7. Both Brantlinger and Arata discuss the pessimistic attitude towards Empire of late Victorian writers. Patrick Brantlinger, *Rule of Darkness: British Literature and Imperialism, 1830–1914* (Ithaca: Cornell University Press, 1988). Stephen Arata, *Fictions of Loss in the Victorian Fin de Siècle: Identity and Empire* (Cambridge: Cambridge University Press, 1996).

8. Joseph McLaughlin observes, "The Holmes corpus arises as a response to a new imperialist frame of mind, one becoming less confident about the spread of English, European, or Western culture from the civilized center toward the savage periphery and more anxious about the incursive flows that travel back to London through these imperial channels." Joseph McLaughlin, "Writing the Urban Jungle: Metropolis and Colonies in Conan Doyle, General Booth, Jack London, Conrad, and T. S. Eliot" (Ph.D. diss., Duke University, 1992), p. 36.

9. William Wilkie Collins's *The Moonstone*, one of the first detective stories written, is about the theft and violent recovery of a gem from India. Critics speculate that Thuggee plays a part in the plot of *The Mystery of Edwin Drood*. See, for example, Angus Wilson's introduction to the Penguin edition of *The Mystery of Edwin Drood*. In chapter 2, I refer to several Sherlock Holmes stories that have imperial subplots. William Wilkie Collins, *The Moonstone* (London: Fontana, 1972); Charles Dickens, *The Mystery of Edwin Drood* (London: Penguin, 1985).

10. As Edward Said suggests in *Culture and Imperialism*, colonial service and the pursuit of knowledge are yoked together in the stories of Doyle and Kipling. In their writing, "Colonial rule and crime detection almost gain the respectability and order of the classics or chemistry." Edward Said, *Culture and Imperialism* (New York: Random House, 1993), p. 152.

11. Sherlock Holmes is probably the most widely known literary character of all times, and many critics have remarked on his near-mythic quality. Jon Thompson attributes Doyle's success to "his refinement, following Poe, of a new, quintessentially popular genre, featuring a single detective hero within an open-ended, continuous form responsive to public fears, hopes, and anxieties" as well as to "a particular use of language, a realistic style notable for its vivid, precise detail." Jon Thompson, *Fiction, Crime, and Empire: Clues to Modernity and Postmodernism* (Urbana: University of Illinois Press, 1993), p. 61.

12. Critics who have interpreted detective fiction in relation to Empire are Stephen Arata, Joseph McLaughlin, and Jon Thompson. Arata, in his study of fin-de-siècle representation of degeneration and national decline in fiction, argues that "from the perspective of contemporary observers, jingoistic imperialism seems to have been called into existence by decadence, as a counterweight to aesthetic excess" (*Fictions of Loss,* p. 6). The ethos of masculinist adventure was a response to anxieties about enervation. In Arata's view, Sherlock Holmes is a vigorous and masterful character who allays anxieties of the period. He is typical of an emergent figure whom he calls "the 'professional reader,' the man (and it invariable is a man) whose training allows him to extract a useful meaning from a welter of often confusing signs" (p. 4). Arata argues, as I do, that "In private life Doyle passionately defended Britain's imperial prerogatives, yet the Holmes stories are notable for their ambivalence concerning matters of empire" (p. 140). He too suggests in his analysis that domestic and imperial social problems are "solved" after being reconstituted as hermeneutic problems (p. 147).

Joseph McLaughlin considers Doyle's detective stories as one of several turn-of-the-century attempts at "writing the urban jungle," that is, at representing an incursion of the colony into the metropolis. Holmes uses the skills of the frontiersman to secure the "urban jungle" in the face of these incursions: "First, the tales arouse a fear that the foreign has invaded and threatens to contaminate the homeland; then, they introduce the hero Holmes to protect England and regulate the insidious interlopers. Because Britain's empire was so large and diverse, "foreignness" in the Metropolis could take many forms—hence the proliferation of plots which follow this same basic structure. It was a politically useful formula which, for Doyle, worked to produce and reproduce definitions of Britain and its Others" ("Writing the Urban Jungle," p. 72).

Jon Thompson also interprets Holmes as a romantic hero, but one who yokes empiricism with imperialism, rather than bringing the skill of the frontiersman to solve threats to a metropole that is depicted as an imperial frontier. By empiricism, Thompson means not only the ostensibly detached, objective interpretation of phenomenon, but also "an ideology which by definition excludes qualitative, ethical, even aesthetic considerations in favour of abstract quantification, domination, and use of resources, human or natural, in the name of progress or profit" (*Fiction, Crime, and Empire*, p. 66). Doyle treats this ideology, one that derives from the Enlightenment and underpins capitalism, much more favorably than late Victorian writers such as Dickens, Hardy, and Eliot, who are more critical of the values of rationalized capitalism. "Through the figure of Sherlock Holmes, and through the empirical values he championed, Doyle's fiction ratified the principles and ideologies of an imperial, patriarchal Britain.... The values and methodologies of the Enlightenment provided the indispensable conceptual and material conditions for the organization of capitalism and, later, the British Empire; that knowledge created that form of power. Sherlock Holmes's knowledge, his ability to unravel the most intractable puzzles, gives him the power to penetrate the mysteries of London. The same form of knowledge that ultimately produced the empire also produced the figure of the empirical detective hero, Sherlock Holmes" (p. 76).

See also Caroline Reitz, *Detecting the Nation: Fictions of Detection and the Imperial Venture* (Columbus: Ohio State University Press, 2004), for a discussion of the imperial detective fiction of Doyle and Wilkie Collins.

13. The first spy thrillers are William Le Quex's *The Great War in England* in 1897 (1893); E. Phillips Oppenheim's *The Mysterious Mr. Sabin* (1898); Rudyard Kipling's *Kim* (1901); Erskine Childer's *The Riddle of the Sands* (1903); and Joseph Conrad's *The Secret Agent* (1907). See Michael Denning, *Cover Stories: Narrative and Ideology in the British Spy Thriller* (London: Routledge and Kegan Paul, 1987), p. 37.

14. Childer's *The Riddle of the Sands*, credited as one of the first spy novels, begins in London, as does Buchan's first spy novel, *The Thirty-Nine*

Steps. In both, Britain is threatened by the imperialist ambitions of Germany. Erskine Childers, *The Riddle of the Sands* (New York: Penguin, 1978).

15. See Michael Denning's cultural study of spy fiction, *Cover Stories*.

16. I discuss such criticism in this and subsequent chapters. It is beyond the scope of this project to review this criticism exhaustively, but the variety of interpretive lenses through which critics have viewed detective fiction is evident in even a cursory account. Tzvetan Todorov focuses on the structure of detective fiction, arguing that in its classic form it is comprised of two stories: the story of a crime, and the story of its detection, which is the subject of the narrative. In this, detective fiction differs from the thriller (and spy fiction would fall under this rubric), in which the narrative coincides with the action. Although Todorov concedes that genres are distinguished not only structurally, but historically by milieu and behavior, he is much more concerned with the former aspect. Tzvetan Todorov, "The Typology of Detective Fiction," in *The Poetics of Prose* (Ithaca: Cornell University Press, 1977). Christopher Clausen, by contrast, discusses the milieu and behavior typical of the Sherlock Holmes stories. He contends that these stories express Victorian concerns about social order, and portray crime and disorder as following from a failure of individual responsibility rather than of social institutions. Christopher Clausen, "Sherlock Holmes, Order, and the Late-Victorian Mind," in *The Moral Imagination: Essays on Literature and Ethics* (Iowa City: University of Iowa Press, 1986), pp. 51–86. Steven Knight argues that both form and content express "immanent social ideologies," and emphasizes the ideology of individualism united with that of scientific rationality in his interpretation of the Holmes stories. "The captivated readers had faith in modern systems of scientific and rational inquiry to order an uncertain and troubling world, but feeling they lacked these powers themselves they, like many audiences before them, needed a suitably equipped hero to mediate psychic projection.... Doyle's ability to popularize and naturalize rational individualism runs through his stories and is central to their success." Stephen Knight, *Form and Ideology in Crime Fiction* (Bloomington: Indiana University Press, 1980), pp. 67–68. Richard Alewyn places the detective story in the tradition of Romanticism: "Romanticism saw reality as the detective novel does: an everyday and peaceful deceptive surface, with abysses of mystery and danger underneath." He thus views the detective as a romantic artist, able because of his extraordinary talent and eccentric character to make sense of the bizarre. Richard Alewyn, "The Origin of the Detective Novel," in *The Poetics of Murder,* ed. Glenn W. Most and William W. Stowe (New York: Harcourt Brace Jovanovich, 1983), pp. 62–78. Catherine Belsey argues, like Knight, that the Sherlock Holmes stories do

argue the power of positivist science, but she sees the figuring of female sexuality in Doyle's detective fiction as an expression of the limits of Enlightenment rationality. Catherine Belsey, *Critical Practice* (London: Methuen, 1980). Psychoanalytic critics have drawn parallels between the interpretation of dreams and the solution of detective puzzle (Albert Hutter, "Dreams, Transformations and Literature: The Implications of Detective Fiction," in *The Poetics of Murder*), as well as between the apprehension of the "primal scene" and the detective story (Geraldine Pederson-Krag, "Detective Stories and the Primal Scene," in *The Poetics of Murder*).

17. McLaughlin notes with regard to Doyle's *The Sign of Four* that in addition to expressing concerns about the incursion of menacing foreign peoples and things, "[Small's] story raises another threat of invasion—that of the English colonist who has lived for years in the colony before returning to England. For many late Victorians, there is an anxiety about how foreign service has transformed the English-born into a group of strangers" ("Writing the Urban Jungle," p. 98). He points out that most of the colonizers in this novel are depicted as venal and corrupt.

18. Peter Brooks, *Reading for the Plot: Design and Intention in Narrative* (Cambridge, Mass.: Harvard University Press, 1992 c1984), p. 123.

19. Freud speaks in *Inhibitions, Symptoms and Anxiety* of the infant's anxiety about separation from the mother.

20. See especially Raymond Williams, *The Country and the City* (London: Chatto and Windus, 1973); Stuart Hall and Tony Bennett, eds., *Popular Fiction: Technology, Ideology, Production, Reading* (London: Routledge, 1990); and Denning, *Cover Stories*.

21. "In the late nineteenth century, a particularly strong relationship developed between education, the juvenile press and the imperial propagandists. Arguably the most fertile ground for their shared agenda was the 'story of Empire.' The high tide of British imperialism corresponded with the expansion of history in the school curriculum, the growth of respectable periodicals, and the perception of a need to reinvigorate public morale and national pride. At the same time the expansion of literacy and fears of degeneracy prompted a concern that conveying the imperial discourse to a wider audience was essential." Kathryn Castle, *Britannia's Children: Reading Colonialism Through Children's Books and Magazines* (Manchester, U.K.: Manchester University Press, 1996), p. 4.

22. See Beth Kalikoff, *Murder and Moral Decay in Victorian Popular Literature* (Ann Arbor: UMI Research Press, 1986), and Richard Altick, *Victorian Studies in Scarlet* (New York: Norton, 1970).

23. Thompson, *Fiction, Crime, and Empire*, p. 62.

24. David Spurr, *The Rhetoric of Empire: Colonial Discourse in Journalism, Travel Writing, and Imperial Administration* (Durham: Duke University Press, 1993), p. 3.

25. Robert MacDonald, *The Language of Empire: Myths and Metaphors of Popular Imperialism, 1880–1918* (Manchester, U.K.: Manchester University Press, 1994), p. 20.

26. MacDonald, *The Language of Empire*, p. 21.

27. MacDonald notes, "By the turn of the century the audience for imperial propaganda was widening: ethics originally taught to public school boys was now entering the classrooms of the board schools, and the language of the clubs and the messes was taken up by the popular press. Imperialism was still at heart the faith of the military caste of the upper middle classes, but in the hands of the media it was available to everyone." MacDonald, *The Language of Empire*, p. 205.

28. Spurr, in his study of the rhetoric of Empire in journalism, travel writing, and administration, discusses twelve modes of writing about colonized peoples: surveillance, appropriation, aestheticization, classification, debasement, negation, affirmation, idealization, insubstantialization, naturalization, eroticization, and resistance.

29. John Cawelti, "The Joys of Buchaneering," in *Essays in Honor of Russel B. Nye,* ed. Joseph Waldmeir and David Mead (East Lansing: Michigan State University Press, 1978), p. 13.

30. Homi Bhabha, *The Location of Culture* (New York: Routledge, 1994).

31. Bhabha, *The Location of Culture*, p. 66.

32. Bhabha, *The Location of Culture*, p. 67.

33. I discuss Kristeva's notion of the abject more fully in chapter 2. Julia Kristeva, *Powers of Horror: An Essay on Abjection* (New York: Columbia University Press, 1982).

34. See Thomas Richards, *The Imperial Archive: Knowledge and the Fantasy of Empire* (London: Verso, 1993).

35. Many critics point this out, including Thompson and Arata.

36. Williams alludes to an ideological function of the detective many scholars have identified, that of being an agent of rational, "scientific" method. He points to this aspect of detective fiction not as a general articulation of rationalist discourse, but specifically in the context of urban geography. The detective's method becomes a way of imaginatively managing the urban space of industrial capitalism. The detective is the "type" who "solves" the particular expression of a general problem. Later, in the early twentieth century, the detective novel became a more "closed" novel of manners. According to Williams, this literary representation of a totality of social relations underwent a

shift when the detective novel placed itself in the space of the country house novel, evolving into the bourgeois detective story. The country house came to be no longer the seat of landed gentry but a space cut off from the culture and history of a living community. In detective novels it became a place where a group of people with tenuous and unknown relationships met; a crime took place; and then the detective was able to decode the ephemeral relations of the group in an abstract way. No longer did one have a complex and contradictory totality; rather, the novelistic world became a highly stylized and seamless totality, welded together by the magical figure of the detective.

37. The twentieth-century detective novel is noted by many critics for its formal regularities and conventions: its country house setting, a cast of stereotypical characters, a detective who is the paragon of "reason" and the powers of logical detection and is frequently a bit eccentric, and a murderer who is often the least likely of all the characters to have done the deed. Such consistent features make it easily delineated as a genre. In the nineteenth century, the period of its emergence, the definition of detective fiction as a genre is more difficult. Raymond Williams suggests two ways of approaching the problem of defining genre. He writes, "For any adequate social theory, the question (of genre) is defined by the recognition of two facts: first, that there are clear social and historical relations between particular literary forms and the societies and periods in which they were originated and practiced; second, that there are undoubted continuities of literary forms through and beyond the societies and periods to which they have such relations." Lukacs's discussion of the nineteenth-century novel, the epic of bourgeois society, and its relation to a social "totality" provides one way to think of detective fiction and its configuration of social relations. Lukacs has argued that the nineteenth-century novel was, at least until 1848, able to grasp and present the complex and contradictory totality of bourgeois social relations. Georg Lukacs, *Essays On Realism* (Boston: MIT Press, 1981). The mystery/detective novel of the nineteenth century is not precisely a "bourgeois epic," but Lukacs's scheme is helpful in an assessment of the politics of this emergent form. The mystery/detective novel emerged as a relatively open form in which the thematics of Empire, of "rational" knowledge and the force of the unconscious, and of the alienation that attended industrialization, were all registered.

38. Even as the detective story rehearses the supremacy of order and reason, it reveals the cultural anxieties of Victorians. Stephen Knight emphasizes precisely this tendency of the Sherlock Holmes stories at once to voice these anxieties and to allay them by sleights of narrative. "It seems clear enough that the early Holmes stories realized fears the respectable audience had about

their own weaknesses. Selfishness, greed, sexual tensions might disrupt the carefully poised bourgeois nuclear family. But these forces are not explored fully, not brought out into an analytic, unmasking light. Rather they are appeased by a figure from the very socio-economic matrix that generated the disturbance in the first place, a helping hero who enacts a faith in rational individualism. So the ideological trick is turned, in a way so neat and so transitory that the fears remain and need to be assuaged again, and again—as each monthly issue appears." Knight, "The Case of the Great Detective," in *Critical Essays on Sir Arthur Conan Doyle,* ed. Harold Orel (New York: G. K. Hall, 1992), p. 64.

39. Stephen Knight interprets the character of Sherlock Holmes along similar lines in *Form and Ideology.*

40. Arthur Conan Doyle, "The Adventure of the Sussex Vampire," in *Sherlock Holmes: The Complete Novels and Stories,* ed. Loren D. Estleman (New York: Bantam, 1986), vol. 2, p. 535. This edition will be referred to as *Complete Sherlock Holmes.*

41. See Thomas, *The Imperial Archive.*

42. See Theodor Adorno, "Culture and Administration," trans. Wes Blomster, *Telos* 35 (Summer 1978): 93–111.

43. Steven Marcus has discussed the parallels between Holmes and Freud. The psychoanalyst, like the detective, attempts to plumb a deeper reality by interpreting minute details, traces of psychic events.

44. Denning, *Cover Stories,* p. 46.

45. Allan Hepburn, *Intrigue: Espionage and Culture* (New Haven: Yale University Press, 2005), p. 42.

46. Hepburn, *Intrigue,* p. 52.

47. John Buchan, *The Four Adventures of Richard Hannay* (Boston: David R. Goodine, 1988), p. 19.

48. Buchan, *The Four Adventures of Richard Hannay,* p. 74.

2. IMPERIAL INTRIGUE IN AN ENGLISH COUNTRY HOUSE

1. William Wilkie Collins, *The Moonstone,* 2nd ed. (Oxford: Oxford University Press, 1999).

2. Ronald Thomas, "Wilkie Collins and the Sensation Novel," *Columbia History of the British Novel,* ed. John Richetti et al. (New York: Columbia University Press, 1994), pp. 500–1.

3. Lillian Nayder, "Robinson Crusoe and Friday in Victorian Britain: 'Discipline,' 'Dialogue,' and Collins's Critique of Empire in *The Moonstone,*" *Dickens Studies Annual* 21 (1992): 213–31.

4. Ronald Thomas, "Minding the Body Politic: The Romance of Science and the Revision of History in Victorian Detective Fiction," *Victorian Literature and Culture* 19 (1991): 233–54.

5. Ian Duncan, "*The Moonstone*, the Victorian Novel, and Imperialist Panic," *Modern Language Quarterly* 55, no. 3 (1994): 297–319.

6. Tamar Heller, "Blank Spaces: Ideological Tensions and the Detective Work of *The Moonstone*," in *Wilkie Collins*, ed. Lyn Pykett (New York: St. Martin's, 1998).

7. Jenny Sharpe, *Allegories of Empire: The Figure of Women in the Colonial Text* (Minneapolis: University of Minnesota Press, 1993). In a brilliant exposition of the treatment of gender in colonial fiction, Sharpe shows how the trope of the Englishwoman as victim of sexual violence functioned discursively.

8. Chris GoGwilt, "The Victorian Blot: Wilkie Collins, *The Moonstone*, and the Concept of Culture," chapter 2 of *The Fiction of Geopolitics: Afterimages of Culture from Wilkie Collins to Hitchcock* (Stanford: Stanford University Press, 2000).

9. Michel Foucault, *Discipline and Punish: The Birth of the Prison* (New York: Vintage, 1979).

10. David A. Miller, *The Novel and the Police* (Berkeley: University of California Press, 1988).

11. David Arnold, "The Colonial Prison," *Subaltern Studies*, vol. 8, ed. David Arnold and David Hardiman (New Delhi: Oxford University Press, 1994), pp. 148–87. In many of the stories of Empire that I examine, disciplinary power fails to operate—either it has broken down, or it has never gained a hold. Here one does not have docile, normal bodies that fit smoothly and obligingly into the productive and reproductive economy of the metropolis. The detective and the spy penetrate to the dark spaces of Empire, illuminating and bringing order to them.

12. The "Thugs" were a confraternity who roved India from the fourteenth to the nineteenth century, practicing ritual murder as part of their worship of the goddess Kali. Between 1831 and 1837, Lord Bentinck's appointee Captain William Sleeman mounted an aggressive campaign against Thuggee, rounding up over three thousand men, and effectively suppressing the cult. See *Encyclopædia Britannica Online*, s.v. "thug," http://www.britannica.com/eb/article-9072311/thug. Also see S. Shankar's discussion of colonial representations of thuggee in *Textual Traffic: Colonialism, Modernity and the Economy of the Text* (Albany: State University of New York Press, 2001). I use the word *fable* to emphasize that, as Shankar argues, the "facts" about thuggee were circulated in the writings of colonial administrators in such a way that they came to be given the status of truth. Also, an interpretive framework

of "fanaticism" was imposed on killings in which ritual elements may have played an unremarkable part. Shankar presents a credible interpretation of the killings as subaltern acts of resistance.

13. Edward Said found this pattern of representation to be characteristic of Victorian writing and explores it in relation to *Mansfield Park* in *Culture and Imperialism* (New York: Vintage, 1993).

14. John M. MacKenzie, *Propaganda and Empire: The Manipulation of British Public Opinion, 1880–1960* (Manchester, U.K.: Manchester University Press, 1985). Other serials of this genre include *Boys of England, Union Jack, Sons of Britannia, The Young Briton, The Young Englishman, Boys of Empire*, and *Captain*.

15. Kirsten Drotner discusses Victorian children's magazines and their readership in *English Children and Their Magazines 1751–1945* (New Haven: Yale University Press, 1988). For a discussion of the shaping of imperial sensibilities through journalism and textbooks, see Kathryn Castle, *Britannia's Children: Reading Colonialism Through Children's Books and Magazines* (Manchester, U.K.: Manchester University Press, 1996).

16. See Peter Haining, Introduction, *The Final Adventures of Sherlock Holmes,* by Sir Arthur Conan Doyle (London: Warner, 1993), p. 13.

17. Perhaps this sense of unruliness is especially pronounced because Doyle, writing during a period of rapid imperial expansion, implicitly raises the question of how newly conquered territories are to be assimilated into the Empire.

18. "Uncle Jeremy's Household" indicates the limits of educational efforts. SeeGauri Vishwanathan, *Masks of Conquest: Literary Study and British Rule in India* (New York: Columbia University Press, 1989); J. A. Mangan, "Noble Specimens of Manhood: Schoolboy Literature and the Creation of a Colonial Chivalric Code," in *Imperialism and Juvenile Literature*, ed. Jeffrey Richards (Manchester, U.K.: Manchester University Press, 1989).

19. Antoinette Burton, *At the Heart of the Empire: Indians and the Colonial Encounter in Late-Victorian Britain* (Berkeley: University of California Press, 1988), p. 6.

20. Rozina Visram, *Ayahs, Lascars, and Princes: Indians in Britain 1700–1947* (London: Pluto, 1986).

21. Tzvetan Todorov, "The Typology of Detective Fiction," in *The Poetics of Prose* (Ithaca: Cornell University Press, 1977).

22. Bernard McGrane's account of the four historically distinct constructions of the Other in Europe may be overly schematic and simplistic, but it illuminates the various ways of understanding Miss Warrender's alterity. In ancient and medieval texts and maps, peoples on the margins of Europe were

represented as monsters. This iconography gave way in the Renaissance to a perception of non-Europeans chiefly as non-Christians, and as putative subjects of conversion. During the Enlightenment, as the power of Christianity diminished and Reason became the dominant value, the Other was viewed as ignorant and erroneous. In both the Renaissance and Enlightenment, non-European peoples were seen not as essentially different but rather as devoid of or deficient in the values of the metropole. This attitude shifted in the nineteenth century as a consequence of evolutionary thinking and scientific racism to a view of other peoples as qualitatively various and as different from Europeans. Bernard McGrane, *Beyond Anthropology: Society and the Other* (New York: Columbia University Press, 1989).

23. The *Oxford English Dictionary* defines *ethnography* as "the scientific description of nations or races of men, with their customs, habits, and points of difference." As a quotation by RECLUS in the 1878 *Encyclopaedia Britannica* indicates, "Ethnography embraces the descriptive details, and ethnology the rational exposition of the human aggregates and organizations." I use the word *ethnology* in my discussion because it is used by one of the characters; clearly, the story demonstrates the preoccupations of ethnography as well.

24. Edward B. Tyler, "Primitive Culture," in *High Points in Anthropology,* 2nd ed., ed. Paul Bohannan and Mark Glazer (New York: Knopf, 1988).

25. Chris GoGwilt, in *The Fiction of Geopolitics: Afterimages of Culture from Wilkie Collins to Hitchcock* (Stanford: Stanford University Press, 2000), argues that turn-of-the-century fiction articulates the relationship between geography and world politics.

26. Arthur Conan Doyle, "The Mystery of Uncle Jeremy's Household," in *The Final Adventures of Sherlock Holmes,* ed. Peter Hainig (London: Warner, 1993), p. 47. Subsequent page references will be given parenthetically in the text.

27. In his essay "Governmentality," Foucault defines the term in the following way:

> 1. The ensemble formed by the institutions, procedures, analyses and reflections, the calculations, and the tactics that allow the exercise of this very specific albeit complex form of power, which has as its target population, as its principal form of knowledge political economy, and as its essential technical means apparatuses of security.
>
> 2. The tendency which, over a long period and throughout the West, has steadily led towards the pre-eminence over all other forms (sovereignty, discipline, etc.) of this type of power which may be termed government, resulting, on the one hand, in the formation of a

whole series of specific governmental apparatuses, and, on the other, in the development of a whole complex of saviors.

> 3. The process, or rather the result of the process, through which the state of justice of the Middle Ages, transformed into the administrative state during the fifteenth and sixteenth centuries, gradually becomes "governmentalized."

See Graham Burchell, Colin Gordon, and Peter Miller, ed., *The Foucault Effect: Studies in Governmentality: With Two Lectures by and an Interview With Michel Foucault* (Chicago: University of Chicago Press, 1991), pp. 102–13.

28. David Scott, *Refashioning Futures: Criticism After Postcoloniality* (Princeton: Princeton University Press, 1999).

29. Talal Asad, *Anthropology and the Colonial Encounter* (New York: Humanities, 1973).

30. Peter Pels provides an excellent review of scholarship on the topic in "The Anthropology of Colonialism: Culture, History, and the Emergence of Western Governmentality," *Annual Review of Anthropology* 26 (1997): 163–83.

31. Peter Pels and Oscar Salemink, eds., *Colonial Subjects: Essays on the Practical History of Anthropology* (Ann Arbor: University of Michigan Press, 1999). See especially the essays by Pels, Raheja, and Dirks.

32. Pels and Salemink, "Introduction: Locating the Colonial Subjects of Anthropology," in *Colonial Subjects,* pp. 26, 28.

33. In *Dominance Without Hegemony: History and Power in Colonial India* (Cambridge, Mass.: Harvard University Press, 1997), Ranajit Guha argues that contrary to the processes of hegemony that obtained in the West, colonial rule was exercised by domination and not consent.

34. A character such as Miss Warrender would have had real-life counterparts in the expatriate colonials who for one reason or another could be found at "the heart of the Empire," to borrow from the title of Antoinette Burton's book on the experience of Indians in late Victorian England. In *At the Heart of the Empire*, Burton suggests that "either because they were part of permanent communities with long histories and traditions in the British Isles, or because they were travelers or temporary residents in various metropoles and regions throughout the United Kingdom, a variety of colonial 'Others' circulated at the very heart of the British Empire before the twentieth century" (p. 6).

35. Ann Stoler, *Race and the Education of Desire: Foucault's History of Sexuality and the Colonial Order of Things* (Durham: Duke University Press, 1995).

36. In *Camera Indica: The Social Life of Indian Photographs* (Chicago: University of Chicago Press, 1998), Christopher Pinney discusses the use of

photographic documentation in some of the ethnographies of India in the late nineteenth and early twentieth centuries.

37. Edgar Thurston, *Castes and Tribes of Southern India* (Madras: Government Press, 1909).

38. See Patrick Brantlinger, *Rule of Darkness: British Literature and Imperialism, 1830–1914* (Ithaca: Cornell University Press, 1988), pp. 199–224.

39. Ranajit Guha, in his essay "The Prose of Counterinsurgency," argues that historical writing tended to invalidate the political agency of the insurgent. His essay is discussed in a later chapter of this book more fully. Ranajit Guha, "The Prose of Counterinsurgency," in *Selected Subaltern Studies*, ed. Ranajit Guha and Gayatri Chakravorty Spivak (New York: Oxford University Press, 1988), pp. 45–84.

40. In "The Case of the Great Detective," Knight interprets the Sherlock Holmes stories as above all concerned with the alleviation of Victorian social and cultural anxieties by a ratification of the principles of scientific knowledge and order.

41. See Joseph McLaughlin's Writing the Urban Jungle: Reading Empire in London from Doyle to Eliot (Charlottesville: University Press of Virginia, 2000), which includes a chapter on *A Study in Scarlet* and another on *The Sign of Four*.

42. See Richard Thomas, *The Imperial Archive: Knowledge and the Fantasy of Empire* (London: Verso, 1993).

43. See Miles Taylor, "Imperium et Libertas? Rethinking the Radical Critique of Imperialism During the Nineteenth Century," *Journal of Imperial and Commonwealth History* 19, no.1 (1991): 1–23.

3. SHERLOCK HOLMES AND "THE CESSPOOL OF EMPIRE": THE RETURN OF THE REPRESSED

1. Joseph McLaughlin also notes that colonials—and he includes the colonizers and the colonized—are represented as suspect characters in Doyle's stories. However, McLaughlin does not attempt to make sense of the pairing of desirable and undesirable colonials, as I do. Rather, he argues that the "foreign" is figured as dangerous and corrosive altogether. Joseph McLaughlin, *Writing the Urban Jungle: Reading Empire in London from Doyle to Eliot* (Charlottesville: University Press of Virginia, 2000).

2. Critic Nigel Leask focuses on anxieties in earlier literature of Empire in *British Romantic Writers and the East: Anxieties of Empire* (Cambridge: Cambridge University Press, 1992). Ali Behdad, in *Belated Travelers: Orientalism in the Age of Colonial Dissolution* (Durham: Duke University Press,

1994), and Patrick Brantlinger, in *The Rule of Darkness* (Ithaca: Cornell University Press, 1988), point to the anxious elements in late Victorian imperial culture. Homi K. Bhabha and Sara Suleri are two postcolonial critics who accentuate and offer theoretical accounts of the troubled moments in colonial discourse. Homi K. Bhabha, *The Location of Culture* (London: Routledge, 1990); Sara Suleri, *The Rhetoric of English India* (Chicago: University of Chicago Press, 1992). Ann Stoler and Frederick Cooper argue for the salience of colonial tensions and contradictions, and Stoler demonstrates the complexities of imperial formations in her studies of Dutch rule in Indonesia. Frederick Cooper and Ann L. Stoler, "Tensions of Empire: Colonial Control and Visions of Rule," *American Ethnologist* 16 (1989): 609–21. Stoler in particular discusses the category of "poor whites" in her work on Indonesia.

3. Pierre Nordon, *Conan Doyle: A Biography* (New York: Holt, Rinehart and Winston, 1966); Julian Symons, *Conan Doyle* (London: Whizzard, 1979); Arthur Conan Doyle, *Memories and Adventures* (Oxford: Oxford University Press, 1989).

4. See Arthur Conan Doyle, *A Study in Scarlet,* in *Sherlock Holmes: The Complete Novels and Stories,* 2 vols., ed. Loren D. Estleman (New York: Bantam, 1986), vol. 2. This collection is referred to below as *Complete Sherlock Holmes.*

5. Doyle, *Memories and Adventures,* pp. 128–29.

6. Doyle, *Memories and Adventures*, p. 142.

7. Arthur Conan Doyle, *The Great Boer War* (New York: McClure, Phillips, 1901).

8. Doyle, *Memories and Adventures*, p. 192.

9. Doyle, *Complete Sherlock Holmes,*vol. 2, p. 492.

10. Doyle, *Complete Sherlock Holmes,* vol. 2, pp. 499–500.

11. John Comaroff discusses the representation of Boers by English missionaries at the turn of the century in "Images of Empire, Contests of Conscience: Models of Colonial Domination in South Africa," *American Ethnologist* 16 (November 1989): 661–85.

12. Doyle, *The Great Boer War,* p. 185.

13. Doyle, *Complete Sherlock Holmes,* vol. 1, p. 511.

14. Doyle, *Complete Sherlock Holmes,* vol. 1, p. 526.

15. See Percival Spear, *Master of Bengal: Clive and His India* (London: Thames and Hudson, 1975), p. 105.

16. Quoted in Spear, *Master of Bengal,*p. 119.

17. Quoted in Carol Lansbury, *Arcady in Australia: The Evocation of Australia in Nineteenth-Century English Literature* (Carlton, Australia: Melbourne University Press, 1970), pp. 54–55.

18. Doyle, *Complete Sherlock Holmes*, vol. 1, p. 511.

19. Tom Nairn, *The Break-Up of Britain: Crisis and Neo-Nationalism* (London: New Left, 1977).

20. E.M. Forster, in *Howard's End* (London: Arnold, 1973), was again to treat the country house as a signifier of a stable and traditional order in a world of flux. Once again, it is Empire that is behind the Wilcox's money, which enables them to maintain Howard's End.

21. Doyle, *Complete Sherlock Holmes*, vol. 1, pp. 511–12.

22. Stephen Arata says of such characters in Doyle's fiction, "What we can call the 'maimed colonial' is in fact a recurring figure in the Holmes stories. Returned from the outposts of Empire, these men become the locus of crime and corruption." See Stephen Arata, *Fictions of Loss in the Victorian Fin De Siècle: Identity and Empire* (Cambridge: Cambridge University Press, 1996), p. 140.

23. See David Arnold, "European Orphans and Vagrants in India in the Nineteenth Century," *Journal of Imperial and Commonwealth History* 7, no. 2 (January 1979): 104–27; Ann Stoler, "Rethinking Colonial Categories: European Communities and the Boundaries of Rule," *Comparative Studies in Society and History* 1 (1989): 134–61; Waltraud Ernst, "The European Insane in British India, 1800–1858: A Case Study in Psychiatry and Colonial Rule," in *Imperial Medicine and Indigenous Societies* (Manchester, U.K.: Manchester University Press, 1988), pp. 27–44; and Kenneth Ballhatchet, *Race, Sex, and Class Under the Raj: Imperial Attitudes and Policies and Their Critics 1793–1905* (New York: St. Martin's, 1980), all of whom discuss "poor whites" in the colonies.

24. Henry Mayhew, *London Labour and the London Poor*, selections, ed. Victor Neuberg (London: Penguin, 1985).

25. Whether these poor whites could be denominated an "imperial lumpenproletariat" with any degree of precision is a question that requires further consideration. Marx famously described the "lumpenproletariat" in *The Eighteenth Brumaire of Louis Napoleon Bonaparte*, giving the term its peculiar connotation. Karl Marx, *The Eighteenth Brumaire of Louis Bonaparte*, in *Karl Marx: Surveys From Exile*, ed. David Fernbach, trans. Ben Fowkes (New York: Vintage, 1974), p. 197. As Peter Stallybrass argues, the "lumpenproletariat" appears as a category in Marx's analysis precisely when class interest can no longer explain the character of a political formation. Peter Stallybrass, "Marx and Heterogeneity: Rethinking the Lumpenproletariat," *Representations* 31 (Summer 1990): 69–95. The "indeterminate fragmented mass" that Marx describes so fancifully is united solely by Bonaparte's efforts, and not because of any essential commonalty. In his analysis, Marx enunciates a vision of class struggle that is situated squarely in the realm of the political—the field

of an articulation of interests—rather than within the framework of a scientific teleology. To take Stallybrass's argument a step further, this aggregate of marginal characters is constituted as a "class," as subjects of representation, *in the name of Empire*. Marx does not develop this point in any detail himself, but he suggests that Bonaparte assumes in a farcical fashion Napoleon's imperial mantle. Bonaparte is able to rally this class that has no name in the name of a category, empire/nation, that has no class, or ostensibly transcends class. The "poor whites" of the British Empire were articulated in similar fashion to the project of imperial domination. No simple model of representation can explain support by poor whites for imperialism, for class interest is confused if not disorganized by imperial interest and ideology formulated in racial terms.

26. See especially the work of Ann Stoler and David Arnold.

27. See David Arnold, "White Colonization and Labour in Nineteenth Century India," *Journal of Imperial and Commonwealth History* 2, no. 2 (January 1983): 139.

28. See Arnold, "European Orphans and Vagrants," p. 104.

29. Quoted in Ballhatchet, *Race, Sex, and Class Under the Raj,* p. 125.

30. Quoted in Arnold, "European Orphans and Vagrants," p. 120.

31. See Arnold, "European Orphans and Vagrants," p. 124.

32. See Rudyard Kipling's *Kim* (London: Penguin, 1987), and "The Man Who Would Be King," in *Selected Stories*, ed. Andrew Rutherford (London: Penguin, 1987), pp. 111–40.

33. See material on the Vagrancy Committee in the Maharashtra State Archives in Bombay.

34. Ann Stoler describes the efforts of white plantation employees in colonial Sumatra to organize themselves into a union at the turn of the century. Ann Stoler, "Rethinking Colonial Categories," *Comparative Studies in Society and History* 1 (1989): 142.

35. Stoler points out that the nexus of "racist ideology, fear of the Other, preoccupation with white prestige, and obsession with protecting white women from sexual assault by Asian and black males were not simply justifications for continued European rule and white supremacy. They were part of a critical class-based logic, statements not only about indigenous subversives, but directives aimed at dissenting European underlings in the colonies—and part of the apparatus that kept potentially subversive white colonials in line." See Stoler, "Rethinking Colonial Categories," p. 138.

36. Louis Althusser, in *Lenin and Philosophy,* trans. Ben Brewster (New York: Monthly Review, 1971), uses the word *interpellate* to describe the process by which subjects are induced by ideology to take up certain positions and behaviors.

37. See J. Edward Chamberlain and Sander Gilman, eds., *Degeneration: The Dark Side of Progress* (New York: Columbia University Press, 1985).

38. Sigmund Freud, "The Uncanny," in *The Standard Edition of the Complete Psychological Works of Sigmund Freud,* vol. 17, ed. James Strachey, trans. Alix Strachey (New York: Norton, 1959).

39. Freud, "The Uncanny," p. 234.

40. Julia Kristeva, *Powers of Horror: An Essay on Abjection* (New York: Columbia University Press, 1982), p. 4.

41. Both Julia Kristeva and Mary Douglas focus on the body to elaborate upon the concepts of abjection and pollution, but they do so in profoundly different ways. For Kristeva, the abject body is somehow "there," outside the symbolic order, but disturbingly proximate to it. Douglas regards the body as an entity that is always *socially* invested with significance. According to her, because the body has a complex structure, and because it is so fundamental to individual experience, its boundaries and lines serve as a powerful symbolic map for charting social experience. Yet for her, these parameters are culturally infused with meaning: no condition or element of the body is "dirty" as such. While the body is not the only important signifier of social meaning, Kristeva's and Douglas's accounts suggest that it is a particularly powerful one. More interestingly, they depart from conventional readings of the body as a model of social harmony and emphasize that it can signify danger and horror. See Kristeva, *Powers of Horror,* and Mary Douglas, *Purity and Danger: An Analysis of the Concepts of Pollution and Taboo* (London: Routledge, 1966).

42. Kaja Silverman's extremely suggestive discussion in *Male Subjectivity at the Margins* provides a way of accounting for the return and doubling of abject colonials in Doyle's stories. She interprets the appearance in post World War Two American films of psychically and physically damaged male characters as a cultural expression of the marking of male subjectivity by a historical trauma. See chapter 2 of Kaja Silverman, *Male Subjectivity at the Margins* (New York: Routledge, 1992).

43. Doyle, *Complete Sherlock Holmes,* vol. 1, pp. 3–4.

44. Joseph McLaughlin, in *Writing the Urban Jungle,* provides an excellent discussion of Watson's predicament and of the characterization of London as an "urban jungle."

4. THE FICTION OF COUNTERINSURGENCY

1. Ranajit Guha, "The Prose of Counter-Insurgency," in *Subaltern Studies,* vol. 2 (Delhi: Oxford University Press, 1983), p. 2.

2. Guha, "The Prose of Counter-Insurgency," p. 77.

3. Guha writes, "There is nothing that historiography can do to eliminate such distortion altogether, for the latter is built into its optics. What it can do, however, is to acknowledge such distortion as parametric—as a datum which determines the form of the exercise itself, and to stop pretending that it can fully grasp a past consciousness and reconstitute it. Then and only then might the distance between the latter and the historian's perception of it be reduced significantly enough to amount to a close approximation which is the best one could hope for." Guha, "The Prose of Counter-Insurgency," p. 33.

4. See Patrick Brantlinger's chapter on Mutiny fiction in *Rule of Darkness: British Literature and Imperialism, 1830–1914* (Ithaca: Cornell University Press, 1988).

5. I draw again on Brantlinger's analysis.

6. Arthur Conan Doyle, *The Sign of Four,* in *Sherlock Holmes: The Complete Novels and Stories,* ed. Loren D. Estleman (New York: Bantam, 1986), vol. 1, pp. 187–88.

7. Stephen Arata suggests that the ideological tensions that Doyle must bridge make the stories ambivalent in their representation of Empire: "Jonathan Small's (actions) serve to illuminate the criminality of Empire itself.... As Small's experience underscores, the problems of Empire prove to be endemic to the system and not the result of the immoral acts of individuals. In Doyle's empire, everyone is a thief and noone can easily be blamed." Stephen Arata, *Fictions of Loss in the Victorian Fin de Siècle: Identity and Empire* (Cambridge: Cambridge University Press, 1996), pp. 139–41.

8. Diana Loxley, *Problematic Shores: The Literature of Islands* (New York: St. Martin's, 1990), p. 132.

9. Charles Dickens, "The Perils of Certain English Prisoners," in *The Works of Charles Dickens: National Library Edition,* 22 vols. (New York: Bigelow, Brown, n.d.), vol. 13, pp. 207–68.

10. See Brantlinger's chapter on "The Well at Cawnpore" in *Rule of Darkness* for a discussion of how the story rewrites the events of the Indian Mutiny.

11. Dickens, "The Perils of Certain English Prisoners," p. 241.

12. Lillian Nayder presents a nuanced analysis of the class politics of this story in "Class Consciousness and the Indian Mutiny in Dickens's 'The Perils of Certain English Prisoners,'" *Studies in English Literature 1500–1900* 32, no. 4 (Autumn 1992): 689–705.

13. Because the narrative is presented as a reminiscence recorded by Davis's "mistress," the reader wonders whether Davis has actually been able to traverse the barriers of class and marry Marion. The narrative suggests this

possibility only to deny it; at the time the tale is told by the illiterate Davis and transcribed by Marion, she has indeed married Captain Carton, has joined the ranks of the aristocracy, and has rescued "her poor, old, faithful, humble soldier," now presumably her devoted servant. The story thus effects a dual closure: the poor white marine accepts his subordinate position, and the single Englishwoman is circumscribed within the bounds of marriage to a member of the officer class.

14. Frantz Fanon, *The Wretched of the Earth* (New York: Grove, Weidenfeld, 1963), pp. 129, 136.

15. The views of the imperial lumpenproletariat with regard to their marginal position in European enclaves is difficult to ascertain from historical records. David Arnold argues that while members of this class enjoyed a certain prestige and privilege by virtue of their race, they resented their degraded status vis-à-vis affluent Europeans: "there was a general feeling that they were ill-used by the colonial rulers without being able to protest effectively." Arnold, "European Orphans and Vagrants in India in the Nineteenth Century," *Journal of Imperial and Commonwealth History* 7, no. 2 (January 1979): 105.

16. Arthur Conan Doyle, "The Green Flag," in *The Green Flag, and Other Stories of War and Sport* (London: Smith, Elder, 1900), pp. 1–24.

17. James Lawrence describes the incident in *The Rise and Fall of the British Empire* (London: Little, Brown, 1994).

18. Pierre Nordon describes this episode in *Conan Doyle: A Biography* (New York: Holt, Rinehart and Winston, 1966). He cites a letter from Conan Doyle to his mother Mary Doyle in which Conan Doyle describes a visit to a village that had been invaded by the Mahdi or "Dervishes" (pp. 41–42).

19. Doyle, "The Green Flag," p. 1.

20. Doyle came to support home rule some years later.

21. Doyle, "The Green Flag," pp. 17–18.

22. Doyle, "The Green Flag," p. 20.

23. In *Inventing Ireland*, Declan Kiberd recounts the mutiny in 1920 of the Connaught Rangers, a company of Irish soldiers in the Punjab. His narrative is uncannily reminiscent of Doyle's "The Green Flag": "News of the burning of rural Irish towns and proscription of hurling matches prompted one soldier, Joe Hawes, to tell his comrades that 'we were doing in India what the British forces were doing in Ireland.' Refusing to parade, about thirty members of 'C' company shouted 'up the rebels!' Their tearful commanding officer reminded them in an eloquent speech of their great reputation, won over thirty-three years; but Hawes stepped forward to say that while those exploits had been done for England, this latest one for Ireland would be counted the greatest

honour of all. They said they would shoulder no more 'until all British troops had been removed from Ireland' and they flew a makeshift tricolour." The smartof cultural and political oppression is pitted here against the imperatives of military discipline. In this context, "Irishness" is redefined by the rebels themselves as a disciplined solidarity with the oppressed Indians. This incident made explicit the paradoxical nature of Irish service in the British Empire. It occurred after the writing of "The Green Flag," and so the latter is not precisely "about" the mutiny of the Connaught Rangers, but the sentiments expressed by Joe Hawes were very much in the air. The correlation between Irish and Indian subjection was made orally and in print by Eamon de Valera, Michael Davitt, Sean T. O'Kelly, Aurobindo Ghosh, and Mahatma Gandhi, among others. Such prominent figures as Margaret Noble, Annie Besant, and Dadabhai Naoroji embodied this connection, crossing continents and taking up the nationalist causes of India and Ireland respectively. See Kiberd, as well as Howard Brasted and G. Douds, "Passages to India: Peripatetic MPs on the Grand Indian Tour 1870–1940," *South Asia* 2 (1979): 91–111.

24. Doyle, "The Green Flag," pp. 3–4.

25. The same bifurcation of allegiances could be found in any context where natives were recruited into the imperial army.

26. The Fenian bombings of the 1880s exemplify a threat posed by colonial subjects, in this instance the Irish, to law and order within England. These events spawned journalistic representations of Irishmen as dangerous terrorists who could strike at the very heart of the nation. See Phillip Thurmond Smith, *Policing Victorian London: Political Policing, Public Order, and the London Metropolitan Police* (Westport, Conn.: Greenwood, 1985); and L. Perry Curtis, *Apes and Angels: The Irishman in Victorian Caricature* (Washington, D.C.: Smithsonian Institution Press, 1971).

27. Doyle was in fact president of the Boy's Empire League, which was founded at the time of the war, and enjoyed a membership of 10,000. See John Mackenzie, *Propaganda and Empire: The Manipulation of British Public Opinion, 1880–1960* (Manchester, U.K.: Manchester University Press, 1985).

28. Doyle, *The Great Boer War* (New York: McClure, Phillips, 1901), p. 62.

29. Doyle, *The Great Boer War*, p. 439.

30. As Renan pointed out a century ago, however, none of these adequately explains what makes a nation. Ernest Renan, "What Is A Nation?" in *Nation and Narration,* ed. Homi Bhabha (New York: Routledge, 1990), pp. 8–22.

31. See Curtis, *Apes and Angels,* as well as Carlyle's essay "Occasional Discourse On the Nigger Question," in *Thomas Carlyle, The Nigger Ques-*

tion; John Stuart Mill, The Negro Question, ed. Eugene August (New York: Appleton Century Crofts, 1971).

32. Boaventura de Sousa Santos, *Toward A New Common Sense: Law, Science and Politics in the Paradigmatic Transition* (New York: Routledge, 1995).

33. According to Santos, it is characteristic of modernity that two tendencies are harmonized, the "pillar of regulation"—actuated by the principles of the state, market, and community—and the "pillar of emancipation"—realized through the aesthetic-expressive rationality of the arts and literature, the cognitive-instrumental rationality of science and technology, and the moral-practical rationality of ethics and the rule of law. Santos asserts that at present the aesthetic-expressive rationality of the arts and literature holds out the most promise for emancipatory social praxis. An examination of the fiction of imperial intrigue, however, suggests that that is equally subject to a regulatory tendency overdetermined by the cognitive-instrumental rationality of science and technology and the moral-practical rationality of ethics and the rule of law. Santos, *Toward a New Common Sense*, p. 23.

34. W. H. Auden, "The Guilty Vicarage," in *The Dyer's Hand and Other Essays* (New York: Vintage, 1989), p. 158.

35. Christopher Clausen, "Sherlock Holmes, Order, and the Late-Victorian Mind," in *The Moral Imagination: Essays on Literature and Ethics* (Iowa City: University of Iowa Press, 1986), p 65.

36. Jon Thompson, *Fiction, Crime, and Empire* (Urbana: University of Illinois Press, 1993), pp. 60–79.

37. I have drawn on Janet Adam Smith, *John Buchan: A Biography* (London: Rupert Hart-Davis, 1966), and Smith's shorter account, *John Buchan and His World* (New York: Scribner, 1979).

38. Juanita Kruse, *John Buchan and the Idea of Empire: Popular Literature and Political Ideology* (Lewiston, U.K.: Edwin Mellen, 1989), p. 44.

39. Robin Winks, in his excellent introduction to *The Four Adventures of Richard Hannay*, notes that Buchan is in the literary lineage of Robert Louis Stevenson and Arthur Conan Doyle rather than Henty and Haggard, with whom he is often compared. Robin Winks, Introduction to *The Four Adventures of Richard Hannay*, by John Buchan (Boston: David R. Goodine, 1988).

40. Winks counters the charges often made against Buchan that he was anti-Semitic, racist, and jingoistic, arguing that it is a mistake to identify Buchan with his fictional character Hannay, and moreover, that Buchan presents even-handed, if not favorable portraits of Africans and of Germans in his novels and his history of World War I. Other critics such as Tim Couzens argue more convincingly that Buchan's use of racial stereotypes was fairly derogatory.

41. Kruse, *John Buchan and the Idea of Empire,* pp. 53–54.

42. Kruse, *John Buchan and the Idea of Empire,* p. 29.

43. John Buchan, *Prester John* (Oxford: Oxford University Press, 1994), p. 81. Subsequent page references are given parenthetically in the text.

44. T. J. Couzens, "'The Old Africa of a Boy's Dream'—Towards Interpreting Buchan's Prester John," *English Studies in Africa* 24, no. 1 (1981): 1–24. Couzens examines the stereotypes and prejudices in *Prester John,* arguing that black characters are represented as lazy and deceitful, incapable of abstract thought, eat "beastly food," and so on. The import of Buchan's strategies of representation is that Africans are not fit for self-rule. "Buchan's ideal is a kind of Club, a small elite ruling over Uncle Tom's Lodge, fine imperialists, who are more guided by patriotism than private gain, and who are above all good administrators" (p. 18). Couzens provides an interesting account of some of the local rebellions that Buchan must have known about.

45. David Daniell, Introduction to *Prester John,* by John Buchan (Oxford: Oxford UP, 1994), p. xi.

46. Craig Smith makes the interesting argument about the struggle between British imperialism and African resistance, that "they collide and collaborate in the dynamic of homoerotic desire and homosexual panic which structure the formation of maleness in *Prester John.*" Craig Smith, "Every Man Must Kill the Thing He Loves: Empire, Homoerotics, and Nationalism in John Buchan's *Prester John,*" *Novel* 28, no. 2 (Winter 1995): 173–200.

47. David A. Miller, *The Novel and the Police* (Berkeley: University of California Press, 1988) p.2 ; Mark Seltzer, *Henry James and the Art of Power* (Ithaca: Cornell University Press, 1984) p. 19.

48. Edward Said, Introduction to *Kim,* by Rudyard Kipling (London: Penguin, 1987), pp. 7–46.

49. T. J. Couzens, "'The Old Africa of a Boy's Dream': Towards Interpreting Buchan's *Prester John,*" *English Studies in Africa* 24, no. 1 (1981): 1–24

50. Once again we see the usefulness of an "imperial archive." See Richard Thomas, *The Imperial Archive: Knowledge and the Fantasy of Empire* (London: Verso, 1993).

51. Jonathan Swift, *Gulliver's Travels,* ed. Robert A. Greenberg (New York: Norton, 1970).

52. Joyce Cary, *The African Witch* (New York: Harper and Row, 1963).

53. John Buchan, *A History of the Great War* (London: Thomas Nelson, 1921), pp. 316–17.

54. Buchan, *Greenmantle,* in *The Four Adventures of Richard Hannay,* p. 183. Subsequent page references are given parenthetically in the text.

55. Winks suggests that this was a capacity required of a historian, and of anyone who sought to know himself. Winks, Introduction to *The Four Adventures of Richard Hannay*, p. xx.

56. Janet Adam Smith writes, "With the real Aubrey Herbert in view—an aristocrat who looked like a tramp, a master of languages, a champion of minority views, a hopelessly short-sighted man who had got himself into the B.E.F in 1914 by putting on khaki and joining a battalion of the Irish Guards as it swung out of Wellington Barracks, who was invited by the Albanians of America to command the regiment they had raised—Buchan had little need to invent." Smith, *John Buchan*, p. 265.

57. Cawelti, "The Joys of Buchaneering," in *Essays in Honor of Russel B. Nye*, ed. Joseph Waldmeir and David Mead (East Lansing: Michigan State University Press, 1978), p. 27.

58. See Marianna Torgovnick, *Gone Primitive: Savage Intellects, Modern Lives* (Chicago: University of Chicago Press, 1990).

59. Cawelti suggests that "one of the key features of this fascination [with entering the identity of colonized people] is a lurking fear that these peoples' traditional cultures which have been destroyed or transformed by imperialistic power, possessed some deeper insight into the meaning of life." Cawelti, "The Joys of Buchaneering," p. 28.

60. Winks, Introduction to *The Four Adventures of Richard Hannay*, p. xvi.

5. INTERMEZZO: POSTCOLONIAL MODERNITY AND THE FICTION OF INTRIGUE

1. I have taken this discussion from my entry on "Decolonization" in Prem Poddar and David Johnson, eds., *A Historical Companion to Postcolonial Literatures in English* (Edinburgh: University of Edinburgh Press, 2005).

2. Dilip Parameshwar Gaonkar, "On Alternative Modernities," *Public Culture* 11, no.1 (Spring 1999): 1–18. Gaonkar offers a helpful resume of the Western bourgeoisie's understanding of the cognitive and social dimensions of what it means to become modern: "On this account, the cognitive transformations include or imply the growth of scientific consciousness, the development of a secular outlook, the doctrine of progress, the primacy of instrumental rationality, the fact-value split, individualistic understandings of the self, contractualist understandings of society, and so on; the social transformations refer to the emergence and institutionalization of market-driven industrial economies, bureaucratically administered states, modes of popular government, rule of law, mass-media, and increased mobility,

literacy, and urbanization. These two sets of transformations are seen as constituting a relatively harmonious and healthy package. This is the idealized self-understanding of bourgeois modernity historically associated with the development of capitalism in the West that called into existence not only a distinctive mode of production but also a new type of subject—an agent who was set free from constraints imposed by tradition to pursue its own private ends and whose actions were at once motivated by acquisitiveness and regulated by '(this) worldly asceticism.'" According to Gaonkar, there were a range of critical responses to this vision of modernity, including those of the Romantics and the avant-garde.

3. Karl Marx, "The Future Results of the British Rule in India," in *Surveys from Exile,* ed. David Fernbach (New York: Vintage, 1974).

4. Marx, "The Future Results," pp. 306–7.

5. Mahatma Gandhi, "Hind Swaraj, Modern Civilization, and Moral Progress," in *The Moral and Political Writings of Mahatma Gandhi,* ed. Raghavan Iyer (Oxford: Clarendon Press, 1986), pp. 199–264.

6. Jawaharlal Nehru, *The Discovery of India* (Oxford: Oxford University Press, 1989), chapter 2.

7. See Isaiah Berlin, "The Counter-Enlightenment," in *The Proper Study of Mankind: An Anthology of Essays,* ed. Henry Hardy and Roger Hausheer (New York: Farrar, Straus and Giroux, 1998).

8. Theodor Adorno and Max Horkheimer, *Dialectic of Enlightenment* (New York: Continuum, 1972).

9. Adorno and Horkheimer, *Dialectic of Enlightenment,* p. 39.

10. Robert Young, *White Mythologies: Writing History and the West* (New York: Routledge, 1990), p. 11.

11. Young, *White Mythologies,* p. 8.

12. Dipesh Chakrabarty, "Radical Histories and Question of Enlightenment Rationalism: Some Recent Critiques of Subaltern Studies," *Economic and Political Weekly,* April 8, 1995, pp. 751–59.

13. Dipesh Chakrabarty, "Marx after Marxism: History, Subalternity and Difference," *Meanjin* 52 (1977): 421–34.

14. Partha Chatterjee, *Nationalist Thought and the Colonial World: A Derivative Discourse?* (Minneapolis: University of Minnesota Press, 1986), pp. 14–15.

15. Dipesh Chakrabarty, *Provincializing Europe: Postcolonial Thought and Historical Difference* (Princeton: Princeton University Press, 2000), p. 6.

16. According to Chakrabarty, historicism, the premise that peoples occupied different positions on a universal path of progress, has relegated postcolonial subjects to a state of deferred arrival, or of belatedness.

17. Charles Tilly, "Epilogue: Now Where?" in *State/Culture: State-Formation After the Cultural Turn,* ed. George Steinmetz (Ithaca: Cornell University Press, 1999), pp. 407–19.

18. Pierre Bourdieu, "Rethinking the State: Genesis and Structure of the Bureaucratic Field," in Steinmetz, ed., *State/Culture,* p. 56.

19. Thomas Blom Hansen and Finn Stepputat, *States of Imagination: Ethnographic Explorations of the Postcolonial State* (Durham: Duke University Press, 2001), p. 4. This collection of essays, as well as the edited volume *State/Culture: State Formation After the Cultural Turn,* exemplifies the new mode of ethnographic and cultural analysis of the state.

20. Hamza Alavi, "The State in Post-Colonial Societies: Pakistan and Bangladesh," *New Left Review* 74 (July–August 1972): 59-80.

21. Mahmood Mamdani, "The Politics of Civil Society and Ethnicity: Reflections on an African Dilemma," *Political Power and Social Theory* 12 (1998): 221.

22. Partha Chatterjee, "Beyond the Nation? Or Within?" *Social Text* 16, no. 3.56 (Fall 1998): 57–69.

23. Hansen and Stepputat, Introduction to *States of Imagination.*

24. Timothy Mitchell, "Society, Economy and the State Effect," in Steinmetz, ed., *State/Culture,* p. 88.

25. James Scott, *Seeing Like a State: How Certain Schemes to Improve the Human Condition Have Failed* (New Haven: Yale University Press, 1998).

26. Scott, *Seeing Like a State,* p. 77.

27. Alejandro Colas, *Empire* (Cambridge: Polity, 2007). See especially the final chapter, "After Empire," for a discussion of these debates.

28. Colas, *Empire,* p. 168.

29. Michael Hardt and Antonio Negri, Preface to *Empire* (Cambridge, Mass.: Harvard University Press, 2000), p. xiii.

30. Arjun Appadurai, "Global Ethnoscapes," in *Modernity at Large: Cultural Dimensions of Globalization* (Minneapolis: University of Minnesota Press, 1996).

31. Les Roberts et al., "Mortality Before and After the 2003 Invasion of Iraq: Cluster Sample Survey," *Lancet,* November 20–26, 2004, pp. 1857–64.

32. Gilbert Burnham et al., "Mortality After the 2003 Invasion of Iraq: A Cross-Sectional Cluster Sample Survey," *Lancet,* October 21–27, 2006, pp. 1421–28.

33. Robert Cooper, "The New Liberal Imperialism," *Observer,* April 7, 2002, http://observer.guardian.co.uk/worldview/story/0,11581,680095,00.html.

6. POLICE AND POSTCOLONIAL RATIONALITY IN
AMITAV GHOSH'S *THE CIRCLE OF REASON*

1. Amitav Ghosh, *The Circle of Reason* (London: Abacus, 1987).

2. Robert Young examines the ways in which colonial discourse analysis enables the "questioning of Western knowledge's categories and assumptions" in *White Mythologies: Writing History and the West* (New York: Routledge, 1990), p. 11.

3. "Police fiction" is a translation of the French *roman policier*. Here I use the term to include detective and spy fiction, fiction of intrigue that celebrated the capacities of the rational sleuth to deduce the particulars of a crime or mystery. See Julian Symons's *Bloody Murder: From the Detective Story to the Crime Novel: A History* (London: Faber and Faber, 1972), for an excellent overview of the genre.

4. Fredric Jameson, "Totality as Conspiracy," in *The Geopolitical Aesthetic: Cinema and Space in the World System* (Bloomington: Indiana University Press, 1992), p. 39.

5. Arundhati Roy, *The God of Small Things* (New York: Random House, 1997).

6. Michael Ondaatje, *Anil's Ghost* (New York: Knopf, 2000).

7. Rohinton Mistry, *Such a Long Journey* (New York: Vintage, 1992).

8. *The Shadow Lines* interweaves in a seamless narrative the stories of two families whose lives straddle London and Calcutta. Amitav Ghosh, *The Shadow Lines* (New York: Penguin, 1991). *In an Antique Land* is the account of an anthropologist who traces the connection between an Egyptian and an Indian merchant. Amitav Ghosh, *In An Antique Land: History in the Guise of a Traveler's Tale* (New York: Vintage, 1992).

9. Like *The Shadow Lines* and *In an Antique Land*, it raises, albeit less explicitly, questions of migrancy, cultural displacement, and ambivalence.

10. See Pasquale Pasquino, "Theatrum Politicum: The Genealogy of Capital-Police and the State of Prosperity," in *The Foucault Effect,* ed. Graham Burchell, Colin Gordon, and Peter Miller (Chicago: University of Chicago Press, 1991), pp. 105–18.

11. One could argue that in Europe the narrowing of the purview of "police" occurs as a disciplinary society evolves and the processes whereby power regulates the population become more and more invisible. As what Foucault calls disciplinary power establishes its sway, only overt threats to order appear as a matter of "police." At this point the regulation of the population becomes so naturalized that it no longer appears to be a concerted project of enlightened, rational administration.

12. See, for example, David Arnold's study of colonial medicine in India. David Arnold, *Colonizing the Body: State Medicine and Epidemic Disease in Nineteenth-Century India* (Berkeley: University of California Press, 1993). See also Lata Mani, "Contentious Traditions: The Debate on Sati in Colonial India," in *Recasting Women: Essays in Indian Colonial History*, ed. Kumkum Sangari and Sudesh Vaid (New Brunswick, N.J.: Rutgers University Press, 1989).

13. Ranajit Guha, "Dominance Without Hegemony and Its Historiography," *Subaltern Studies*, vol. 6, ed. Ranajit Guha (Delhi: Oxford University Press, 1994), pp. 210–309. Hegemony, in Gramsci's formulation, implies domination and consent; according to Guha, there was little consent on the part of colonized peoples.

14. See Foucault's essay "Governmentality," in Burchell, Gordon, and Miller, eds., *The Foucault Effect*, pp. 87–104.

15. The breaking off of East Pakistan from West Pakistan and the formation of Bangladesh occurred in 1971, with the military intervention of India on the side of Bangladesh.

16. See Gopal Balakrishnan, "The National Imagination," *New Left Review* 211 (1995): 16–69; Partha Chatterjee, *The Nation and Its Fragments: Colonial and Postcolonial Histories* (Princeton: Princeton University Press, 1993); Benedict Anderson, *Imagined Communities* (London: Verso, 1983).

17. Chatterjee, *The Nation and Its Fragments*, p. 204. Chatterjee also makes the interesting point that the postcolonial state attempted to distinguish itself by embracing a project of national planning and "development" (p. 4).

18. Kant argues for the free exercise of reason, but paradoxically, inverts the distinction between its private and public use so that free thought does not pose a political challenge to the rule of Frederick the Great. Immanuel Kant, "An Answer to the Question: What is Enlightenment?" in *What is Enlightenment? Eighteenth-Century Answers and Twentieth-Century Questions,* ed. James Schmidt (Berkeley: University of California Press, 1996).

19. See Ranajit Guha, *A Rule of Property for Bengal: An Essay on the Idea of Permanent Settlement* (Paris: Mouton, 1963); Nicholas Dirks, "Casts of Mind," *Representations* 37 (Winter 1992): 56–78; and "Reading Culture: Anthropology and the Textualization of India," in *Culture/Contexture: Explorations in Anthropology and Literary Studies,* ed. E. Valentine Daniel and Jeffrey M. Peck (Berkeley: University of California Press, 1996), pp. 275–95; David Arnold, ed., *Imperial Medicine and Indigenous Societies* (Manchester, U.K.: Manchester University Press, 1988); Lati Mani, "Contentious Traditions: The Debate on Sati in Colonial India," in Sangari and Vaid, eds., *Recasting Women;* David Arnold, "Bureaucratic Recruitment and Subordination

in Colonial India: The Madras Constabulary, 1859–1947," in Guha, ed., *Subaltern Studies*, vol. 6, pp. 1–53.

20. Gayatri Spivak, *A Critique of Postcolonial Reason* (Cambridge, Mass.: Harvard University Press, 1999), p. 7.

21. Karl Marx, "The Future Results of the British Rule in India," in *Surveys from Exile,* ed. David Fernbach (New York: Vintage, 1974). Marx views the transformation of Indian society as brutal but necessary.

22. Dipesh Chakrabarty explores the contradictory relationship of India to the West in his articles and in *Provincializing Europe: Postcolonial Thought and Historical Difference* (Princeton: Princeton University Press, 2000).

23. See Antonio Gramsci, "State and Civil Society," in *Selections from the Prison Notebooks,* ed. Quintin Hoare and Geoffrey Nowell Smith (New York: International, 1971).

24. See Tapan Raychaudhari, "The Pursuit of Reason in Nineteenth Century Bengal," in *Mind, Body, and Society: Life and Mentality in Colonial Bengal,* ed. Rajat Kanta Ray (Calcutta: Oxford University Press, 1995).

25. Raychaudhari, "The Pursuit of Reason," p. 47.

26. See Sumit Sarkar, "Rammohun Roy and the Break with the Past," in *A Critique of Colonial India* (Calcutta: Papyrus, 1985), p. 10.

27. Sarkar, "Rammohun Roy," p. 8.

28. Sarkar argues for the need to analyze links between British free traders, often the bearers of utilitarian ideas, and men like Rammohun who combined zamindari with moneylending and business enterprise.

29. I am indebted to Nick Dirks for this point.

30. Ghosh, *The Circle of Reason,* p. 83. Subsequent page references will be given parenthetically in the text.

31. In this novel, as in *The Shadow Lines,* East Bengal is represented as a place of backwardness and irrationality. The prevalence of this trope suggests that the postcolonial nation produces its own quasi-Orientalist discourse of otherness. I am grateful to Dipesh Chakrabarty for pointing this out.

32. See Jawaharlal Nehru, *The Discovery of India,* ed. Robert Crane (Garden City, N.Y.: Anchor, 1960), p. 17.

33. In celebrating the hand loom, the novel invokes a Gandhian vision of national progress in counterpoint to the Nehruvian one.

34. Partha Chatterjee, *Nationalist Thought and the Colonial World: A Derivative Discourse* (Minneapolis: University of Minnesota Press, 1986).

35. Salman Rushdie, *Shame* (New York: Henry Holt, 1983).

36. Robin Cohen, *Global Diasporas: An Introduction* (Seattle: University of Washington Press, 1997).

37. See Nancy Armstrong, *Desire and Domestic Fiction* (New York: Oxford University Press, 1987); and Partha Chatterjee, "The Nation and Its Women," in *The Nation and Its Fragments.*

38. See Anannya Bhattacharjee, "The Habit of Ex-Nomination: Nation, Woman, and the Indian Immigrant Bourgeoisie," *Public Culture* 5, no. 1 (Fall 1992): 19–43. Bhattacharjee describes what happens when this figure is exposed as a fiction by the fact of domestic violence.

39. See Gerd Hardach, Dieter Karras, and Ben Fine, *A Short History of Socialist Economic Thought* (New York, St. Martin's, 1979), pp. 9–12.

40. See Ranajit Guha, "The Prose of Counter-Insurgency," in *Selected Subaltern Studies*, ed. Ranajit Guha and Gayatri Chakravorty Spivak (New York: Oxford University Press, 1988).

41. This is the declared agenda of the journal *Public Culture*. See http://www.publicculture.org/about.

42. See Arjun Appadurai, *Modernity at Large: Cultural Dimensions of Globalization* (Minneapolis: University of Minnesota Press, 1996).

43. See Dilip Parameshwar Gaonkar, "On Alternative Modernities," *Public Culture* 11, no. 1 (Spring 1999): 1–18.

44. Chatterjee's analysis of "civil society" sheds light on this complicity. Chatterjee argues that in formerly colonized countries, civil society—by which he means "those characteristic institutions of modern associational life originating in Western societies that are based on equality, autonomy, freedom of entry and exit, contract, deliberative decision making, recognized rights and duties"—is the preserve of a small segment of "citizens," whereas the legal-bureaucratic apparatus of the state reaches a "population." See Partha Chatterjee, "Beyond the Nation? Or Within?" *Social Text* 16, no. 3.56 (Fall 1998): 57–69.

7. "DEEP IN BLOOD": ROY, RUSHDIE, AND THE
REPRESENTATION OF STATE VIOLENCE IN INDIA

1. Benedict Anderson, *Imagined Communities: Reflections on the Origin and Spread of Nationalism* (London: Verso, 1983, 1991).

2. Fredric Jameson, *The Geopolitical Aesthetic* (Bloomington: Indiana University Press, 1992), p. 39.

3. Arundhati Roy, *The God of Small Things* (New York: Harper Perennial, 1998), p. 289. Subsequent page references will be given parenthetially in the text.

4. Aijaz Ahmad, "Reading Arundhati Roy Politically," *Frontline* 14, no. 15 (July 26–August 8, 1997): 103–8.

5. James Scott, *Seeing Like a State: How Certain Schemes to Improve the Human Condition Have Failed* (New Haven: Yale University Press, 1998), p. 22.

6. Tzvetan Todorov, "The Typology of Detective Fiction," in *The Poetics of Prose* (Ithaca: Cornell University Press, 1978).

7. Arundhati Roy, "The Greater Common Good," http://www.narmada.org/gcg/gcg.html.

8. Salman Rushdie, *The Moor's Last Sigh* (New York: Vintage, 1997), p. 59. Subsequent page references will be given parenthetically in the text.

9. Salman Rushdie, "India at Five-O," *Time*, August 11, 1997, pp. 40–42.

10. Thomas Blom Hansen, "Governance and State Mythologies in Mumbai," in *States of Imagination: Ethnographic Explorations of the Postcolonial State,* ed. Thomas Blom Hansen and Finn Stepputat (Durham: Duke University Press, 2001), pp. 221–22.

11. Hansen, "Governance and State Mythologies in Mumbai," p. 235.

12. Hansen identifies varying attitudes toward the state during this politically fraught period. Justice Srikrishna, whose own stature and careful stewardship of the commission lent the state credibility, takes the view that the state is a higher moral entity that requires of its representatives exemplary ethical behavior and "a sense of duty toward the nation" (Hansen, "Governance and State Mythologies in Mumbai," p. 242). This notion is a crucial founding myth of the nation, and Hansen argues that the commission served the purpose of revivifying it. The rhetoric around the Terrorism and Disruptive Activities Act investigation and prosecutions represented the state as operating secretly and ubiquitously to save the nation from its enemies: this is the discourse of the "security state" that has become dominant globally, especially after the September 11, 2001, attacks in New York and Washington, D.C. Finally, Hansen argues, ordinary people held a much more pragmatic view of the state: "the commission of inquiry appeared as a somewhat inconsequential sign of 'the state,' a manifestation of authority that simply was expected to restore the public order that had been upset by the riots" (p. 243). We see in these different perceptions of the state a belief in its ethical imperative, a view of a practical mode of operation, and an acceptance of its opaqueness.

13. Arjun Appadurai, "Dead Certainty: Ethnic Violence in the Era of Globalization," *Public Culture* 10, no. 2 (Winter 1998): 225–47.

14. Homi Bhabha, "On Minorities: Cultural Rights," *Radical Philosophy* 100 (March/April 2000): 3.

15. See Arundhati Roy, *The Cost of Living* (New York: Modern Library, 1999).

16. Duncan Ivison, *Postcolonial Liberalism* (Cambridge: Cambridge University Press, 2002), p. 33.

17. Arundhati Roy, "Let Us Hope the Darkness Has Passed: India's Real and Virtual Worlds Have Collided in a Humiliation of Power," *Guardian*, May 14, 2004, http://www.guardian.co.uk/comment/story/0,3604,1216532,00.html.

18. Salman Rushdie, "India's New Era." *Washington Post*, May 14, 2004, p. A25.

19. Roy, "Let Us Hope the Darkness Has Passed."

8. "THE UNHISTORICAL DEAD": VIOLENCE, HISTORY, AND NARRATIVE IN MICHAEL ONDAATJE'S *ANIL'S GHOST*

1. I want to thank Amy Carroll for pointing this out, and for helping me think through this essay.

2. Gyanendra Pandey, "In Defence of the Fragment: Writing About Hindu-Muslim Riots in India Today," *Representations* 37 (Winter 1992): 27–55.

3. David Scott, *Refashioning Futures: Criticism After Postcoloniality* (Princeton: Princeton University Press, 1999), p. 4.

4. Stanley Tambiah, *Ethnic Fratricide and the Dismantling of Democracy* (Chicago: University of Chicago Press, 1986), p. 21.

5. Pradeep Jeganathan, "After a Riot: Anthropological Locations of Violence in an Urban Sri Lankan Community" (Ph.D. diss., University of Chicago, 1997).

6. E. Valentine Daniel, *Charred Lullabies: Chapters in an Anthropology of Violence* (Princeton: Princeton University Press, 1996).

7. Tambiah, *Ethnic Fratricide*, p. 1.

8. Jeganathan, *After a Riot*, pp. 51–52.

9. Jeganathan, *After a Riot*, p. 231.

10. Daniel, *Charred Lullabies*, p. 6.

11. Daniel, *Charred Lullabies*, p. 6.

12. According to Jeganathan, there is a certain coherence in Daniel's account, both in the invocation of "horror" and in the attribution of an act of political resistance to an estate Tamil who stabs his English employer.

13. Daniel, *Charred Lullabies*, p. 208.

14. Michel Foucault, "Truth and the Juridical Form," in *Power*, ed. James D. Faubion, trans. Robert Hurley et al. (New York: New Press, 2000).

15. Foucault, *Power*, p. 5.

16. Foucault, *Power*, p. 4.

17. Michael Ondaatje, *Anil's Ghost* (New York: Knopf, 2000), p. 151. Subsequent page references will be given parenthetically in the text.

18. vv19. *Merriam-Webster's Collegiate Dictionary*, 11th ed., s.v. "interlinear."

20. See Tambiah, *Ethnic Fratricide,* on the JVP and the government's repression of Marxist insurgents after 1971.

21. Dominick LaCapra, *Representing the Holocaust: History, Theory, Trauma* (Ithaca: Cornell University Press, 1994).

22. LaCapra, *Representing the Holocaust,* p. 125.

23. Arif Dirlik, "Postmodernism and Chinese History," *boundary 2* 28, no. 3 (2001): 45.

24. Cited by Tom LeClair in his review of *Anil's Ghost* in the *Nation,* June 19, 2000.

25. Giorgio Agamben, *Homo Sacer: Sovereign Power and Bare Life,* trans. Daniel Heller-Roazen (Stanford: Stanford University Press, 1998).

26. Agamben, *Homo Sacer,* p. 72.

27. Agamben, *Homo Sacer,* p. 83.

28. Kalliopi Nikopoulou, review of *Homo Sacer,* in *SubStance* 29, no. 3 (2000): 124–31, 125

29. Hardt and Negri have been criticized for their lack of attention to the modern forms of sovereign power and institutional structures that persist in the postmodern, postcolonial present. Certainly, nation-states maintain more conventional modes of sovereignty when it comes to repressive apparatuses such as armies, police, and border patrols.

30. Brian Massumi, *Parables for the Virtual: Movement, Affect, Sensation* (Durham: Duke University Press, 2002).

31. Massumi, *Parables for the Virtual,* p. 27.

32. I am grateful to Sujata Moorti for pointing to this privileging, one that is typically diasporic, of the affective over the historical.

CONCLUSION: "POWER SMASHES INTO PRIVATE LIVES":
CULTURAL POLITICS IN THE NEW EMPIRE

1. "A Writer by Partition: Salman Rushdie Interviewed by Michael Enright," *Queen's Quarterly* 112, no. 4 (Winter 2005): 554.

2. United Nations Department of Social and Economic Affairs/ Population Division, *World Population Prospects: The 2004 Revision,* volume 3, *Analytical Report,* Table 5.1, p. 86.

3. "A Writer by Partition," p. 2.

4. Tariq Ali's chapter "The Story of Kashmir," in *The Clash of Fundamentalisms: Crusades, Jihads and Modernity* (London: Verso, 2003), provides a brief historical overview that is handy for better understanding the setting and events of the novel. Ali sketches the history of modern Kashmir, recounting its rule

by the Dogras after the middle of nineteenth century, with the supervision of a British resident; the reign of Hari Singh in the mid-twentieth century; the rise of Sheik Abdullah and anti-British nationalism; Hari Singh's decision to join India; a Pakistan-based move to "liberate" Kashmir; and India's appeal to the United Nations, which advocated a plebiscite that never took place. Pakistan went to war with India in 1948 and the partition of Kashmir followed; Pakistan occupies part of it, having established a de facto "line of control." Ali briefly sketches the subsequent rise of the JKLF, a secular, Kashmiri nationalist group that fought for a separate homeland and rejected Pakistani and Indian control. The JKLF was gradually outflanked by groups of Islamic militants backed by Pakistan, who continue to wage war with Indian troops who occupy the valley.

5. Mridu Rai, *Hindu Rulers, Muslim Subjects: Islam, Rights, and the History of Kashmir* (Princeton: Princeton University Press, 2004).

6. Salman Rushdie, *Shalimar the Clown* (London: Jonathan Cape, 2005), p. 110. Subsequent page references will be given parenthetically in the text.

7. Doris Sommer, *Foundational Fictions: The National Romances of Latin America* (Berkeley: University of California Press, 1991).

8. While Rushdie's earlier novels are clearly national allegories of the type discussed by Fredric Jameson, *Shalimar the Clown* can be read as an allegory of global geopolitics. Each of the parts of novel is named after a character—India, Boonyi, Max, Shalimar the Clown, and Kashmira—who is associated with a historically and geopolitically specific location. Broadly speaking, Shalimar the Clown represents Kashmir, but in its fiercely angry, violent aspect; he becomes an international terrorist. Boonyi, his wife, is originally named Bhumi, or earth; she clearly represents Kashmir in its beautiful and then tragic aspect. Max Ophuls, originally a Jewish economist from Strasbourg, goes to England as a refugee, becomes an American ambassador to India, and then later is the secret head of antiterrorist operations in the United States; he represents the West, a conflation of Europe and America. Max's multiple associations bespeak a thoroughly postnational identity. If Max is an allegorical figure for the "West" and especially the United States, he at the same time straddles the "insider/outsider" split as well as replicates the Kashmiri characters' liminal status. Kashmira bears the original name given to India, and is the illegitimate daughter of Max and Boonyi; the novel ends with a return to Kashmira and her story. Read allegorically, Max's seduction of Boonyi raises the spectre of the United States' exploitation of Kashmir and of India. Plied with food, drugs, and tobacco by Max's dogsbody, Edgar Wood, Boonyi becomes grotesquely obese. Interpreted once again along allegorical lines, Boonyi's degradation can be read as criticism of consumerism and cupidity after the era of liberalization: the East is seduced by Western wares. If *Shalimar the Clown,* the story of Boonyi and Shalimar's love and marriage,

constitutes a national romance that bridges ethnic and religious differences, then the liaison between Max and Boonyi constitutes a sort of globalized concubinage, one that destroys the national romance.

9. See, for instance, Biju Mathew and Vijay Prashad, "The Protean Forms of Yankee Hindutva," *Ethnic and Racial Studies* 23, no. 3 (Spring 2000): 516–34.

10. The notion that one must look beyond the nation, rather than imagining, or in order to imagine, a transformed civil society within India, is one that some critics have questioned. Partha Chatterjee cautions against a tendency to applaud the emergence of a postnational global order, and argues that it is the old categories that tie together local structures of the community and the nation-state—the family, civil society, political society, the state—that most strongly shape people's lives in postcolonial India. He could be addressing Rushdie when he writes, "The virtual neighborhood, where context-generating feelings of solidarity can be produced among people spatially located in different places, is at present confined to relatively small diasporic groups in which the most active component is probably the exiled intellectual." He urges us instead to look within the nation, and argues instead for the further development of what he calls political society, a space of mediation between civil society and the state, for secular and progressive politics to be advanced. Partha Chatterjee, "Beyond the Nation? Or Within?" *Social Text* 16, no. 3.56 (Fall 1998): 57–69.

11. The point that this embrace of cosmopolitan originates in bourgeois privilege is one that Timothy Brennan makes in *Salman Rushdie and the Third World: Myths of the Nation* (London: Macmillan, 1989).

12. Saskia Sassen, *Losing Control? Sovereignty in an Age of Globalization* (New York: Columbia University Press, 1996).

13. I am grateful to the anonymous reader of my manuscript for this and the subsequent quoted comment.

Index

8, 144, 176; and postcolonial
fiction of intrigue, 139; and
power, 208–10; and rational
administration, 143, 176; representation of, 130, 167, 169;
scholars' attention to, 129–30;
violence of, 201, 202
Postcolonial subjects, and modernity,
140
Postmodernism: and New Empire,
133; and postcolonial fiction of
intrigue, 139; and power, 209,
210, 264n29
Postnational subjects, 223
Poststructuralism, 127, 128, 194
Poulantzas, Nicos, 130
Power: abuse of state power, 168;
of affect, 212; and anxieties
about hegemony, 63; bifurcated, in postcolonial state,
131; and *homo sacer*, 207–8,
215; imperial, 63, 96; and
international institutions, 132;
and masculinity, 78; and New
Empire, 134, 218; political,
101–2; and postcolonial fiction
of intrigue, 11; and postcolonial state, 208–10; postmodern
modalities of, 209, 210, 264n29;
and representation of European
bodies, 78; self-representation of
governmental, 50; and shaping
of knowledge, 48; and social
interests, 129; U.S. as dominant
imperial power, 7, 123, 132,
134; will to power, 4, 217. *See
also* Disciplinary power
Preemption principle, 7
Prester John (Buchan): and code
of counterinsurgency, 112–13,

120; and identity, 119–20; and
imperial servants, 106; and
insurgency, 13, 86, 104, 107,
110–13, 114, 115, 117; and
knowing the Other, 108, 115–16,
120; and landscape, 109–10;
and nature, 114; and pursuit
of knowledge, 109; and racial
stereotypes, 110, 114, 254n44;
and surveillance, 108, 109, 114–
15; and syncretic Christianity,
113–14
Prevention of Terrorism Act, 190
Process of signification, 23
Profit interests, 153, 154
Pseudo-sciences, 148
Psychoanalytic critics, on detective
fiction, 237n16
Psychoanalytic theory: and returned
colonials, 64, 83. *See also* Freud,
Sigmund
Public Culture, 165

Race: Buchan's racial stereotypes,
105, 106, 110, 114, 254nn40,
44; duality of racialized citizenry,
130–31; mythology of racial
superiority, 76, 77, 249n35;
racial coding as "Other," 82,
101, 104; racist ideology, 95,
249n35
Rai, Mridu, 220
Raychaudhuri, Tapan, 146, 148
Religion: Christianity, 113–14,
243n22; Enlightenment rationality as corrective to, 147; and
fanatic religious fervor, 38; and
insurgency, 111, 112, 113–14,
116–18; and Kashmiriyat, 220;
Kierkegaard on, 20; Marxists'